Carrying My Father's Torch

CAROLINA ACADEMIC PRESS AFRICAN WORLD SERIES
Toyin Falola, Series Editor

*Africa, Empire and Globalization:
Essays in Honor of A. G. Hopkins*
Toyin Falola, editor, and Emily Brownell, editor

African Entrepreneurship in Jos, Central Nigeria, 1902–1985
S.U. Fwatshak

*An African Music and Dance Curriculum Model:
Performing Arts in Education*
Modesto Amegago

*Authority Stealing:
Anti-Corruption War and Democratic Politics
in Post-Military Nigeria*
Wale Adebanwi

*The Bukusu of Kenya:
Folktales, Culture and Social Identities*
Namulundah Florence

Carrying My Father's Torch: A Memoir
Kalu Ogbaa

Contemporary African Literature: New Approaches
Tanure Ojaide

*Contesting Islam in Africa:
Homegrown Wahhabism and Muslim Identity in Northern Ghana, 1920–2010*
Abdulai Iddrisu

*Converging Identities:
Blackness in the Modern African Diaspora*
Julius Adekunle and Hettie V. Williams

*Democracy in Africa:
Political Changes and Challenges*
Saliba Sarsar, editor, and Julius O. Adekunle, editor

*Diaspora and Imagined Nationality:
USA-Africa Dialogue and Cyberframing Nigerian Nationhood*
Koleade Odutola

*Food Crop Production, Hunger, and Rural Poverty in
Nigeria's Benue Area, 1920–1995*
Mike Odugbo Odey

*Esu:
Yoruba God, Power, and the Imaginative Frontiers*
Toyin Falola

*Ghana During the First World War:
The Colonial Administration of Sir Hugh Clifford*
Elizabeth Wrangham

Globalization: The Politics of Global Economic Relations and International Business
N. Oluwafemi Mimiko

*A History of Class Formation in the Plateau Province of Nigeria, 1902–1960:
The Genesis of a Ruling Class*
Monday Yakiban Mangvwat

*Horror in Paradise:
Frameworks for Understanding the Crises of the Niger Delta Region of Nigeria*
Christopher LaMonica and J. Shola Omotola

Imperialism, Economic Development and Social Change in West Africa
Raymond Dumett

In Search of African Diasporas: Testimonies and Encounters
Paul Tiyambe Zeleza

*Intercourse and Crosscurrents in the Atlantic World:
Calabar-British Experience, 17th–20th Centuries*
David Lishilinimle Imbua

*Julius Nyerere, Africa's Titan on a Global Stage:
Perspectives from Arusha to Obama*
Ali A. Mazrui and Lindah L. Mhando

*Local Government in South Africa Since 1994:
Leadership, Democracy, Development, and Service Delivery in a Post-Apartheid Era*
Alexius Amtaika

*Narratives of Struggle:
The Philosophy and Politics of Development in Africa*
John Ayotunde Bewaji

Perspectives on Feminism in Africa
'Lai Olurode, editor

Pioneer, Patriot, and Nigerian Nationalist:
A Biography of the Reverend M. D. Opara, 1915–1965
Felix Ekechi

Satires of Power in Yoruba Visual Culture
Yomi Ola

The Tiv and Their Southern Neighbours, 1890–1990
Emmanuel Chiahemba Ayangaôr

The Vile Trade:
Slavery and the Slave Trade in Africa
Abi Alabo Derefaka, Wole Ogundele, Akin Alao, and Agustus Ajibola

The Women's War of 1929:
A History of Anti-Colonial Resistance in Eastern Nigeria
Toyin Falola and Adam Paddock

The Yoruba Frontier:
A Regional History of Community Formation,
Experience, and Changes in West Africa
Aribidesi Usman

Women, Gender, and Sexualities in Africa
Toyin Falola and Nana Akua Amponsah, editors

Carrying My Father's Torch
A Memoir

Kalu Ogbaa

Carolina Academic Press
Durham, North Carolina

Copyright © 2014
Kalu Ogbaa
All Rights Reserved

Library of Congress Cataloging-in-Publication Data

Ogbaa, Kalu.
 Carrying my father's torch : a memoir / Kalu Ogbaa.
   pages cm
 Includes bibliographical references and index.
 ISBN 978-1-61163-494-5 (alkaline paper)
 1. Ogbaa, Kalu. 2. Ogbaa, Kalu--Family. 3. Nigerian Americans--Biography. 4. Immigrants--United States--Biography. 5. College teachers--Connecticut--New Haven--Biography. 6. Igbo (African people)--Biography. 7. Fathers and sons--Nigeria. 8. Nigeria--History--1960---Biography. 9. Nigeria--History--Civil War, 1967-1970 10. Christian biography--Nigeria. I. Title.

E184.N55O35 2013
270.092--dc23
[B]

2013029996

CAROLINA ACADEMIC PRESS
700 Kent Street
Durham, North Carolina 27701
Telephone (919) 489-7486
Fax (919) 493-5668
www.cap-press.com

Printed in the United States of America

To
My father, Mazi Stephen Ogbaa Ikpo
And
My mother, Mrs. Ogonnaya Ogbaa Ikpo
For giving me life and the torch

Contents

Series Editor's Preface	xiii
Introduction	xv

Part One · *A Father's Influence*

Chapter 1 · Why We Wrestle	3
Chapter 2 · My Ancestors	15
Chapter 3 · My Birth and Early Incidents in My Life	19
Chapter 4 · Becoming a Christian	31

Part Two · *The Educational Matches*

Chapter 5 · The Primary School Years	41
Chapter 6 · Beyond the Village	65
Chapter 7 · War Days in Biafra	79
Chapter 8 · Postwar Reconstruction	97
Chapter 9 · Starting a Career and a Family	121

Part Three · *My American Experience*

Chapter 10 · Coming to America for Graduate Studies	151
Chapter 11 · Back Home with the Golden Fleece	173

Part Four · *My Second Coming to America*

Chapter 12 · The Sabbatical Leave Years	221
Chapter 13 · From Permanent Residency to Citizenship	239
Chapter 14 · A Second Chance on Marriage	257
Chapter 15 · Southern Life	267
Conclusion	279
Acknowledgments	283
Index	285

Series Editor's Preface

The Carolina Academic Press *African World Series*, inaugurated in 2010, offers significant new works in the field of African and Black World studies. The series provides scholarly and educational texts that can serve as both reference works and readers in college classes.

Studies in the series are anchored in the existing humanistic and the social scientific traditions. Their goal, however, is the identification and elaboration of the strategic place of Africa and its Diaspora in a shifting global world. More specifically, the studies address gaps and larger needs in the developing scholarship on Africa and the Black World.

The series is intended to fill gaps in areas such as African politics, history, law, religion, culture, sociology, literature, philosophy, visual arts, art history, geography, language, health, and social welfare. Given the complex nature of Africa and its Diaspora, and the constantly shifting perspectives prompted by globalization, the series also meets a vital need for scholarship connecting knowledge with events and practices. Reflecting the fact that life in Africa continues to change, especially in the political arena, the series explores issues emanating from racial and ethnic identities, particularly those connected with the ongoing mobilization of ethnic minorities for inclusion and representation.

Toyin Falola
University of Texas at Austin

Introduction

This book tells the story of my struggles—with my homeland and its colonial past, with ethnic differences and violence that produced the Nigeria-Biafra War, but most of all with my father, a man who himself lived through and was shaped by these struggles. At this stage of my life, I can say that I am my father's son, and that I have taken up his torch to new places. I now live in America, where I have tried to realize his dream of using Western education and values to overcome the poverty and turmoil of life in postcolonial Nigeria. I am also Igbo, and that ethnic identity, passed on from father to son, has had an enormous influence on me, from customs, dispositions, and values that still affect who I am, to a stake and role in the bloody Nigerian civil war. Finally, like my father, I am Christian, which has helped me get a universal perspective on my country's and my own personal history.

Christianity has been a source of solace and reconciliation, which has helped me to come to terms with the difficulties of my homeland and my struggles with my father, who was both an exacting taskmaster and beloved ideal. This memoir tells the story of how I, a young Igbo boy, took on the ideals of my father and found my way from a situation of poverty, postcolonial malaise, and ethnic violence to a new life as a university professor in America. It is a story that tells how the burden of carrying my father's torch has given me the freedom of a new life, one that remains haunted by the traumas of its past, but which embraces the blessings of its present and future.

My father himself wrestled with the idea of adapting to the sociocultural, political, and religious changes that occurred in Igbo society because of the British invasion of their land between 1902 and 1906. After some futile resistance to the changes, he became one of the first to join the church white missionaries founded in our clan. He first became a Roman Catholic Mission (RCM) convert, and later a convert of the Church of Scotland Mission (CSM). He studied up to Standard II, which enabled him to serve as an interpreter in his village church for the white missionaries. He played music for the church band and led other native Christians when they went on open-air and camp crusades. My father loved schooling, and he would have gone beyond the level of education he attained if there had not been a devastating incident that prevented him from achieving his educational goal.

According to him, Scottish missionaries and British officials invited him to train as a police constable, so he could help maintain law and order in his clan and to run some errands for them. He had received enough basic literacy training in English to train for those roles. He could read and write letters for his fellow villagers (and later in my lifetime, he could write agreements for them). As he prepared to go for the training, his elder sister refused to let him go, threatening to die if my father left their home for anywhere else. In obedience to his sister's wishes, Father declined the invitation, and the ruling white men gave the opportunity to another villager. However, six months later, the sister died, and Father lost the opportunity to become a leader in a white man's employment but not the will to become a village leader in other village affairs.

He perfected his wrestling match prowess and strategies and became a wrestling champion in his village and clan. In addition, he became a parent-teacher association (PTA) chairperson and secretary, respectively, alternating the two roles with another literate man from a neighboring village, when the Scottish missionaries established a primary school between our village of Umuchiakuma and the neighboring Amammiri village. Other roles he played in the village and clan because of his basic formal school education in his time taught him the importance of acquiring a Western education. So he vowed to train all his children, especially the boys, in school. When other parents failed to encourage their children to attend school, he insisted that his own children had to go, with or without his material support. He would punish me if I failed to do my homework or come out on top of my classes in every test and exam I took. I did not understand why he was doing that to me at my young age. But after I became a college graduate, he told me the reason he had dropped out of school and never became the police constable for which he wanted to train. He thus failed to realize his dream. It seemed to me that he was vicariously living through my achievements as an educated person.

Now that I live permanently in America and have grown older and perhaps wiser with sons and grandsons both in the United States and Nigeria and my father is no longer alive, I feel the urge to write my story, which includes recalling and examining the events of the uneasy relationship I had with him very early in my life. I fear that some of my sons, who detect some of my father's character traits in me, misunderstand me occasionally as I did my father. Some days, he would show me the greatest love a father could show to his most beloved son, but on other days, he would spank me or talk to me harshly because of some mistakes I made, including those I considered minor. On such days, I wondered if he loved me at all. No, my father could never overlook any of my mistakes and avoid punishing me for them. To my mother, a demure and obedient Christian wife, what my father was doing to me then was a show of tough love to his beloved son. From time to time, she would remind me of what the Holy Bible says:

> Honor thy father and thy mother: that thy days may be long upon the land which the Lord thy God gives thee (Exodus 20:12).

On his own part, my father would constantly exert his paternal authority over me and recite a similar biblical passage after punishing me, lest I forget to obey or honor him as if he were God:

> My son, forget not my law; but let thine heart keep my commandments:
> For length of days, and long life, and peace, shall they add to thee (Proverbs 3: 1-2).

As time went by, I learned to listen carefully to my father and to do whatever he asked me to do without questions. Nevertheless, that is not to say that I appreciated the rocky father-son relationship between us early in my life.

"How could I, the last born of four children, be the one that he always sent to run all his errands? Why couldn't he ask Brother Ikpo to run some of the errands for him as I did?" I asked myself. But I dared not ask such questions openly, fearing he would spank me for my effrontery.

It was after my father realized that I was trying to neither disobey him purposely nor impugn his parental authority that he began to act in a way that surprised me pleasantly. He showed me some measure of kindness that seemingly cleared some of my doubts. One day, he invited me for a private talk in his house where my mother and Brother Ikpo could not hear us.

"Do you know how special you are to me?" he began.

"No, I don't," I said, for I did not understand what he was getting at, and my eyes began to cloud up with tears.

"Yes, you are! I see you as a very perceptive, mentally sharp, and physically agile, son. I trust you as the only one who can deliver my messages accurately to people. And, I see you as being capable of carrying my torch when I become unable to do most of the tasks I'm now doing in our home and community."

I had never before known my father had so much trust and regard for me as his beloved. I was overjoyed and wondered if Father had always been preparing me for a big role all along without showing any hint of his intentions.

"Why do you think I call you *Ikenga nna ya* (Father's right hand man) whenever you please me or bring honor to our family?" he asked. "Always remember the Bible passage I read in our last family prayer meeting. 'Chasten thy son while there is hope, and let not thy soul spare for his crying' (Proverbs 19:18). I only chasten you to make you stronger—and to keep you from suffering at the whims of fortune which will sometimes bring hard times to you and your life."

As a result of our discussion, I began to work harder than before to maintain his trust and thereby become my given name, Kalu, which means God of thunder and war, and my praise name, *Ikenga nna ya*, which means his father's right hand man.

It is for the sake of my children and grandchildren's understanding of me as a father and grandfather, as well as for the benefit of all struggling young people that I write my story so they can stop doubting their bright future in life. For both reasons, I feel it is important that I tell the story of my life, which begins with my family upbringing, colonial education, and my professional life: my story, which echoes the story of all the poor and needy, who have strived to get out of poverty and become successful in life at the long last. I hope my story—indeed our collective story of struggles and triumphs—will inspire other people who started life poor like me to aim at achieving a better life for themselves in spite of whatever obstacles they face in life.

Part One

A Father's Influence

Chapter 1

Why We Wrestle

One day in the early afternoon, Father seemed happy but somehow anxious. "Hurry up, *Ikenga nna ya*, we are going to be late," he said. I didn't understand why it was so important that he get to Nde Ogbu compound square early for the wrestling matches. But once we arrived there, it became clear to me.

"*Ogbaa nwa Ikpo, Dimgba Eleoha, Osiere uke ya oso, ana m ekele gi oo!*" ("Ogbaa the son of Ikpo, the wrestling champion of Eleoha, and pacesetter for his age grade, I salute you!"), said a tall elder, standing to make way for Father. Other elders followed suit, each hailing my father and bowing.

Father smiled and bowed in return, addressing them by their honorific names. "Hello, *Ogbuefi* (killer of cows) and you *Odoziobodo* (peacemaker of the community)." Then he approached each, slapping the back of their outstretched palms five times, as was their custom. After the ceremonial exchanges, the elders all took seats in their designated stools, arranging their brightly colored clothes such that the other villagers and spectators could have a clear view of their fine wares.

I took my place behind Father, along with the other young pages who accompanied their sires like miniature bodyguards. Then the talking drums began to pound a frenzied, steady rhythm that formally announced the presence of the elders, followed by *ogbu opi*, the flutist, naming each with its melodic language, a stylized mode that paid homage to them for their titular and honorific achievements. In our patriarchal Igbo society, people respect age and revere achievement. They respected my father for his age and revered him for his wrestling victories. He brought honor to our village and clan. "That was many years ago, before you were born," he proudly told me after that day's matches.

I did not fully understand my father's delight watching those matches until I read Chinua Achebe's novel, *Things Fall Apart* (1958). My father's stories all came rushing back. And the more pages I read, the more the life of the novel's main character, Okonkwo Unoka, reminded me of another successful Igbo wrestler and farmer living in another rural Igbo community: Stephen Ogbaa Ikpo, my father. Reading about Okonkwo's life, including the wrestling matches he won, his involvement with Christian missionaries, his own clan's customs and beliefs that so paralleled our own Ihechiowa clan's traditional religion, customs, rituals, and ceremonies, I was struck by the sense of brotherhood shared by such honored men. I became conscious of my link to that brotherhood, which began with my first wrestling match with Ogbonnaya Obi.

Ogbonnaya Obi challenged me to a fight. I was six and had just returned to our compound square from the public latrines, combating the stench and swarm of flies while sitting perched atop a log placed between two heavier forked logs. In our village, where most of us boys roamed the compounds naked, it was a cold December morning of the West African harmattan season of dry, dusty, and chilly days and nights. We'd huddle together around a log fire in an open shed to warm ourselves, pressing our bodies close to the roaring flames, often shoving and pushing others, struggling to reach the heat.

That morning, I'd run through the cold winds that swirled against *udara* trees and taken a position close to the flames when Ogbonnaya nudged between a friend, Geberelu, and me. Ogbonnaya was a neighbor and schoolmate, a stocky, strong, left-handed bully who liked to fight. Without thinking, I elbowed him in the side, shoving him away. He pushed back against me and I jumped on him. Before long, a crowd of spectators had formed around us shouting: "Hit him, hit him!" We grabbed at one another, each attempting to throw the other, wrestling, shoving and struggling until the scene resembled a regular rural wrestling ritual except that it was not between warring clans or villages.

At the time, I did not understand why Ogbannya would want to intimidate and fight me and the other children. I had always been friendly to him as a neighbor and shared pieces of chalk and pencils with him at school. I thought perhaps that he was just stupid, because he struggled with schoolwork I was able to complete easily. But I'd always tried to get along with him, and others, since my father had warned me against fighting in school. Doing so would give my teachers the impression that I lacked good home training. Ogbonnaya may have wrongly assumed that I refused to fight him at school because I was a coward. But he dared not pick a fight with me at home where my father, an elder of the village and reputable wrestler, would see us. But this particular morning, my father was not there.

As we continued to wrestle, he held me tight, twisting my body and pinning my limbs, hoping that I would give up easily. Then, I saw my father striding across the compound to join the crowd. I could not give up and bring shame to my father, Ogbaa *nwa* Ikpo, our village wrestling champion. Ogbonnaya also saw my father, so he too tried harder to win the battle.

We closed in on each other, tightened our grips, and began pushing right, left, forward, and backward until we both fell to the ground, rolling and kicking in the dirt without either winning over the other. I glanced at my father hoping he'd move in to break up the fight. He did not. At last, Onoh Aja, one of our compound chiefs, stepped in and stopped the fight. And lifting both our hands in the air, he said, "*Inyi araale oko*," in our Ihechiowa dialect, declaring that there was neither a winner nor a loser. Then he asked us to hug and shake hands. We reluctantly embraced and then ran to the nearby brook, Iyi Ugwu, to wash the sand and sweat off our slippery bodies.

When I returned home, my father grinned and shook my hand. He then turned and left without saying a word about the fight. Father never said much. Only action. Some days, he would show me the greatest love a father could show to his most beloved son, but on other days, he would discipline me harshly over mistakes I had made, some of which I considered minor. On such days, I wondered if he loved me at all.

The next morning, Ogbonnaya was waiting for me in front of *agbala ogo*, our thatched compound shed, where we had our fight. He was unhappy that I had punctured his image as the strongman and bully and was sporting for a rematch.

"Hey, smart boy. Where do you think you are going?"

"Get out of my way, you big bully," I said.

"Oh no, Kalu. You have to finish what you started yesterday!"

"Get out of my way." I tried to push past him.

"No, you are not going anywhere until I've settled the score with you." He moved to block my way.

I didn't want to fight him before school. But as I turned to leave, he slapped me across the face. I shook my head, rubbed the tears from my eyes, clenched my fist and teeth, and punched him so hard in the belly that he staggered and fell back. I quickly turned and began to walk away, leaving him reeling on the ground. But before I'd taken three steps, he sprang up like a man possessed and ran quickly after me. Before I could spin around to face him squarely, he gave me a sharp blow with his left fist on my right temple. I was dazed. I staggered. Then suddenly, my father appeared. Once again, a crowd had gathered and began egging us on.

"Hit him back, Kalu. Hit him," the crowd shouted.

I steadied myself and faced Ogbonnaya Obi squarely like a man. "Since you really want to fight me this morning, come on. Let's fight," I beckoned him with outstretched hands.

I must have appeared weakened and stunned, because Ogbonnaya grinned and charged to finish me off. I kept a keen eye on him as he closed in. Instinctively, I shoved out my hand, poking him in the eye. As he recoiled in pain, I kicked him away with my right foot. He fell to the rocky ground, smashed the left side of his head, and began bleeding. "Oh God! What have I done?" I asked myself. I'd never seen so much blood and worried that I'd killed him.

But Father was quickly at his side, pulling Ogbonnya up and pressing his thumb on the small gash to stop the bleeding. He sat Ogbonnaya on *ogwo ogo*, a long heavy tree trunk that served as a sitting bench for the villagers, and ordered me to fetch iodine from the house. I sprinted to the house and soon returned, Mother following me with a towel and water carried in a small washbowl.

Father began treating Ogbonnaya's wound, dabbing his head with a moist towel. "Does it hurt you, Ogbonnaya Obi?"

"Yes sir?"

"How much does it hurt?"

"Very much, sir!"

"Do you like it?"

"Not at all, sir!" Ogbonnaya Obi cried out.

"Come here, Kalu."

"Do you like what you are seeing?"

"No sir!" I said, afraid.

"Why not?"

"Because it hurts, sir."

"Does it hurt you or Ogbannaya?"

"Ogbonnaya, sir."

"I thought you would be happy that your enemy is hurting," Father said.

"No, sir, he is my friend; not my enemy." I sobbed quietly.

My father looked at us both. "Never fight again. You are both clansmen. I will whip you both if I catch you fighting."

I was sad that I had hurt Ogbonnaya so badly, even though I hadn't started the fight. I quickly agreed never to fight a clansman again. Ogbonnaya, too, had learned his lesson. Indeed, we eventually became friends and allies that teamed up to fight other bullies. And whenever we fought, we always defeated all our adversaries who, while trying to avoid punches from my right hand, received dangerous blows from Ogbonnaya's left fist. I enjoyed the thrills of our collaborative effort whenever we defeated our opponents in such fights, but I never fully appreciated the lesson of the right hand working collaboratively with the left to achieve victory in all aspects of our community life until I was grown.

At any rate, over time Ogbonnaya and I became good friends. I even ended up helping him with his homework assignments. I had always received good marks at school since Father who had attended some basic literacy and Bible classes, conducted by Scottish missionaries for new Christian converts in our area, had always been there to help me. But Ogbonnaya's father never attended any such classes and thus remained illiterate, leaving Ogbonnya to struggle alone with his schoolwork.

I also discovered that despite our initial differences, Ogbonnaya and I had a lot in common. We were both born and raised during the mid-1940s in Nde Ngwo compound, Umuchiakuma Ihechiowa in Arochukwu District, in the then Eastern Nigeria. We both belonged to the same three-year age bracket for boys and girls, Aduanu. Our village trained the boys and girls to become well-developed men and women in all aspects of our village life. At the time, they raised boys to be strong and aggressive to achieve success in our warlike, agrarian Igbo society. Our village was primarily comprised of subsistence farmers. Consequently, we were regularly involved in land disputes with our Ibibio neighbors from the Akwa Ibom State, especially during seasons of planting and harvesting of farm crops. Hence, all our able-bodied men trained to serve in the security bodies, *nde nche*, that fought to protect our village from attacks by neighboring clans and tribes. Male babies, named Kalu, Kanu, Kamalu, or Akanu (after the Igbo god of thunder and war), were brought up early to be aggressive and qualified to lead in such battles, and as such, becoming of their names.

Hence, Igbo boys learned early in life to engage in wrestling matches and learn from the adult men who wrestled on Afo Market days. Afo Market days were specially set aside from the regular workweek. On Afo Market mornings, the men tapped palm wine and collected yams early from their barns and returned quickly to buy and sell their farm produce in the market square until two o'clock in the afternoon. Then, they would take a break and prepare for the matches while the women, who'd also started the day early harvesting cassava tubers, would bring the harvest home and place them in sacks to ferment for baking, as *foofoo*, while others would peel, grate, and bake them into *garri* (similar to corn meal) for cereal. Children also joined in the work helping to carry the yams, cassava, and other crops home. Monday through Friday, men and women worked from sunrise to sunset while the children went to school and joined them to work on the farms after school. But Afo was a day on which everybody worked less. Instead, they prepared for wrestling matches, playing such roles as animated wrestlers, drummers, cheerleaders, and spectators at the Nde Ogbu compound square, the official arena of the wrestling matches.

Early in the afternoon, the children from Nde Ngwo compound would arrive first with drums, flutes, and small kitchen stools. We would beat the talking drums, *nkwa*, and the flute, *opi*, as a call to those interested in competing with other wrestlers in the arena. As a kind of appetizer to the more strenuous, energy-sapping matches between adults, the younger boys would normally wrestle with one another, which also gave them a forum to show off their own wrestling prowess. Then, adult drummers and flutists would replace the young players when adult wrestling was about to start.

At the opening of the matches, the drummers would kneel on the ground or sit on short stools while the village elders sat on *ogwo ogo* and folding chairs, which their pages brought and placed behind the drummers and on their right and left flanks so they could face the center of the wrestling ground. Other spectators, including prospective wrestlers, would stand in a horseshoe formation around the drummers and wrestlers. Generally, the younger men wrestled between themselves according to their age grades. If any competitor threw his opponent, he stayed in the ring to wrestle other challengers until he was finally defeated, and replaced by others. The crowd acknowledged the last wrestler standing as champion of the particular day, but he would be the first to face other wrestlers' challenges during the next Afo day matches.

Young, up-and-coming wrestlers usually practiced on Nkwo, Eke, and Orie days in their compound squares or on soccer fields at their schools, preparing for the next Afo day wrestling matches at the official village venue. The boys, especially those whose relatives lost the battle during the previous Afo day, trained hard to beat their opponents and bring back honor and glory to their defeated, disgraced, relatives. The practice sessions were just as exciting and real as official Afo day wrestling matches, except that they took place on a smaller scale and with less fanfare. Nevertheless, victories on such practice sessions emboldened the wrestlers to challenge other prospective wrestlers during bigger, official matches.

During the big matches, wrestlers come from all twelve compounds, comprising three agnate blocs, of our village. The wrestlers began their competitions from the compound level to the bloc level before reaching the village level. The village champion would then proceed to compete for one of two Ihe clan titles: Dimgba Eleoha and Dimgba Ikwun. At the time, Ihe clan, which changed to Ihechiowa during the war in 1967, was comprised of twenty-eight villages, which they sub-divided into two blocs: Ikwun Ihechiowa and Eleoha Ihechiowa. Umuchiakuma belonged to the latter bloc. As a successful wrestler, my father progressed from being Dimgba Ezukwu to becoming Dimgba Umuchiakuma, and then rose to the Dimgba Eleoha level, when he defeated the Achara village champion, Isaac Ukoha, the father of Barrister Imo Ukoha. Despite his defeat, Isaac Ukoha befriended my father, and the two wrestling champions remained friends until Mr. Ukoha died. I believe now that my father wanted me to learn from his personal examples, not just from his words. Although I sometimes wished he had used his words more and his examples less.

I was only able to witness my Father wrestle a few times in our village square. Not in competition with others as such, but just to demonstrate to the younger generation of wrestlers how he wrestled with his opponents, defeated them, and eventually became the celebrated village and sub-clan champion.

But on one occasion, as I watched several renowned champions engage each other furiously in the square as if possessed by the sounds of the booming talking drums and the voice of the flutes rising around the ring, I learned a lesson of honor and courage I had never before understood. During the match, I was mesmerized as the wrestlers grabbed, twisted, and shook each other; stretched and grunted as if they were pushing a boulder up a slippery slope. As the contests wore on, it finally came down to two strapping wrestlers. We watched, yelling and pulling for our favorite, a younger nineteen-year-old boy, who, overly anxious to win, lost his balance and fell. The spectators from his opponent's compound suddenly surged into the ring, lifted him onto their shoulders and danced, jeering and mocking amid frenzied shouts of victory, while the victor danced alone in the center of the ring acknowledging the applause of his family and admirers.

But such a loss carried with it more than just hurt pride since it was also during such occasions that the young women looked out for prospective suitors. A bold girl could jump into the ring to embrace a victor and whisper an invitation for a warm bath in her house, which could lead to dating or planning for future marriages. Good marriages were the central symbol of wealth and standing in a clan. And since the defeated wrestler had come from our village, the outcome of that match was so embarrassing for my father the he immediately spun and left the scene in shame.

But as I watched him begin to stride away, the talking drums increased their rhythm and pitch of violence. The urge to fight and win, like a man's desire for a woman, must have gripped my father, because he suddenly turned and sprang into the center of the ring, danced a few steps, and then stopped and looked around him. Shuddering at the violent rhythm of the drums talking to him esoterically, he threw his wrestling paraphernalia, *ikpo mgba*, to the ground in a challenge to anyone who would dare to wrestle him. I worried that he was too old to wrestle. The others were much younger and stronger from what I'd just witnessed.

The drumming abruptly stopped and all eyes were riveted toward him, eager to know who had the audacity to punctuate the order of events. But as soon as the drummers recognized my father, they resumed, but this time in an old familiar tune:

Ogbaa nwa Ikpo, o gara mgba adim uche, o gara mgba,
Nwa Ikpo, o gara mgba adim uche, o gara mgba;
Ngirigi cha, ngirigi cha, ngirigi cha; cha ngirigi, cha ngiricha cha.

(Ogbaa, the son of Ikpo, who wrestles without any doubt of victory;
Son of Ikpo, who wrestles without any doubt of victory, comes to wrestle ...)

Then the women from our compound ran into the ring and formed a circle around him, singing his familiar victory song, lacing it with ear-deafening ululation as their way of encouraging him to wrestle and avenge the disgrace brought to them by their defeated wrestler.

On hearing his fighting song, Father picked up the *ikpo mgba* and threw it to me to hold. I caught it and continued watching nervously for his next move. He danced to the former winner's corner and tauntingly challenged them to a return match. They looked around to one of their accomplished wrestlers of my father's age grade and gave him a sign to take up the challenge on their behalf. The man quickly took off his sleeveless singlet, flung it angrily out of the circle, and leapt into the ring. My father saw him and smiled. Then turned and danced toward the drummers in respect and recognition of the elders, for some of them were retired champions like him. They returned the respect and recognition my father accorded to them and wished him luck.

The drums and flutes wailed in fury, accompanied by more ululation of the women, who were still dancing as the drums played. Mother ran toward me, smiling and clapping and dancing to the rhythm of the song, "*Ogbaa nwa Ikpo, o gara mgba adim uche*," which I had heard her sing to us her children innumerable times. Oh, yes, my father's wrestling prowess was one of the qualities my mother admired. As she told us so many times, Father never lost a wrestling match. When he saw us together, he smiled broadly, then turned and took a few steps angrily toward his opponent, who winced in fear, retreated for a moment before finally standing his ground.

Then Father crouched, scooped some sand off the ground, crushed it between his palms, and blew it into the air. The crowd roared and cheered. "*Ogbaa nwa Ikpo* …" filled the whole arena. Father stood and ran as one possessed by Kamalu, the Igbo god of war and thunder, held his hands up in the air and waved his right open palm insultingly in the face of the other wrestler. The other wrestler charged toward my father, reckless, wild. But Father had expected him to react that way and quickly bent down and swept him off his feet onto his own shoulders, spun him around a few times and let go. The man fell dizzily to the ground. The match was over.

The talking drums and flute wailed loudly, the tune calling out my father by name. Simultaneously, the crowd followed suit, singing "*Ogbaa nwa Ikpo, o gara mgba adim uche*." My mother and I, accompanied by our people from Nde Ikpo agnate family, jumped into the ring to celebrate. Then the drummers changed their tune to address the vanquished man:

Gbekwa akwa ma imegwara, gbekwa akwa ma imegwara;
Ngiri ngiri chacha, ngiri ngiri chacha, cha ngiricha, chacha.

(Stop crying so you can retaliate; stop crying so you can retaliate
Ngiri ngiri chacha, ngiri ngiri chacha, cha ngiricha cha ngiricha)

On the other side, the celebration was still raging as a throng of muscular young men carried my father on their shoulders away from the wrestling arena. Women and children followed them to our compound, where we continued our joyous victory until late in the evening. Mother served the family a specially prepared *egusi* soup with dried *atuma* fish and Norwegian cod, served with pounded yam *foofoo*. She and my father went to bed early and woke up later than usual the next morning, Sunday. My parents seemed to have rediscovered their long-forgotten youthful love. We were happy for them and we all dressed in our Sunday best, went to church and cheerfully thanked God for the happy event.

After the service, I asked Father why he taunted the wrestler in the ring.

"Simple!" he replied. "To prevent him from focusing his attention on me as we wrestled." Then he talked about the art and various techniques to help you to outwit and defeat a wrestler easily. Like knowing whether your opponent is right-handed or left-handed, or easily irritated when taunted, or anxious to defeat you too soon. Furthermore, he explained how wrestling was an important metaphor for the struggles in one's life, a means of understanding various ways of dealing with life's challenges.

I saw the benefits of learning those lessons from my father early in my life. For instance, each time I failed to score highly in our class quizzes and my teachers asked why, I would reduce my involvement in afterschool games and instead stay home to prepare for future quizzes. The result was that each time I did, I succeeded in maintaining my top position in all my classes. And when my parents were unable to send me to high school because they could not afford the tuition, I took another route to preparing for college: I enrolled in a correspondence college program in London that helped me to prepare privately for college, beating my former elementary school classmates, who attended high school but never made it to college. Later in life, I learned to go into hibernation, a covert preparation for a more overt action, as Ralph Ellison defined it in *Invisible Man*. So, whenever I could, I would learn more and more about wrestling from my father to enable me carry his torch into my own life.

Chapter 2

My Ancestors

Akwara Akuma traveled to Arochukwu with his two younger brothers, Abaka and Obaa from Asaga village of the Ohafia clan. Akwara was anxious to consult *Nnechukwu*, the Long Juju (a religious totem of veneration) to find out why his wives were giving births to twins. Considered an abomination by his clan, twins and their mothers were ostracized and exiled into the "evil" forests, a practice that continued until Scottish missionaries established churches in the area and stopped the practice. After offering oblations to *Nnechukwu*, the brothers began their long trek back to Asaga, stopping beside a lake, Iyi Nnam Oji, to refresh themselves. Located in a lush, fertile, forested valley, they decided to stay and settle on the land, farming it as they did in Asaga. In doing so, they founded the Umuchiakuma territory.

Akwara built his home on a corner now known as Nde Akwara compound. Abaka built his home on another corner now called Nde Abaka compound. Obaa, built his own home on what is now known as Nde Uche compound. Over time, the three founding fathers' homes multiplied into twelve compounds, divided into three village blocs: Ekelogo comprising Nde Akwara, Nde Agwu Okpo, Nde Okwun Ama, and Nde Ndu compounds; Ebemogo comprising Nde Abaka, Nde Ogbu, Nde Eji, and Nde Ihuoma compounds; and, Ezukwu comprising Nde Uche, Nde Ngwo, Nde Orugo, and Nde Apia compounds. The village appointed the traditional village chief, *Eze Ogo*, from Ekelogo bloc. The twelve compound chiefs constituted the Eze-in-Council and oversaw all aspects of the village governance, including the activities of all elected and appointive agencies.

Obaa Akuma's son, Ngwo Obaa, founded our compound, Nde Ngwo. Ngwo Obaa's son, Ikpo Ude, is the father of my grandfather Ikpo Ogbonnaya Ude, father of Ogbaa (Stephen) Ikpo, my father. My brother Ikpo and I dropped our ancestral surname Ikpo and stuck to my father's given name Ogbaa, whose personal achievements were greater than the ones made by the other descendants of my grandfather.

On my mother's side, our great, great grandmother Orie Ikechi Ogbuta gave birth to Ovuonu Okorafor, who gave birth to my grandmother Nkwocha Uche, who gave birth to my mother Nwagbara Uche. The name Mother preferred, Ogonnaya, is descriptive of the relationship between her father and her namesake, the woman who raised her in the absence of her deceased mother whom she never knew.

The brothers founded Umuchiakuma in the late 1800s between two existing Ihechiowa villages, Amammiri and Umuye, and two Ohafia villages, Akanu and Nde Uduma Awoke. As agrarian societies, these four competing villages did not want the founders to gain a foothold on their lands. Consequently, our village was established through warfare—conflicts continually arising between the competing factions until 1936, when the district government intervened. Only after the British took charge of Arochukwu and Ohafia districts, then surveyed and registered the land and awarded judgments to our people, did the warfare somewhat abet. Nevertheless, generations of people from neighboring villages, especially Abia Ohafia and Amammiri Ihechiowa, grew up and viewed the judgments awarded to our village as unjust, have continued to dispute our land-claims. Hence, they have left the younger generations of our villagers to continue, both physically and legally, to defend their claims against such disputes.

Despite these sporadic disruptions, our people continued the hard work of maintaining an agriculture-based economy of the village. Indeed, the farm practices of our ancestors proved so successful that, over the years, our village has become a principal agricultural center, supplying food for not only our own families, but also those of the Arochukwu and Ohafia clans. The currency and property they acquired in the past, through either bartering or sales, allowed us to rise economically above most other villages.

Today, unfortunately, our agricultural systems remain un-mechanized, and only a few farmers operate above the subsistence farming level. The problem is only exacerbated by a mindset, strongly held by most farmers, that the quality of living begins and ends with a family's ability to feed and minimally clothe itself. To that end, the prosperity and success of a man is measured by the number of wives and children he has and the number of yam barns he produces. Yam, the king of Igbo crops, enables a rich farmer to acquire titles by holding feasts for his villagers, serving them mounds of pounded yam *foofoo* and *egusi* soup prepared with the meat of cows (*efi*) slaughtered by him. In that way, a man becomes a titled elder, *ogbuefi*, of the village.

Consequently, many village farmers fear that selling their yams will reduce the number of yam barns they own and thereby reduce their fame and standing in the village. Such thinking causes them to hoard their yams instead of selling them off as a means of gaining financial security, which, in turn, might enable them improve the future quality of life for the next generation by, for example, sponsoring their children into secondary and university educations. Most children in the village, particularly when I was a child, never attended school after the age of eleven. Even someone as successful as my father did not have the means to sponsor my education to such several noted secondary schools whose entrance exams I passed simply because he refused to send his crops to market. Nevertheless, with his love and encouragement I found other means and routes to acquire my post-primary school education beyond the village.

Education or not, we all spent our teenage lives working side by side with our parents, tilling the soil to plant seed yams, cocoyam, cassava, *ona*, beans, peas, and other crops, carrying heavy baskets of crops on our heads three to four miles, covering the distance many times a day during harvest seasons. Schoolchildren worked part-time on the farms after school on weekdays, except when they had to play soccer and other sports in school, and all day on Saturdays. Preschool children went with their parents to farm from Monday through Saturday, and everybody rested on Sundays.

In addition to our farm duties, young boys in the village were trained to track and hunt various animals and recognize edible plants and herbs. For extra money, we collected edible snails, wove baskets, thatched roofs, and mended fences. During the holidays, we went to neighboring clans and villages to work for hire on their farms. In this way, I was able to pay my school fees in Standard IV (sixth grade in America), when I was only eleven years old. During one Easter break, I earned eleven shillings, six pence from making yam mounds at Akanu Ohafia. I took ten shillings and paid my tuition for the semester, and one shilling, six pence to buy my first pants, *kappa*, an expensive D-34 green khaki cloth sewed by the famous Amammiri tailor, Nna Ome Joseph, which I wore proudly after school.

With neither radio nor television for entertainment, we participated in sporting activities, such as soccer, track and field, and, above all, wrestling. But we also delighted in other non-regulated sports, like climbing palm and coconut trees that did not belong to our families to harvest the fruit. While most villagers did not consider such pilfering of coconuts or bananas a crime (provided we did not harvest more than we could eat on the spot), we were usually spanked for such thievery when caught. But practically everyone in the village was in on the game. Besides, such punishment was always worth it, since for us, tree climbing and gathering the most coconuts or bananas was a matter of great pride.

    I won many of the competitions. I was always hungry and did everything I could to satisfy my Igbo village hunger. In essence, all the village activities taught me how to become a strong, active boy, who would grow up to face strong competition in life. More importantly, my father's ubiquitous eyes were upon me. Would I live the life of a winner or play a second fiddle to others? Certainly, I always wanted to live like a winner like my father in everything I did within and outside the village. If I did not take a top position in my classes, the thought of my father scolding me for playing a second fiddle haunted and forced me to study harder until I regained my top position.

Chapter 3

My Birth and Early Incidents in My Life

I was born August 21, 1945, Nkwo day, on Ngeleoke farm to Stephen Ogbaa Ikpo, and Ogonnaya Ogbaa Ikpo (nee Nwagbara Uche). On that day, my mother had gone to harvest some yams with my father and siblings, Sister Mgbore, Brother Ikpo, and Sister Nwannennaya. Although the expected date of my delivery was near, nobody advised my mother to stay home and rest since there were no doctors or hospitals in the whole of Ihechiowa clan, let alone in my little Umuchiakuma village. There were, therefore, no scheduled check-ups or modern-day precautions to follow. Instead, pregnant women in the village had to rely on the services of traditional village midwives and healers for their medical treatments, including infant deliveries. And the midwives had calculated that I would be born in September, not August. Besides, unless a pregnant woman felt too sick to work, she normally continued to work on the farm alongside other members of her family until the day she gave birth.

Mother arrived early that morning at the field and began digging, cutting, and pulling yams. Under the stress of such strenuous activity, she suddenly felt the kick and tumble of the baby in her womb.

"Mgbore, come quickly. I'm falling down." She collapsed into the dirt.

"What is wrong, Nne?"

"Help me to the nearby bush, for I feel like peeing."

"Do you want me to call my father?"

"No, no, it isn't my time yet."

"Are you okay, Nne?" Mgbore asked again.

"I'm all right. Just help me to the nearby bush as I asked you before."

Sister Mgbore helped my mother to the bush where she began to urinate uncontrollably. Mgbore, afraid, ran to get help from the other women.

"Why did you agree to come farm when you are this heavy?" a woman Nne Egu asked my mother when she arrived.

"I was feeling well this morning. Besides, I didn't think it was my time since my pregnancy is barely eight moons old." Mother winced again and writhed in pain.

"Go back to your farm and bring us loincloths and rags and a gourd of water, and tell your father to come quickly with you," Nne Eke Ngwo ordered my sister. Mgbore ran as fast as she could to fetch my father and the items.

In the meantime, the women rushed my mother to a nearby thatched shed, *agbala ubi*. They asked Father and Mgbore to leave the items and wait outside.

"Push, push, push!" the women ordered my mother repeatedly.

"I'm pushing. I'm pushing. I'm pushing. Stop yelling at me."

"We'll stop yelling if you push harder."

"Where are my husband and our daughter, Mgbore?"

"Why do you ask? You know they cannot see you like this."

"Am I in trouble?"

"Stop talking and push harder," they command.

"*Uwaaa, uwaaa, uwaaa!*" the baby cried as the women pulled it into the world.

"Thank you. Thank you all." Mother's voice was weak, but proud. "Is it a boy or a girl?"

"It's a boy," the women shouted all together.

"I thank God, for His mercies, and you all for your timely help."

They then invited Father and Mgbore into the shed. They quickly cleaned and covered me with my mother's headscarf and wrapped me with her loincloth. Father was pleased, smiling widely as the women held me up to the light. And while he couldn't accompany Mother home with Mgbore, since he and Brother Ikpo and Sister Nwannennaya needed to stay in the field to finish planting, he worked the rest of the day with a smile. Eventually, they all returned home and joined in the jubilation and merriment to welcome the newborn child into the uncertain world.

Immediately after my mother arrived home, exhausted, two renowned village midwives, Nne Mgbokwu Kalu Ulu of Nde Uche compound (a relation of my father's) and Nne Udo Mgbogo of Nde Okwunama, went to work cleansing both my mother and me. They bathed her with hot water, pressed and massaged her belly to force impurities out of her womb, and gave her hot yam pottage and soup prepared with herbs, red pepper, and smoked fish, which she took for about two weeks before reverting to eating her regular meals. They bathed me, cleaned and dried my navel, and applied locally brewed antibiotics on it. Thereafter, they applied a balmy chalk, *nzu*, all over my body and put me beside my mother on a mud bed, where we rested and slept near a hearth. Nna Abaka Uro, an agnate family elder, took my umbilical cord and afterbirth to a spot behind my mother's house where buried them and marked the spot for the planting of a totemic tree, like coconut or *ube*.

Four days after my birth, the village shaman circumcised me. For the Igbo, circumcision is not simply a folk custom; it is a ritual of purification and reunion of the newborn child in the world of the living with the dead-living ancestors in the spirit world. According to this cosmological belief, Igbo people have their being in three ontological worlds—*ili* (the tomb), the spirit world of the dead-living ancestors, *akpa nnwa* (the womb), the world of the unborn and *eluwa* (the earth), the physical world of the living—all of which constitute the Igbo trinity.

The Igbo belief of the cyclic existence of man's reincarnation stems from their understanding of the connection between the soul of man and the world's spirit. Each aspect of spirit participates with the other, but a transition is required to bring the soul back into the material world. Such a transition takes place through the womb, the holy vessel through which we pass into the human world. The process is unified in the umbilical cord—the link between the three ontological worlds—which after being severed, is buried in the ground along with the afterbirth and foreskin, where they stay with the dead-living ancestors until they are reunited with their owner after they die and are themselves buried. Therefore, the Igbo people regard such ground as sacred: Mother Earth protects them in her womb (the tomb) while they await another reincarnation cycle. For the same reason, the Igbo also insist on taking the remains of their loved ones from foreign lands back to Igbo land for burial. Until such a return is made, a person's spirit would be in a state of what a Catholic might call purgatory.

After circumcision, the village elders proceeded with the naming ceremony. Father named me Kalu after Chief Kalu Okoro, alias Kalu Ebumkpii, of Nde Nsioma agnate family in Nde Ngwo compound, who had sponsored Father's marriage to my mother. Father's younger brother, Ebu Ikpo, however, resented the naming, since, by our custom, a man has to name his first son after his father and the second after his brother. If he bore more sons, he names them after his other brothers, or uncles, male in-laws, and friends. Uncle Ebu felt that Father failed to show him brotherly love when he reversed the order of naming. Father later named his fourth son (born by his second wife) after Uncle Ebu. But the wounds between the two never fully healed.

Igbo naming ceremonies are sacred and highly ceremonial. A similar order of naming applies to female babies, but a father can change the normal order to include important incidents in his life, or according to the values he places on his relationships with his mother, sisters, etc.

During the ceremony, elders pour libations on the floor of the house of the head of the agnate family to open the "doors of the spirit world" through which the dead-living ancestors emerge to associate with their kith and kin in the physical world (a similar ritual of libation is performed during burial ceremonies). After the libations, the elder of the family breaks kola nuts and throws the pieces on the ground to further entice the presence of the ancestors, followed by beating talking drums and blowing traditional flutes while the people to engage in various forms of entertainment, particularly dancing and wrestling.

Such ceremonies, inextricably linked to the cultural essence of the Igbo, who consider not only the shrines of their gods and goddesses sacred, but also every piece of the earth, highly inform the social order of the Igbo peoples. For instance, since people are continuously watched by the ever-present unseen but ubiquitous dead-living ancestors and unborn children in the wombs of women, they believe they are never alone in their earthly existence. Consequent to this belief, the Igbo are usually very careful wherever they are and in whatever they do so as not to desecrate the earth, which is the abode of their forebears. As a sign of their reverence to the land, for example, they usually taste dirt or sand from with their tongues to proclaim their innocence if they are accused of any wrongdoing. In other words, as long as people stand or sit on the ground or floor, so long do the dead-living ancestors expect them to tell the truth even if they were not sworn to any human oath to do so. Doing otherwise would defame the dead-living ancestors and earn such persons the ire and punishment of the gods, goddesses, and dead-living ancestors. Therefore, it is not only important for one to be honest and truthful in their dealings with their fellow human beings as a gesture of keeping their own reputation, but as a way to respect their gods, goddesses, and dead-living ancestors and enjoy their blessings and protection.

This long tradition and deeply felt spiritual connection to the Igbo way of life, however, has often clashed sharply with the steady encroachment of the Westernized belief systems. It was just such a clash that would greatly affect my own story and inform my thinking about life in the years to come.

Shortly before I was born, several of my father's relatives were not happy that he was married only to my mother. Although everyone in the village was happy that Mother was "fruitful and multiplying," they wondered why he did not want to marry more wives, like the rest of the men. Everyone knew he had the wherewithal to manage many wives and to raise as many children as they could bear for him. And, besides, a larger family would give him the adequate labor force he needed to make him a richer farmer. Father, however, had resisted their pressures of polygamy and the benefits it would offer because of he had converted to the Catholic faith.

As a young man, Father had been one of several converts to the Catholic Church in Ihechiowa, renouncing the religion of his father, Ikpo Ogbaa, a great leader and advocate of Igbo traditional religion, so honored by the other villagers that they addressed him as *Oke Ikpo* (Ikpo the great). Consequently, after his conversion, the villagers banished him from compound Nde Ngwo to compound Nde Apia, fearing he might contaminate the Igbo religion, *Igo mmuo*, with the practices of Christianity.

In spite of his banishment (and maybe because of it since Father was always a headstrong man) his early religious fervor, piety, and services to the new Catholic church in our village quickly earned him the love and respect of the Catholic priests. So much so, that after his baptism during which he was named Stephen, they enrolled him in school as an adult where he studied up to Standard II in their elementary school system. The priests then appointed him to serve as an interpreter, both at Saint Mary's Catholic Church in a neighboring village, Umuye, and Saint John's in our own village where he remained an active member for many years. But tribal resentment grew between the converts and the Igbo traditionalist since the Catholic priests condemned all Igbo religious practices, including ostracizing twins and their mothers, offering of sacrifices to the gods and goddesses of the village, and the practice of polygamy, branding all Igbo rituals and ceremonies "the work of the devil." In open-air services and catechism sessions, the priests taught young Igbo children to abandon the ways of their forebears and embrace their own religious dispensation. Many resisted. And some, like my father who was now under great pressure from his fellows to take on other wives, found other options.

After marrying his second wife, Orieji, he became enemy number one in the Catholic Church. Soon after hearing of father's decision to follow the Igbo's tradition of polygamy, Father Kelly, the Catholic priest in charge of the parish in our village, approached my father, returning one evening from his yam barn.

"Stephen Ogbaa?"

"Yes, Father Kelly."

Father Kelly slapped my father and yanked the Saint Stephen medallion off his neck.

"*Chei, Nnam Ikpo!* Oh, my father, Ikpo!" Father exclaimed. Then he stooped low, grabbed Father Kelly and hauled him up on his shoulders, then threw him to the ground and began punching him repeatedly. The priest's followers, led by his village assistant, Dennis Ofor, joined the fray, attacking Father from behind and sending him sprawling into the dirt. The melee continued for a time with Father giving as good as he got. By the time other villagers had broken up the brawl, my father, and Father Kelly and his followers were all bloodied, beaten, and exhausted. But Father Kelly never reported the assault to the police, fearing more the disgrace of being beaten by a "native" in the presence of other black men who, until then, had regarded him as a demi-god who would never stoop to the level of primitive black people from Africa.

That following Monday, Father went to the village of Ebem Ohafia and approached Reverend Collins, head of the Church of Scotland Mission (CSM) schools and churches in Afikpo, Edda, Ohafia, and Ihechiowa clans, to declare his interest in becoming a member of CSM in our village (a more liberal and lenient congregation). My father told him why he was leaving the Catholic Church, and Reverend Collins was overjoyed because he knew of my father's reputation as a devout "fisher of men." He could use my father to wage the war for the souls of men raging between the two young church denominations in our district. Reverend Collins drove my father back to the village and introduced him to the elders of the emerging congregation, including Elder Kalu Chiowa and Mr. Thomas Ikpe Okwuagwu. Father found peace in his new religious home, but the conflict between the Igbo cultural mores and the white man's authority was not over. And the effects of such an autocratic ruling-class would bring more heartache and violence to my family—beginning at the very hearth of our home and then infecting all other aspects of our culture to the very heart of the state.

In the home, Father's decision to abandon the Catholic Church created much discord with my mother, whom he had married as a Catholic in Saint Mary's Church. She was disappointed, sad and angry that Father chose to disregard their marriage vows. But just as important to her, she feared for the souls of their future children. Their first three children had been baptized and christened in the church. Father, however, left the Church before I was born, and Mother resented him for taking what she saw as a blessing and opportunity for eternal salvation away from me. She also feared for some certain damnation that might come my way since I never received the early blessings that my other siblings had. A couple of events that followed seem to justify her trepidation.

In my first year, I was a strong, chubby, happy, and handsome baby. Women from other Ihechiowa villages who came to buy and sell farm produce in our Afo Market Square used to beg Mother to let them carry me so they could admire my thick woolly hair, which she always greased with *elu aki* (fried palm kernel cream). Some of them paid her compliments for taking care of such a good-looking baby, and others even gave her some presents for little Kalu.

One evening, however, while sleeping on my mother's bosom, I turned suddenly in her arms and slipped off the bed. My right leg landed in the log fire left smoldering to warm us during the cold harmattan nights. Despite Mother's quick reaction, picking me up from the floor near the hearth, and running to the neighbors for help, I sustained severe burns on my knee and thigh. Mother was beside herself with grief, crying "Nna m ee, nwa m anwuale; nna m ee, nwa m anwuale; nna m ee, nwa m anwuale ... (Oh, my father! My baby is dead. Oh, my father! My baby is dead. Oh, my father! My baby is dead....)." All the while, she beat her chest, crawling and rolling on the ground until she passed out. When she came to, people had already taken me to a native healer, who assured her that I would survive the burns.

When the wounds healed, I had three large scars on my right knee and thigh that looked like the three points of a triangle which grew bigger and bigger as my body continued to develop. When my father, who was away on business, returned home, he beat my mother severely for her carelessness. Although she became sad and angry to the point of almost losing her joy of motherhood, I remained a joy to her in spite of my injuries. Thenceforward, my mother resolved never to let anything bad happen to me again. Thenceforth, she never allowed anyone, not even my siblings, to carry me as they used to. But Father could never shake the belief that she had somehow been negligent out of her own resentment over his decision to leave the Catholic Church. The tension continued to grow between them.

Then, one afternoon when I was eighteen months old, on Afo Market day, when most villagers stayed home watching wrestling matches or wedding ceremonies in the village square, the tax collectors from Arochukwu district headquarters snuck into the village to arrest tax evaders. Since the collectors did not have a list of the tax evaders in our village, every man became a suspect. The only way one could prove his innocence was to produce his tax receipt on the spot. Since Igbo men did not own or carry wallets in which to carry tax receipts or other documents, the collectors arrested and detained them in the town hall while word went out to their wives or children to look for the receipts. And if tax collectors came looking for evaders and did not find them at home, the wives were arrested and detained until the evaders faced their accusers. Then they would either pay their taxes, or face being jailed at the Arochukwu Police Station.

But on this particular day, Mother was attending a wedding ceremony, clutching me at her side when the tax collectors struck, scattering the crowd who scampered in every direction to hide. Mother hurriedly slung me on her back as she ran through the spinning, jostling crowd thronging the square. Suddenly, she lost her grip and I slipped off her back, falling headlong onto the stony ground, cracking the top of my head open like a melon. And there I lay, silent.

"My precious son Kalu is dead! Oh! God, how can I live without *ezi nwam nwoke*, my precious son?" she wailed and then passed out.

At that point, everyone stopped, even the tax collectors.

"*Kuhiri ya nde dibia, kuhiri ya nde dibia*" (Take him to native healers, take him to native healers), someone shouted. Uncle Ebu grabbed me and ran as a group of women surrounded my mother, fanning her with their loincloths until she revived, then they took her to the compound healers who were tending me.

The head injuries were so severe that I bled through the mouth, nose, and ears. I could not eat or drink for twenty-four hours. My mother did not eat or sleep for a week as she watched over me. She only drank water to replenish her dehydrated state. The healers sucked the drying and congealing blood out with *ami*, a local straw, until I began to show signs of life. Then they placed my head over an earthen jar, *nja*, of steaming water and covered it with a blanket several times a day while I cried excessively. They also mixed a plaster made of herbs, chalky clay (*nzu*), and ground tree bark and applied it to the top of my head. And finally, they force-fed me a hard-boiled, strained herb concoction, guzzled into my mouth. At the end of each regimen of medications, I slept. It took a whole week of such heavy treatments to stop the bleeding through my nose and mouth. But my ears continued to bleed for another six months.

When I finally recovered, the shape of my head had changed. Slightly elongated, it now took on the shape of a mango. Additionally, I developed regular ear infections and sinusitis, which continued to bother me and got worse over the years. The healers called sinusitis *ozu isi*, and prescribed herbal treatments, which helped me until I left the village to pursue higher education. Later on, Brother Ikpo consulted a medical doctor in Enugu who recommended that I take felsic tablets whenever I experienced the sinus pressure. I still experience the discomfort and pain today.

Mother continued to rue both accidents until the day she died, her sorrow only heightened by the violent anger Father heaped on her, as if she had purposely wanted to kill his beloved son. It was an unfortunate situation because despite the love they both had for me, their mutual fear of losing me drove them to hate each other for the decisions each had made in choosing to live their lives. Mother resenting and hating Father for never being there to help out since his duties were split between several households, my father believing all the blame rested on my mother's carelessness and stupidity.

I never blamed either of them. Both incidents were just accidental mishaps. However, I can definitely trace the root cause of the second accident to the tax collectors' unwarranted raid of our village—and because of that, I have always carried a certain disdain for tax collectors. Nevertheless, in the end, I became a lively, boisterous, and energetic young man whom the villagers referred to as *nwa kere ndu*, a child determined to live.

Overall, the emotional and psychological wounds on me and on my mother were deeper than the physical scars I saw on my body every day. From the time the unfortunate incidents took place, my mother felt inadequate, largely because of the physical and emotional abuse from my father, who never missed the opportunity to blame her for everything that happened to me as a baby. But the effect of his mistreatment only brought her and me closer. I suckled her breast until I was three. In an effort to help me wean off, she used to press out juice from bitter-leaf (*olugbu*) and rub it on her nipples. But the bitterness bothered me less than the separation from my beloved mother. I needed to be pacified.

My fondness for Mother infuriated my father. And since she was still angry over their broken marriage vows and the second marriage, she did not sleep with him immediately after the culturally proscribed two years of sexual abstinence following childbirths. In addition, she vowed not to get pregnant and bear another child that might suffer a fate similar to mine. And when she eventually did begin sleeping with him again, she never got pregnant again. The villagers started calling me an ill-fated boy: one who brought such bad luck to his mother that she could not conceive and bring other babies into the world. I was often ridiculed and mocked by the mothers of children I'd play with, especially if I accidentally hurt one of them. Each time they called me names, scoffing and jeering at my luck, Mother took me aside to explain that I was not at fault for her inability to bear children. She would only blame herself.

Nevertheless, I was a lonely child in my pre-teen years. My older sister, Nwannennaya, who should have been my traditional babysitter, was taken away from our family when she was about seven years old. Father gave her to his Christian friend, Teacher Okore of Amodu Ututu, to live with his barren wife, Mgbore Teacher Okore, to serve as her domestic hand. Nwannennaya lived in Ututu until age sixteen when my father finally brought her home to get married in our village at the age of seventeen. Her absence from home was another reason for Mother's continued sorrow, since she needed Nwannennaya for herself to help her with farm work. At any rate, Mother and I used to trek to Ututu on Sunday afternoons to visit with Nwannennaya, and she always felt nostalgic each time we took leave of her and returned to our home in Umuchiakuma.

In spite of what she went through, Mother learned to find contentment toward the end of her life. And her children, who always occupied a special place in her heart, count us blessed with such a sweet and kind-hearted mother. To this day, whenever I see her in photos or recall her in my memories, her spirit of compassion never ceases to amaze me. In fact, since her death in April 2004, whenever I meet those who knew my mother and closely interacted with her have continued to tell me what a wonderful, humble, and quiet human being she was. As her son, I gratefully cherished such eloquent and glowing testimonies about my mother who, even though she was orphaned early in life, and despite her tough struggles in life as well as the spousal abuse she experienced and endured from my father, ended her life's journey on such a contented note. I could not have asked for a better blessing from God who gave me the grace to experience her ever-abiding love and care all through the time she lived with me on earth. It is a love that I will always feel deeply in my heart until I cross the River to meet her in the world beyond, where we will never separate again.

Chapter 4

Becoming a Christian

Scottish missionaries and teachers formally introduced me to several aspects of Western civilization at the church and primary school I attended in Umuama Ihechiowa: Christianity, the English language and literature, and European history and culture. Initially, the new Church of Scotland Mission (CSM) converts and the missionaries built a mud-and-thatch church on a piece of land owned by Nde Orugo and Nde Ihuoma compounds, where the houses of Elder Kalu Chiowa and Onyike Okoro now stand. I was in the younger generation of children whose parents took to the ancient building to worship and receive instructions in Bible Studies and basic literacy. The missionaries also set up a similar structure in the neighboring Amammiri village, where a Presbyterian Church stands today, for the same purpose. Over time, those first two churches served as community centers where members conducted their daily devotional morning and evening prayers in their respective villages until their memberships grew larger.

Later on, Christians from the two villages joined together to build a new church and a classroom bloc on a parcel of land donated by landowners from Amammiri, to accommodate worshipers during combined services on Sundays, and their children in the classrooms on weekdays. Upon completion, the missionaries named the school "CSM Primary School, Umuama," and the church, "Church of Scotland Mission, Umuama," respectively. The missionaries combined the first three letters ("umu" and "ama") from each community, Umuchiakuma and Amammiri, the two villages now united in Christ, as a means of preventing people from either of the villages from claiming ownership of the two CSM institutions. Nonetheless, the priests of both churches prayed fervently that the unity and love, which they had forged between the "natives," would survive their departure of the two villages, in particular, and Nigeria in general.

While the Scottish missionaries were busy building a prayer house in our village and later a church and primary school at Umuama,

Catholic missionaries were also exerting great efforts to convert as many people as they could to their own church. They built a mud-and-thatch house of prayer for evening mass on land in Umuchiakuma donated by Nde Abaka. The building also served as a junior primary school. Later, they built a new primary school opposite the CSM church and primary school at Umuama on a piece of land that Umuchiakuma villagers donated to the Catholics in the late 1940s. Hence, they named the school Saint John's Catholic School, Umuchiakuma. Still, the schoolchildren and their parents attended high mass on Sundays at Saint Mary's Catholic Church, Umuye. On those days, one could see Catholics going south from our village to the neighboring Umuye village to attend mass, and the Protestants going north to Umuama CSM Church for their own Sunday worships. In between the two groups were European missionaries (from Scotland and Ireland) in charge of the two church denominations scrambling daily to convert the "benighted" souls of West African (Igbo) men, women, and children with the hope of saving them from burning in hell fire.

The raging "crusades" in my village not only divided the villagers into Christians and heathens, or believers and non-believers, but also into Protestants and Catholics. In addition, the disagreements between the two Christian denominations were so boisterous and hateful that non-Christians called all the Christians "*Nde Uka*"—literally meaning "quarrelsome people"—and referred to Christians then and now as "*Onye uka.*" Consequently, from about 1844, the beginning of missionary activities in Igboland, the sermons from the Bible are interpreted in Igbo as "*Uka Chukwu*" or "*Okwu Chukwu*" ("Word of God"), because the traditional Igbo saw the preachers as people who were always ready to engage others in impassioned debates, with or without invitation. Consequently, in the eyes of the traditional Igbo, Christianity was *not* a peaceful organized religion. And when I became educated enough to study the history of the holy wars between Christians (Crusaders) and Muslims (Jihadists), I, too, had my doubts. Like my forebears, I began to wonder whether either religion, both of which claimed Abraham as the father of their faiths, were indeed as peaceful and superior to our own traditional religions as foreign missionaries portrayed them to our people when they first came to Igboland and other West African countries.

Despite my initial doubts, however, I much admired the beauty and values of Christianity compared to many of the beliefs of my people's traditional religion. For example, the Church accepted and loved the hitherto ostracized twins, and their mothers, seeing them as blessings from the Almighty and Merciful Father in Heaven. Missionary doctors quarantined and treated lepers and sufferers of other deadly diseases like chickenpox and smallpox instead of pushing them into exile as was the traditional custom. And in some areas of Igboland where the *osu* caste system existed, such people were warmly welcomed as God's children into the new churches and given Western education. Indeed, some descendants of these same "outcasts" were in the first batch of students sent overseas to receive higher education. And at the end of their academic programs, many returned to the country and served as highly placed ordained ministers, civil servants, doctors, engineers, lawyers, accountants, and district commissioners. In 1960, when Nigeria attained its political independence from Great Britain, many of the *osu* and their descendants took control of the high positions British officers vacated as they finally left Nigeria. Since then, no Igbo person dares to use the horrible slur *osu* in public. On the contrary, people continually try to curry economic and political favors from them. Over time, as the local villagers have become well educated and embraced the values of Christianity, they have largely done away with their superstitious beliefs. Such superstitions, however, still exist.

As a toddler, my parents took me to prayer meetings in the Umuchiakuma prayer house and later at the CSM church and primary school at Umuama. Hence, unlike some of my friends and fellow students in institutions of higher learning, both at home and abroad, who claim they became Christians when they were teenagers or adults, I was a Christian from birth. Mother got up early every morning, before daily chores, and brought us children to Father's house for family prayers, or took us to the old village prayer house for community prayers. We prayed before and after our meals. Father discussed the differences between our *pagan* neighbors and us, admonishing us never to allow them to overcome us with their evil ways.

But, even in my pre-teen years, I was skeptical of such admonition coming from him because I saw nothing but goodness and love in some of them, especially my adoptive namesake, Chief Kalu Ogoro, who always gave me mouth-watering dried meat and smoked fish to eat, although Father didn't approve. I could never quite believe that a person like Chief Ogoro would be condemned to hell. I saw him feed the poor and hungry. I saw him take care of orphans and widows in our compound. I saw him make peace between villagers who fought themselves over land disputes. I saw him serve as an oral historian of our village. And, I saw him organize our people to carry out many community development projects in our compound, village, and clan. I believe that most of those roles he played could have been done in the name of Christ if he had been a Christian. Could doing all that without converting to Christianity earn him a place in hell? Because of these observations, I continued to struggle with such religious conflicts well into my adult life.

Furthermore, I often wondered whether my father really believed that our non-Christian kith and kin were all evil, as such, or if he was merely regurgitating the admonitions he heard preached from the pulpit of the white missionaries. But I dared not pose that kind of "heretical" question to my father, Stephen Ogbaa Ikpo, the great man of faith, without incurring his furious anger for not "honoring my father and mother, the first law with the promise of long life." Nevertheless, since my education has enabled me to think critically and objectively—I have never shied away from confronting some Western attitudes I found prejudicial to everything African. But I also agree with some Western evaluations of things African, which seem good or bad, acceptable or unacceptable, when they are measured objectively by universal standards.

My Christian education began with learning "The Lord's Prayer," "The Ten Commandments," Psalm 23, and Mathew 5: 3-11 ("The Beatitudes)," all of which I memorized and recited during prayer meetings and Sunday school classes, in addition to taking quizzes and exams designed to test my Biblical Knowledge. My classmates and I studied, from Primary 1 through Standard II, all our courses in the traditional Igbo language, and then in English from Standard III through Standard VI. As we moved through the grade levels, our primary school education became bilingual.

But despite acquiring a wonderful bilingual gift of language, there were times when such an understanding didn't help in translation. For example, for many years, I did not understand the true meaning of the familiar Bible passages Psalm 23, Verse 5: "Thou preparest a table before me in the presence of mine enemies: thou anointest my head with oil; my cup runneth over." Which was translated in Igbo as "*I naedo table n'iru n'anya ndi nakpagbu m: I tewo isi m mmanu; iko m bu inwebiga ihe oke.*" I could not imagine how Jesus, my Lord and Savior, could literally prepare a table in the presence of my enemies without the enemies attacking us violently. I wondered, "Could it be because I did not understand then the omnipotence, omniscience, and omnipresence of Christ?"

But about the year 1968, while we the Igbo people, who became Biafrans, were fighting the Nigeria-Biafra War, I began to apprehend the import and tenor of the phrase as David used it contextually in the Psalms. Even when I had studied English idiomatic expressions and learned that preparing a table meant setting meals on a table, I barely understood that Jesus made it possible for us Biafrans to withstand the brutal assault of our Nigerian enemies, whom Great Britain and the USSR assisted militarily and diplomatically, even though they outnumbered us. Under heavy fire, we managed to survive by eating anything we could find around us. It was also then that I realized how David, the psalmist whom Saul pursued daily, was able to eat anything to survive while simultaneously evading his capture. David's survival meant that he had to be vigilant, to keep his eyes open at all times as Saul pursued him. The idea became clearer to me when I carefully analyzed the Biafran mantra: "The price of liberty is eternal vigilance. Biafrans, be vigilant." This mantra was repeatedly broadcast to us on Radio Biafra. Its Igbo translation, "*Onye ndi iro gbara gburugburu naeche ndu ya nche mgbe dum; umu Biafra, unu araghula ura,*" provided a more poignant metaphor to me, for "*unu araghula ura*"—means literally "you should not sleep," which is to say, "always keep your eyes open." Jesus Christ also admonished his disciples to "watch and pray always" so they could avoid being caught off guard by the enemy or tempter.

> *Holy, holy, holy! Lord God Almighty!*
> *Early in the morning our song shall rise to thee:*
> *Holy, holy, holy! Merciful and mighty,*
> *God in three Persons, blessed Trinity.*

One morning after singing our devotional song, I asked Father: "How can three *persons* count as one *being*? When I tied three sticks together to form a bunch, then untied the bunch and counted them, the number equaled three." I shook my head in disbelief, wondering why the white man, who wrote the song about the blessed Trinity, could fail such a simple problem of addition, for 1+1+1 does not equal one.

Father shook his head and looked at me intently. "The Trinity should be seen as God the Father, God the Son, and God the Holy

Ghost, three persons in one God. But remember, the three persons are not human beings like us; they are ghosts or spirits without physical bodies.

> *Holy, holy, holy! All the saints adore thee,*
> *Casting down their golden crowns around the glassy sea;*
> *Cherubim and seraphim falling down before thee,*
> *Which wert, and art, and evermore shalt be.*

"Okay. So why are the first two *persons* Father and Son—suggesting that they are males?" I said.

"But they call the third person a ghost without suggesting its gender." I was still puzzled because some of the ghosts they told us about in Igbo folktales appear in human form like us. Besides, I wondered privately why God the Father, God the Son, and God the Holy Ghost were all males, living without a female being among them as in human families.

Father moved uneasily in his chair before finally answering. "Although I cannot explain the concept to you in a way you will understand, the Holy Spirit can. If you pray to Him and accept the concept of the 'blessed Trinity' by faith, the answers will come to you, as they did for me after praying, for I, too, expressed similar doubts to the missionaries. Believe the scriptures through faith, they told me, and not by human reasoning." Then he stood and walked over to the wall where he kept his religious books and brought on back to the table and opened it. "This is the image of Jesus they showed me," he pointed. On the page was a picture of Jesus at his baptism. A white dove, symbolizing the Holy Spirit, my father said, perched on His head. "This image helped me to understand how the three parts of God worked as a whole. Jesus as man (God the Son) connected to God the Father through the dove (God the Holy Ghost). All of these parts work together to make the Trinity."

> *Holy, holy, holy! Though the darkness hide thee,*
> *Though the eye of sinful man eye thy glory may not see,*
> *Only thou art holy; there is none beside thee,*
> *Perfect in power, in love, and purity.*

Still not persuaded by his explanation, I nevertheless was willing to give this illogical math a second chance since in our traditional Igbo folktales ghosts were evil beings that haunted people's homes.

Whereas Christians represented "the ghost" as a good spirit, I yearned to be free of the terrors that constantly haunted me about evil spirits visiting suffering and terror upon me. Therefore, the Christian ghost was a convenient tale for my childhood imagination. In my adult years, I came to understand that the differences in religious beliefs and practices between the White Christians and Black Traditionalists were created by the Christian missionaries as a way to make their culture appear superior to ours. Indeed, the white missionaries used every cunning device at their disposal to convince our villagers that their traditional religious culture was inferior, inculcating and reinforcing such ideas during Sunday school and in the classrooms. We had to accept them unquestionably, or endure their punishments, both physical and mental.

Holy, holy, holy! Lord God Almighty!
All thy works shall praise thy Name in earth, and sky, and sea;
Holy, holy, holy! Merciful and mighty,
God in three Persons, blessed Trinity.

I often wondered where at the seeming lack of mercy after watching another student suffering under the whip or berated by the white men of the cloth. At those times, I pictured the white dove feathers bloodied and stained, yearning to escape the sorrow of the earth.

On the other hand, I loved to hear that Jesus loved me, a small, weak, child and that he, my Lord and Savior, was strong enough to protect me from all harm and danger, because I belonged to him. The miracles and healings he performed on other people as recorded in the Bible confirmed his powerful love and mercy.

Jesus loves me! this I know, For the bible tells me so;
Little ones to Him belong, They are weak but He is strong.

Yes, Jesus loves me! Yes, Jesus loves me!
Yes, Jesus loves me! The bible tells me so.

Jesus loves me! He who died, Heaven's gate to open wide;
He will wash away my sin, Let His little child come in.

Jesus, take this heart of mine, Make it pure and wholly thine;
On the cross you died for me, I will try to live for thee.

I believed salvation awaited me after death. But I was too young to die, even if it did mean that I would go to heaven through the gate, which Jesus' death opened wide for me and everyone else, whose sins his blood washed away. The story of the little boys—between ages one and four—whom King Herod killed after the Magi told him that they were looking for the newborn Jesus only deepened my fear. Herod had hoped that the next king would come from his lineage. But when the Magi did not come back to tell him where they found Jesus, he carried out the mass killing of babies under four years old.

I was baffled, frightened, wondering why God, the father of Jesus, the lover of little ones—the omnipotent, omnipresent, and omnipresent God—would not prevent the destruction of those children. I wondered, as I grew a little older, however, if maybe Jesus had not yet attained his Christhood to prevent the murders; or if, maybe, the Trinity considered the world too sinful for those little babies to live in; or maybe, after death, life in heaven was more lovely and better for them. Whatever the case might have been, I did not want to die and go to heaven, leaving my mother behind here on earth. I asked myself, "Who would take care of her in my absence if I died young?" To date, I am scared every time I hear of any mass killings of children, like the murders that fellow Nigerians committed against Igbo children during the Northern riots, and later in Biafra, where Nigerian military authorities used starvation as a "legitimate weapon" of war during the Nigeria-Biafra War. At the time, I considered the genocidal massacre of the Igbo in Nigeria as comparable to those innocent children that King Herod murdered en masse. Any such mass killings of children, no matter who they are and in what parts of the world they occur, are unacceptable. And despite my fears and doubts, I have continued my Christian journey and quest, always holding to the knowledge that Jesus loves me. My faith and belief in the story of his precious blood being shed on the Cross of Calvary for me, and all people, continues to inspire me as I walk through this world of evil, carried by His lesson of brotherly love.

Part Two

The Educational Matches

Chapter 5

The Primary School Years

The harmattan winds blew hard that morning shaking the thatched roof like a piano keyboard exposing us to the chill outside. Sand and debris scoured the outer walls, biting and nipping at the structure like a thousand termites as I got up and stoked the log fire on the hearth while Mother slept. She had gotten used to the harsh harmattan seasons, but I was still a child, not yet acclimated. As I warmed myself at the hearth, a hard knock came at the door. It was my brother. He appeared anxious.

"Good morning Brother Ikpo. It appears you don't feel the cold outside," I said.

"Good morning Brother Kalu," he said. "I have brought you some good news from Father. You will start school today; so get ready, and I'll take you there."

"Does Mother know about this?" I asked, surprised by this sudden decision.

"I don't know. But father asked me to tell you. They must have discussed it."

"Must I go with you this cold morning or can I wait until the day gets a little warmer?"

"Yes, you have to start this Monday morning. So, go take a bath quickly, eat your breakfast, and come to Father's house to change into the school uniform he bought for you."

"Did father buy me a new uniform, or am I going to wear one of your old ones?"

"Just get ready and come and see what it is," Brother Ikpo said. Then he turned to leave.

I quickly woke Mother to prepare breakfast. "Good morning Nne. Brother Ikpo brought me some good news from Father. He said that I was going to start school today. Did you and Father discuss this?"

"Good morning, Kalu." She rubbed her eyes and shook her head. "No, your father did not tell me. But I'm happy that he is sending you to school, even though I think you might be too young to start school." She sounded worried, and much less enthusiastic than I.

"Is that the reason Father did not discuss it with you? Do you not want me to go to school?"

"Yes, I want you to go." She nodded. "But I worry that the older boys will beat you up."

"No, they won't! If they try to beat me, I'll scratch and bite them. And then I'll run to Brother Ikpo to protect me. When they see him, they will not fight me."

"Will you be studying in the same classroom with him?" Mother asked.

"I don't know, but I hope so."

"Very well, then." She patted my shoulder. "Now let me help you get ready so you won't be late."

Although I wanted to attend school, the cold morning kept me from quickly getting ready. I wanted to spend a little more time warming my hands over the glowing hearth. Finally, Brother Ikpo dragged me out into the winds to school. Father had ordered it, and so it would be. We stopped in front of a big on the house school compound where I'd register. Brother Ikpo pointed to a big man coming toward us and whispered. "When we meet that man, you should say to him 'Good morning, sir.'"

I nodded, and we moved forward.

"Good morning, saa," I said as we approached.

"Good morning, son. And how are you today?"

"I am well, saa. But I am not your son."

"Oh? Whose son are you?"

"I am Kalu *nwa* Ogbaa."

"I know your father. He is my good friend."

"But I've never before met you. What's your name, saa?"

"I am Teacher Okore, the headmaster of this school. Tell your father that I send greetings to him when you get home."

My boldness in front of the Headmaster embarrassed Brother Ikpo. As soon as the Headmaster turned to leave, Brother Ikpo grabbed my lapel and whisked me quickly away to the Infant 1 classroom for registration. I was barely four years old. My encounter with Headmaster Okore of Uburu Ihe marked the beginning of my educational experience at the CSM Primary School, Umuama.

At that time, the school did not admit the children according to age—nobody knew precisely how old they were anyway since most of the parents were functional illiterates who did not keep records of their children's birthdays. Moreover, unlike the Catholics, Scottish missionaries did not emphasize infant baptism in their churches, which would have enabled schoolteachers to obtain records of the births of their prospective pupils from their baptismal certificates. In the absence of such records, the teachers devised another means of ensuring that the children were old enough to begin their primary school education.

"Come here son. What's your name?" Teacher Anyunku asked.

"My name is Kalu."

"What's your father's name?"

"His name is Ogbaa, Sitivin Ogbaa."

"Can you place your right arm over your head and touch your left ear with your fingers? He took my right arm to place it across my head. I snatched my arm away, ran to Brother Ikpo, and hid behind him.

"No, no; go back! He won't hurt you. I'll be waiting for you here," Brother Ikpo yelled, exasperated.

"Why does he want me to put my arm across my head and touch my ear?"

"Because he wants to know how old you are before he admits you into his class."

Apparently, children who were able to follow these simple directions were big enough to register. So, I walked back to the teacher and attempted to do as he asked. But I could not reach. No matter how hard I tried, my hand would not touch my ear. The teacher asked Brother Ikpo to take me to his class because he could not leave the school then to take me home. Disappointed, and feeling that I'd failed my family, I followed Brother Ikpo to his class. At the end of the day, however, Teacher Anyunku said that I had behaved well enough, paying close attention to the classroom activities, and that he would talk to the headmaster and see if I might still qualify to return.

The next day, Brother Ikpo and I arrived early to the school, and Teacher Anyunku informed me that I would be allowed to stay on a trial basis. Once again, I paid close attention to all the classroom activities, and at the end of the day, I was officially admitted as his pupil. I was happy and proud, and loved going to school each day with Brother Ikpo, who became my babysitter and friend in the absence of my parents and two sisters.

I know now that the teachers allowed me to stay in school that first day to avoid offending my father because he was a powerful member of the Parent-Teacher Association. I also believe that my father pushed me to attend school so early because my immediate elder sister, Nwannennaya, who should have been my babysitter at home, lived in Amodu Ututu and therefore could not attend to me. The school and my brother, therefore, became my babysitters.

In the evenings after school, Brother Ikpo and my father taught me how to read and write above my grade level to ensure that I'd pass all exams. By the end of the school year, my test scores were high enough that they promoted me to Standard I, skipping me over Infant II. In essence, I began early to study rigorously and seriously in all my primary school classes. From January 1, 1949 through December 10, 1957, when I passed the Eastern Nigeria Regional Standard VI Examination, I studied with a sense of competitive energy that I could only compare to my zeal for wrestling. Indeed, I was the first pupil to pass the Standard VI Examination with distinction from the CSM Primary School, Umuama Ihe. But at the time, there I was only a handful of students who even graduated. Enrollment in each of our schools ran between ten and fifteen students per class. Enrollments figures in the upper classes—Standards III and IV—were even lower.

Three factors contributed to the low enrollment rates. First was the establishment of two primary schools in the same area—a CSM school and an RCM school—which competed for students from two relatively small neighboring villages with a combined population of about 5,000 inhabitants. Second was the lack of importance villagers placed on the idea of a Western education. As a result, many parents did not encourage their children to attend, nor lend support to them if they expressed a desire for scholarly pursuits. As a subsistence farming community, many parents preferred to use their children as laborers to cultivate food crops. In addition, some parents sent their older children to live with relatives who ran trading businesses in Eastern Nigerian towns. Finally, in those days students paid school tuition and fees right from Infant 1 through Standard IV. While some were able to pay theirs in full, early in January of each year, others only registered with a promise to pay later in the term, perhaps after their parents sold some of their farm produce. Students who did not eventually pay were released. That was why Brother Ikpo, who paid his own fees, was the only student left to study in Standard IV in 1950.

Consequently, as the only student registered for his level, the headmaster decided to place Ikpo students in Standard III, receiving separate assignments in English, Arithmetic, and History, but studying Bible, Natural Science, and General Studies with Standard III students. Brother Ikpo found the arrangement discouraging, singled out, as he was, to repeat a class he had already passed. He was especially disappointed when he scored lower than some of his Standard III classmates. Yet, Ikpo persevered and graduated to Standard V in 1950, transferring to Eleoha CSM Primary School at Achara Ihe.

Such disruptions were not uncommon. Inadequate funding interrupted our studies every semester because the school fees that the few students paid were not enough to cover teachers' salaries. And since many of the pupils who registered were unable to pay registration fees on opening day, it was common for them to miss several days of study while their parents tried to arrange payments with the schools. Early one Monday morning, I was one of those.

Driven out of our classrooms, four of us, Eni *nwa* Udo, Acha Ndu, Okore Ikpo and I, decided to team up and as a group to ask our parents for the school fees. We had just left the school compound when Eni saw Father coming our way. He nudged and pointed.

"Kalu. Look who's coming down. Today must be your lucky day."

I was excited and proud to be the first. He smiled as I approached.

"Kalu. Why are you and the other boys not in class?"

"Eni, Acha, Okore and I were sent out today to collect the school fees from our parents, Father." I smiled and looked around at the others. "And I am the first, and the luckiest since you are here."

"And you wanted me to give you the fees here and now?" Father angrily drew me to his side.

"Yes sir."

"*Tawam, tawam!*" He whacked me left and right on my head.

I ducked and fell to the ground.

"Get up immediately and run as fast as you can back to school," he thundered.

I staggered up, shock and dismayed, then turned and sprinted away. However, instead of running to the school compound, I ran past it and into the forest behind a nearby farm.

"Come back here, you fool." Father's voice boomed behind me. "Is that the direction of the school?"

But I kept running, faster and faster until my leg got weary, my breath ragged. I finally took cover behind some shrubs where Chief Eke Ogbonnaya's house now stands. Exhausted and gasping for breath,

I huddled, shivering in the shrub, listening for Father. Suddenly, I felt the grip of his large hand on my shoulder as he pounced, dragging me from the bushes.

"*Tawam, tawam!*" He slapped me twice. "Did you think you could hide from me?" he asked.

"No, sir," I whimpered. "I'm sorry, sir. Please, Father. Please forgive me. Please, please let me go."

"Forgive you? No, I won't forgive a disobedient child like you. I will take you first to school to receive your punishment and then, when you come home after school, we'll talk."

I knew what he meant. You talk as much with your hand as your tongue, I thought as he dragged me along the road back to the compound. When he finally pushed me inside the classroom, Teacher Ogbaga from Ohafia and my classmates were startled.

"*Look a'm. Look a'm, dis boy. He no wan' com' to school as I tell a'm to do. Instead, he de run away. Look a'm. Look a'm. Look a'm …*" Father stuttered in Pidgin English as he fumed and pointed.

The entire class burst into laughter.

"Order!" yelled Teacher Ogbaga.

There was dead silence in the room. The other students settled back down into their seats and look to the front of the room. Then he turned to Father.

"Thank you, sir, for bringing him to me. I will deal with him later." He turned to me and pointed. "Now back to your seat!"

Father shot one last angry look my way before storming out of the classroom. Out the window, I could see him striding across the compound toward the headmaster's office. I was scared.

I sat absent minded through the remaining classes of the day wondering what further punishment I would suffer at the hands of my father. But when I returned home that evening, he acknowledged neither my presence nor my greetings. Neither did he punish me. And as time wore on without any other mention of the incident, I began to wonder what had transpired between him and the headmaster that day. Had my father been coming to pay my fees when I rudely accosted him on that fateful morning? Did he pay my school fees to the headmaster after dragging me disgracefully to my classroom? Did he tell the headmaster to never, ever again send his boy to collect in his name? Whatever the answer, I was glad that they never drove me out of school again to collect fees from my father. Nevertheless, I was teased and taunted by some of my schoolmates who mimicked Father's angry words back to me from time to time: "*Look a'm; look a'm. Dis boy. He no wan' com' to school ...*" They eventually stopped, however, once my friends, including Ogbonnaya Obi, and I fought them for my honor, beating them roundly into silence. Besides, I had my best revenge each time I achieved the highest scores on our quizzes and exams.

Teachers and students alike always respected my academic accomplishments, coming in at the top of my classes every term of my studies at Umuama. I worked hard to achieve the successes, encouraged and motivated by my desire to please and honor my father, who spent many hours, along with Brother Ikpo, helping me with homework and studies. They served as my audience whenever I read aloud assigned passages from Igbo and English primers. They corrected me when I made mistakes and applauded me when I read the passages correctly. They listened to me as I chanted the multiplication and addition tables printed on the back covers of my exercise books. They reviewed my class assignments the teachers marked with red chalk on my slate, or with red ink in my exercise books. If I scored 100% on a test, Father applauded, long and loud. If I scored lower, he threatened to withdraw me from school and put me to work with him on his farms. The choice was clear: work harder on my class assignments and stay in school. To fail would mean working long hours with my parents during the tropical wet seasons with no chance to change my future. I'd be stuck in the Igbo village forever. Brother Ikpo, who was as committed to doing his homework assignments as I, made sure I was prepared for every test.

 At the end of each term (like a marking period in American grade school system), parents, teachers, and pupils gathered in the school's assembly hall on the last day of classes to hear the headmaster read aloud the names of the first, second, and third highest scores in each class. The program opened with a reading from the Bible, a short prayer, and the singing of a song from an Igbo hymnbook. Then everyone sat down and anxiously awaited the announcements. The headmaster read the names of the three highest achievers in each class, beginning from the lowest and moving to the highest. The students would stand for recognition while the parents in the audience would cheer and clap. As rewards, the third highest achiever received three handclaps and one broom bundle, the second received six handclaps and two broom bundles, and the first received nine loudest handclaps and three broom bundles, as rewards.

My first year's academic honors were twofold: one, for ranking highest in Infant One class, and, two, for receiving double promotion from Infant I to Standard I. When Father realized how much I had accomplished, he could not contain his joy. He immediately jumped out of his seat and ran to the stage, pleasing me with a big hug. After the ceremony, he took me to the village square and bought me some fried deer meat from "Bar David Oke," which became a ritual he repeated almost every term until I graduated Standard VI. Following my first year's achievements, every teacher desired to have me in his or her class so they could get a share of the honor from playing a part in my intellectual harvest, as it were.

That was how I came to live with Teacher Arunsi Ikoro, our school choirmaster. Parents and pupils loved him for being such a handsome, light-skinned, slender-bodied, happy gentleman. Every time he conducted the choir, choristers imagined themselves singing in the company of the Seraphim, who surround the heavenly throne of God, always singing "Holy, holy, holy ..." to the blessed Trinity, the song they memorized and performed during choir competitions between the three CSM primary schools from Umuama, Achara, and Obinto in Ihe clan.

I am not sure if Teacher Ikoro chose me over my peers for my voice or for my academic performance in the classroom, or both. Nevertheless, he approached my father to ask if he could take me on as his houseboy, in return for which he promised to train my voice, and to teach me privately after school so I could excel academically. Father was honored to be the only parent whose son the famous choirmaster chose to take on. I did not know at the time that Father had also sent Brother Ikpo to study with a teacher from Ututu when I was a baby. It was father's way to ensuring his sons would excel in their scholarly careers. But there was a bigger price to pay than what he accounted.

My mother, as expected, was vehemently opposed to the idea, even though the new school was less than one mile away. She, however, would not express her opposition openly to my father because she knew that he would interpret it as her desire to prevent their son from achieving a better socio-academic advantage. I knew that was not the case. Because of the special bond between us, I read the sorrow in her eyes as a desperate fear of separation. She'd already lost her second daughter, Nwannennaya, who was taken from her without her consent some time before to live with the barren wife of my father's friend in Ututu. Father had also sent Brother Ikpo to live with Teacher Ogbonnaya Uyo of Ututu in 1946 and 1947 without her consent. Now he was sending Kalu away, her favorite little beauty. She stared vacantly down the street and listened meekly, tears welling up, as Father gave his consent to Teacher Ikoro.

When Mother later told me the story of her losses at the hand of Father, I wondered how my father was unable to imagine the impact of what he was doing to my mother, and our family cohesion. Was he punishing her for a crime he suspected she secretly committed against him? If so, why couldn't he tell her directly about it? Mother, just as confused, said she never knew the reason. Consequently, she was often depressed, living in a state deep anguished brooding. And she appeared sadder than at any other time I had known her. So much so that I, too, became depressed, holding in a hatred for my father that was only suppressed by a deeper fear of his authority and stature. I had to love him unconditionally, and he took it for granted that all was well within his family. But not all was well.

Before I left for my new home, I wanted to try to clear the air with Mother. So the evening before my departure, we talked.

"How can I cope without you, Kalu? Your sister Nwannannaya is living at Ututu, and your brother Ikpo is studying in Calabar."

"Don't cry, Nne. Even though I'll not be with you under the same roof as I used to every day, I will always love and pray for you daily," I said.

"No, life will not be the same again for both of us after you are gone." Her voice cracked.

"I know that, Nne, but you can visit me on Sundays after church services and we'll see each other every Afo Market day in the village whenever I come to buy groceries for my master."

Mother heaved a sigh of relief, flashed her beautiful white teeth, and hugged me tightly. She knew I was not going to be away from her long. She also knew that I kept promises I made to her in the past. We knelt down and prayed God to protect each of us wherever we might be. I believed that God would hear the prayer and protect her for my sake.

"Could this departure from home be the first stage of my formal separation from my mother's lovely care and protection?" I wondered. I hesitated a little bit before I ran to hug her.

"Please, go. I'll be alright." Her voice trembled as she wiped a tear from her eyes.

While I was happy to live with the teacher, I felt sick and sad leaving behind my dear mother emotionally wrecked and lonesome at home. Tears rolled down my cheeks as I pondered what the outcome of my new adventure in life would be. After taking a few steps away toward the door, I turned to steal a final view of my unhappy Mother. "Only time will tell," I mused silently to myself. Then I moved on in my father's company to Teacher Ikoro, who was anxiously awaiting our arrival in the school compound.

Teacher Ikoro was one of the seven teachers who taught at Umuama. Six of them, including the headmaster, taught regular subjects, while the seventh taught students handcrafting: making brooms, mats, baskets, nets, and ceiling sheets with palm fronds and bristles and special canes, or learning to carve simple wooden ornaments out of soft wood we collected locally from nearby forests.

The teachers' quarters were comprised of three large fenced-in, double-bedrooms and one single-bedroom mud-and-thatch house with kitchens, pit latrines, and urinals. In the three large backyards, teachers grew vegetables, yams, and other tuberous plants like cocoyam and *ona*. Teacher Ikoro occupied the only one-bedroom house, whose backyard was very close to the road, Umuchiakuma villagers used to travel to and from their farms. The headmaster occupied one of the double-bedroom houses, whose backyard was next to the Amammiri to Arochukwu. Four other teachers and their houseboys occupied the remaining two double-bedroom houses. The handwork teacher lived in Amammiri, which was less than one mile away from the school.

When Father and I arrived, Teacher Ikoro met us outside.

"Welcome, sir. How are you today?"

"I am well, thank you," Father replied.

"And how are you today, Kalu?"

"I am well, sir. Thank you."

"But you look sad. Is anything wrong?"

"No, sir; I'm alright." I averted my eyes looking down at the floor.

"Well, here is Kalu," Father said. "Please, take good care of him as you promised."

"Thank you, sir, for bringing him to me. I will take very good care of him."

Father shook hands with the teacher and me, and then left me to his care as my master. As soon as Father left, Teacher Ikoro took me to his bedroom and showed me where I should hang my schoolbag and uniform. He then gave me a new straw mat and pillow. I would sleep in the parlor, he said. Then he explained my daily chores: doing the dishes, sweeping and dusting the rooms, and warming the stew and soup pots in the mornings, afternoons, and evenings, and carefully putting them away in the kitchen chop box, to be kept locked securely at all times. Lastly, he showed me how to clean the hurricane lamp and globe. After his demonstration, he asked me to clean the lamp while he watched. I was to light the lamp at 6:30 p.m. every day, but he would be the one to put it out at night, after he had graded his students' written assignments and prepared for his next day's classes. Over the next few days, I observed him cook the meals, after which he allowed me to practice cooking under his supervision until I learned to cook them on my own.

Once I demonstrated my ability to cook, he left the house chores for me to do alone. He neither helped me to do my homework assignments, nor trained my voice so that I could sing better as he promised to my father. In addition, he fed me only cassava *foofoo* (pounded cassava dough) three times a day. Rarely did he allow me to share the yam pottage he asked me to prepare for him. I felt deprived, considering that my father gave us the yams for the pottage, and my mother gave us the *garri* and cassava to prepare the *foofoo*. Over the next two years I lived with Teacher Ikoro, I never had the company of the other houseboys my age except during brief recesses from class, unlike other teachers' houseboys who lived in the double-bedroom houses and enjoyed the companionship of their fellow houseboys.

The only time I was in their company was when we walked together to fetch water from Iyi Amammiri. On those occasions, we shared our experiences of living with our masters. I was unhappy indeed, when the other boys told me about all the new clothes their masters had given to them. I, on the other hand, had been given only one old, torn sleeveless shirt in the two years I lived with my master. The more I thought about my condition, the more depressed and careless I became with my daily chores.

One day while cleaning the hurricane lamp, I accidentally broke the globe. When I reported the accident to my master, he whipped me on my palms, locked me out of the house, and ordered me to weed the grasses on our backyard garden. Moreover, he threatened that unless I removed all the grass from the entire garden, he would not let me into the house to drink or eat anything. He stayed home waiting for me to either come to the house and beg for food or announce that I had finished the task he had given me. He figured that I could not leave the house without passing through the front door.

I worked and worked for hours until I got too tired and hungry to continue. Finally, I broke a hole in the fence and ran home to my mother. She did not question me as to what had forced me to come home so unexpectedly. Instead, she saw I was tired and hungry, so she quickly prepared and served me my favorite yam pottage, which I devoured like a hungry dog. Then she wondered at my loss of weight, which she assumed had been a result of my growing taller. But after the meal, I told her about my experiences in my master's house and she realized that hunger had caused my apparent loss of weight. Immediately, Mother grew angry and, for the first time in her married life, she was ready to confront Father for exposing her youngest child to the cruel treatment of Teacher Ikoro. I cried and begged her not to confront him. I told her that instead of doing so herself, I would go to my father and tell him why I ran away home from my master.

When I met my father and told him what had happened in Teacher Ikoro's house, he looked into my sorrowful eyes, saw my grief, and gently drew me to his bosom.

"Don't cry. It's okay my dear son."

I felt better. Later on, he confessed that he was surprised that I never wore any clothes other than those he bought for me all those many months ago. Like my mother, he had mistaken my loss of weight for a growth spurt. After we talked, he sent me away and I happily ran to tell my mother what transpired between Father and me.

"You look happy, Kalu. What did your father say to you?"

"Oh, I told him all about my ordeal at my master's house," I said.

"Was that all?"

"No. He hugged me lovingly and said 'Don't cry.' All will be well, my dear son.'"

Mother was overjoyed, and happier still that I was able to persuade my father to allow me stay home with her. She would never know the irony of the story: Father had once admonished me to tell him the truth always, for Jesus said: "Ye shall know the truth and the truth shall set you free." Apparently persuaded by the veracity of my story, my father had to set me free from the house bondage.

The following day, Teacher Ikoro came to apologize to my parents for what he had done, and to ask if I could go back to live with him again. My father told him that while he accepted his apology, Kalu was not going to live with him or any other teacher again, no matter the benefits I could lose for not living with any of them. After his unsuccessful mission, Teacher Ikoro left our home and returned to his house in the school compound. He returned my school bag and uniform to me through a boy who was living with another teacher in the school. Not long after, the same boy who returned my belongings also left his master and made complaints of maltreatment to his parents, which were similar to those I made against my master.

The year, 1955, was pivotal in my personal and academic life, just as it was for our Umuama CSM Primary School. In late December 1954, the Board of Education at Arochukwu proposed to grant our school and the neighboring Saint John's RCM School, Umuchiakuma, permission to offer classes up to Standard V on a trial basis. Toward the end of 1955, the board would conduct competitive exams for students in both schools to determine which of them got permission to offer classes up to Standard VI, beginning in January 1956. I had just passed Standard IV in December 1954, and was wondering whether I should attend Eleoha Ihe CSM Primary School at Achara or Ihe Central School at Obinto the following month, unaware that the government had made the proposal to both school authorities. My father called me to his house to discuss which school I would prefer to attend. When I arrived, he began the discussion with an announcement.

"Kalu *nwa m*, my son. The government has just granted your school permission to offer classes up to Standard Five, beginning from January 1955. Would you want to continue your education at Umuama or transfer to either Eleoha Ihe, as Brother Ikpo did, or to Ihe Central as Uko Ekpesu and others did?" he asked.

"No, no. I want to continue at Umuama," I answered.

"Well then, you will continue at Umuama but note well that there will be a lot of competition in your new class," he cautioned.

"Why? Will it be more than what I've already faced in the past? You don't have to worry about that, for I will work hard, as always, to beat the other students in our exams," I assured him.

"Yes. I believe you'll do well in your school. I'm just thinking of how well you'll do in the competitive exams that the government will conduct between your school and Saint John's."

"Oh, that one? Don't worry about it! I'll beat any of them any day and in any subjects they'll test us. Let them bring it on."

"Oh, *Ikenga nna ya*, I believe you. But don't be too confident. Just make sure you study as hard as you used to, and I know you'll do well and make me proud as usual."

Father called me *Ikenga nna ya*, "His father's strength," whenever I did anything that pleased him or made him proud. Then he shook hands with me. "Go tell your mother about your decision. We'll buy all the school supplies you'll need before the school starts in January."

Father didn't know that students from both schools had already been having informal competitions in sports and academic exercises in which we, the Scottish pupils, beat the Catholics. Now that representatives of the Board of Education were going to conduct such competitions, I was going to work even harder to beat my worthy opponents again. When I told Mother about the conversation with Father, she was overjoyed that I would continue my education in our village for another year before moving on to pursue my academic dreams beyond our village and clan.

When the school reopened in January 1955, they gave us a new headmaster, Mr. Eleke Nwankwo, and Mr. Okwaraeke Kalu as the Standard V teacher. Both of them came from Ututu, and they both liked my academic prowess and my vivacious personality. Mr. Nwankwo brought with him new developmental plans for the school, which included making it compulsory for all male students to live in the school dormitory so he and his staff could supervise our academic work closely. We stayed in dormitories from Sunday evening through Friday afternoon, returning home on Saturdays to wash our clothes, assist our parents with their farm work, and collect groceries. We'd attend church services from home between 8:00 a.m. to 12:00 p.m. and return back to the dormitory before 6:00 p.m.

Our dormitory life was set up as a boot camp, but it taught us good academic and behavioral discipline: We had to wake up at 5:00 a.m., run and exercise for fifteen minutes, take a morning bath, quickly eat our breakfast, dress up and get ready for inspection before marching to the school's assembly ground for morning inspection. If they found anyone's bed not made, or not putting away their food and utensils in their chop boxes properly and storing them neatly under his bed, they either flogged him on the buttock, or gave him a good portion of a grassy field to cut and rake after school. During the inspection, we had to show our well-manicured finger and foot nails, well-brushed teeth, and well-trimmed and combed hair to the teacher in charge of the dormitory inspection. If a student did not show evidence of excellent hygienic practices, they punished him severely for not remembering to put into practice the motto, "Cleanliness is next to Godliness."

I carried out all my dormitory activities with diligence because of the prior training I received while living with Teacher Ikoro. Occasionally, my dormitory mates, who were attracted to the smell of my cooking, begged me to give them portions of my meals. But I only granted the requests of those who were willing to contribute to the condiments I needed to do the cooking.

In addition to the private dormitory activities, we took part in morning prayers and inspection that students from other classes went through every day. After our fifteen-minute outdoor morning exercises on the soccer field, we began study in the classrooms until 2:00 p.m., when classes ended. Then we headed back to the dormitory to eat lunch and observe a one-hour siesta, played soccer and other sports from 3:30 p.m. to 5:30 p.m., and ate dinner from 6:00 p.m. to 6:30 p.m. Thereafter, we attended night classes from 6:30 p.m. to 9:00 p.m., and finally went to bed at 9:15 p.m. in the dormitory, after night prayers.

Since I always stayed well ahead of the others in my academic studies, the headmaster gave me some additional responsibilities. He created a small garden for the school, which contained a rain gage, a thermometer, and a weathercock for measuring average daily temperatures, directions of the wind, daily amount of rainfalls, and for recording the days when we had sunshine or rainfall each week. My task was to take the measurements and records in all those areas, and report them to the headmaster on Monday mornings. In addition, I collected attendance registers from all class teachers on Fridays and checked to ensure the records of the students' attendance or non-attendance as presented to the headmaster were accurate. If they were not, I would point the mistakes out to him, and he, in turn, would deal privately with the teachers who made the mistakes. He rewarded me by exempting me from doing the weekly maintenance duties, such as working on the school gardens, scrubbing teachers' houses with charcoal, or mending the school fences.

The combination of rigorous life we led in the dormitory, the tough classroom exercises we did by day, the extra night classes we attended by night, and the close relationship I had with the headmaster prepared me for the regular class tests and exams we took in our school. They also helped me to excel in the competitive exams the Board of Education in Arochukwu conducted for our two village schools. Consequently, when we took the exams in November 1955, I was the only student from both schools who scored 100% in all three areas of the exams: Arithmetic, English, and General Knowledge. Students from our school, the CSM Primary School, took the first and second positions in order of merit, but the highest scorer from Saint John's Catholic School, took a distant third position. The Board's representative, Mr. Okoro (who was a member of the CSM in Arochukwu), was so pleased at the results that he revealed the results privately to our headmaster before releasing them officially.

When the headmaster announced the results to the rest of our teachers, they were extremely happy but not surprised because of my consistent high performance in all the exams I took in our school. What was surprising, though, was that I beat everybody in both schools in a test that someone, who came from outside the two schools, set and graded. Moreover, because I had maintained the first position in our internal Standard V promotion exams as well, I had no doubt that the Board was going to grant our school the permission to establish the first Standard VI class in the two village schools. Beginning from that happy month of November 1955, I prepared myself mentally and psychologically for the forthcoming year of my studies at Umuama.

However, two incidents that year eventually turned my joy into sorrow. First, the Board of Education granted the approval to establish the Standard VI class to Saint John's instead of my beloved Umuama CSM Primary School, in spite of my high performance. The Board purportedly based their decision on the recommendation their representative, Mr. Okoro, whose daughter served as Standard IV class teacher in our school in 1955 At that time, none of us understood why he would not want his daughter's school to be the first to receive approval to run a Standard VI program, which puzzled all of us. Nevertheless, the Board promised that our school would start its own Standard VI program a year after Saint John's. When the news broke, both parents and students were devastated. Nobody gave us a persuasive reason why our school lost the award to St John's, whose students performed less than we did in the competitive exams. Yet, although some students knew beforehand that Mr. Okoro's daughter and our headmaster were friends, none of us had any inkling that their relationship had something to do with our unfortunate situation until after they announced the Board's recommendations. It later dawned on us that Mr. Okoro did that to punish Mr. Nwankwo for committing fornication with his daughter and refusing to marry her. Mr. Okoro felt that Mr. Nwankwo would have taken credit for bringing our school the Standard VI program if it was granted to our school. He could not do that when the approval was given to Saint John's.

Under the circumstance, however, the headmaster gave each Standard V student the opportunity to either repeat the class in 1956 and then move to Standard VI in 1957 or transfer to Achara or Obinto to do Standard VI in 1956. Some students took the latter option, but my father insisted that I stay back and repeat Standard V at Umuama, despite my distinguished academic performance. I was devastated. But what could I do? Father's word was law in our home.

The second incident happened the first week of January 1955. That morning, Father sent all the members of the family to the Igboro farm while he stayed behind to work on our village Motor Park. He promised to join us later. The months of December and January were peak earnings months, and he was now trying to pay for both of his sons to attend school. Villagers who lived, and practiced business abroad, usually came home to celebrate Christmas and Second Yam festivities with kith and kin in December, heading back when the festivities were over. It was the business of my father and his fellow passenger seekers—*nde ocho pasinja*—to load and offload the goods of passengers from the produce and cargo trucks that passed through our village. Usually, there were more passengers and goods than available trucks, and therefore, many passengers queued early to avoid missing their schedules, some even advancing money to Father to reserve their passage.

That morning, Father stopped at a public toilette before going to work at the park, when a group of people drinking palm wine in a bar invited him to come and drink with them. He refused, telling them he had to relieve himself first. On his way back, they offered him the drink again, saying that it was not courteous of him to refuse the first morning gift offered to him that day. Out of respect, Father took a sip of the palm wine, thanked them, and walked away without knowing that they had spiked the wine with poison. We later found out that the poisoner had been sent to kill Father by a man with whom Father had fought for a civil service position for Brother Ikpo in Arochukwu District. Even before he reached the Motor Park, Father fainted, falling to the ground. Several kind passersby quickly lifted him off the ground and took him to his house.

Relatives at the house urgently called the traditional healers to revive and heal him. However, his condition was so bad that our uncles sent for us to return quickly so we could see him before he passed away. When we received the news, we were all shocked and scared. We returned home immediately and searched for renowned healers to give him better treatment. We were tense as we watched the healers try to revive him. Finally, he regained some consciousness.

Although he did not die that day, he remained sick for over a year. Even after taking him to Arochukwu General Hospital for further treatment, the doctors could never make an accurate diagnosis of his illness and were unable to cure him. Instead, they suggested we take him home where he could die in peace, with family members by his side. Hoping against hope, we brought him home and hired other traditional healers to treat him. They gave him all the medicinal concoctions he could take, but his condition continued to deteriorate. In the meantime, I continued to attend school, working from home and becoming more sad and angry as time went by.

Early one morning, Father's condition grew worse. He could no longer speak clearly or move his limbs. They summoned members of our immediate and agnate families to offer final prayers to God before he passed on. When I came and saw him so helpless, I fainted. After I recovered, I noticed that they had moved me to an uncle's house. Mother was sitting beside me, sobbing. I jumped up.

"Where is my father? Where is my father? Where is my father?"

"Calm down, he is not dead, yet," said Uncle Timothy.

"What do you mean he is not dead, *yet*?"

"He is breathing. At least for now."

"Is he going to die?"

"Only he and his Maker can answer that."

"Oh! God, don't let him die, at least not now." I broke down.

"It's alright son." Mother sobbed. "I am here for you." She drew me to her side and held me so tight, as if to say, "You, too, should not leave me here alone."

I wiped away my tears, held her close, and started comforting the woman I realize would be widowed, soon. For the first time, I felt like an adult—one brought up to be strong for his mother—for she had experienced more anguish, pain, and loneliness, resulting from the deaths of those she loved than I could know.

When I went back to see my father in his house, I found my headmaster, Mr. Eleke Nwankwo, arguing with my uncles. He turned to me when he saw me approaching.

"Kalu Ogbaa. Did I not teach you and your classmates a lesson on tuberculosis?"

"Yes, sir, you did." I knew where this line of questioning was going.

"And you could not see its symptoms on your father?"

"No, sir, I never thought of it."

"If you never did, then what is the purpose of your education?"

"I don't know, sir." I looked down in shame. The thought of not applying the benefit of my education to save Father's life overwhelmed me. I began to cry. "I'm sorry," I said to both my beloved headmaster and my father. I turned away, head bowed in shame, when the headmaster drew me to his side.

"I am sorry for being harsh with you. It's just hard for me to see a good man like your father die because of the ignorance and carelessness of your people. Your father is suffering from tuberculosis, but he could be cured of it."

"Thank you, sir. But how?" I asked.

"We must take him to an infectious disease hospital," he answered. "By the way, didn't you tell me that your elder brother Ikpo works in Enugu? There is an IDH in Enugu. Your father must be rushed there immediately."

I turned to look at Father. Tears rolled down his near lifeless cheeks. I ran to his bedside, knelt down and prayed. "Oh! God. Spare my father's life for the sake of my mother and me." I started sobbing again. Then Father slowly lifted his right hand toward my face as if to wipe my tears away. "Father! Oh, Father. Thank you, Jesus."

My headmaster, Mr. Nwankwo, turned to the crowd gathered for Father's anticipated death. "You must rush him immediately to the IDH in Enugu. Now!"

"Rush him there for burial or for healing? Does a dead man take medication?" someone asked.

"If you don't take him to Enugu and he dies, I will call the police from Arochukwu to arrest all of you for murder," Headmaster Nwankwo shouted.

At the mention of the police, several distant family members ran out of our home fearing an arrest. The remaining group began to discuss how they would collect enough money to send my father by truck to Uzuakoli to catch the train to Enugu where Brother Ikpo would receive them, along with the letter from the headmaster instructing Brother Ikpo how to proceed with getting the proper care for Father's deteriorating condition.

The money was collected and Father was rushed to Enugu where the British doctors cured Father of the disease (with the assistance of Igbo nurses whom Brother Ikpo tipped with 70 pounds sterling saved for my secondary school education).

At the end of the 1956 school year, the school board relieved Mr. Nwankwo of his position as headmaster of the CSM Primary School, Umuama. Allegations had risen accusing Mr. Nwankwo of fornication with Miss Agnes Okoro, the daughter of the education officer whose recommendation caused the Board of Education to deny our school the right to offer the first Standard VI program. I felt especially sad since Mr. Nwankwo had been such a beloved influence in my life. We had grown even closer after his intervention had saved my Father's life. So close, indeed, that he trusted me to help him convince a weary population of our villagers to take advantage of a gift from Queen Elizabeth II of England, who, after visiting Nigeria, offered millions of cans of condensed milk to our students, which we had never seen or even tasted before.

After the Headmaster Nwankwo collected our school's share, he ordered all the pupils to bring firewood to school for boiling the milk. When the milk was ready, he invited us to come and drink it before he distributed unopened cans to us to take home to our parents. No one volunteered because they feared the British wanted to poison schoolchildren as a way of controlling the population of Nigeria. To show us it was safe, the Headmaster Nwankwo drank some of the milk to show it safe, and invited us again to come forward and drink. When no one came forward, he pointed to me.

"You, Kalu Ogbaa, come and drink it from my cup. It won't kill you."

I stepped forward, worried, fearful, and then took a sip. The milk was delicious. I happily drank more. If I must die, I figured, it would at least be with my beloved headmaster. Once the others realized that it was safe, they all stepped forward and gladly drank of the sweet milk. Headmaster Nwanko winked at me and smiled. I felt that somehow I was repaying his service to my father. But there was a larger cost to be paid, and it related directly to my education.

Father returned home from the hospital late in 1956, but he was never as physically healthy as he was before January 1955. And because of his continued illness, he was physically unable to make enough money to sponsor my secondary school education at either Hope Waddell Institute, Calabar, or the Government College, Afikpo, both of which I had secured admission, hoping to begin my studies in January 1957. Brother Ikpo was also unable to help, having spent his savings paying for Father's treatment at Enugu. Consequently, my inability to attend secondary school prevented me from studying math and science courses at the secondary school level, which became a deficiency in my higher education (and continues to affect my life in other ways to this day). My heart was nevertheless filled, though touched with a bittersweet tint, since Father had survived the attack of a deadly disease like tuberculosis.

Finally, in January 1957, the Board of Education authorized the Umuama schoolteachers to start offering a Standard VI program. Some of our former Standard V graduates, who had gone to Achara and Obinto to complete their Standards V and VI programs, came back to repeat Standard VI with us. One of them, Eke Uwakwe, who had passed Standard VI in 1955 in Achara and also at Obinto in 1956, came back to repeat the class with us in 1957, hoping to pass Standard VI with the highest score in our class and garner a recommendation to study at the Boys Vocational School (BVS), Ididep. The BVS students were a pool of highest achievers drawn from Standard VI classes of all the CSM primary schools in Eastern Nigeria, and trained as "C" teachers. Successful candidates taught in various primary schools of the presbytery at the end of their training. Uwakwe believed he could beat me in the selection exams because of his previous experiences at the two primary schools he'd attended. But the memory of my Father's struggles and his fighting spirit strengthened me, and the discipline I'd learned as a wrestler enabled me to come out on top of everybody in our class, especially Eke Uwakwe, in the 1957 Standard VI final exams. Next stop, BVS.

The supervising teacher of the Arochukwu/Ohafia School District, Mr. Agwu Kalu Ogwe, conducted interviews for admission into the BVS. Normally, candidates from each school were paired and interviewed together. Each school presented only two candidates for admission. But since this was our school's first interview opportunity and we were unaware of such limits, all eleven students who had passed the exam presented themselves for the interview. Mr. Ogwe was amused when he saw us approaching, all proud and happy. He looked again at the reports our school headmaster had sent to him and smiled.

"Who is Kalu Ogbaa?" he asked.

"I, sir." I stepped forward.

"Who is Eke Uwakwe?"

"I, sir." Eke Uwakwe came forward.

Then Mr. Ogwe looked over the rest. "As all of you should have known, your school, like any other school, is entitled to one candidate only for the Boys Vocational School education. Based on your school's overall academic reports, Kalu Ogbaa is the only candidate I am recommending to represent Umuama in this year's admission exercise." He paused, briefly. "I have also noted the case made for Eke Uwakwe. I will forward his case to the Synod, and if they permit me to send two candidates from your school, then he will be the second person. The rest of you should go home and try your luck on something else."

"Thank you, sir. I assure you that I will represent my school well just as I did when our school competed with Saint John's RCM School in 1955 for the establishment of a Standard VI class in our village." I had to mention the 1955 competition because he had personally congratulated me on my performance there. I stood tall, looking him in the eye.

"Thank you, Kalu. I still remember how proud all of us felt about your achievement in that competition. I wish you good luck in your new school and challenges."

Father and I thanked him again before we left the interview room. Father was particularly grateful that he had not let the recommendation letter for Eke Uwakwe affect his good judgment on my BVS selection. The other unchosen candidates went home disappointed, while Eke Uwakwe and his sponsor, Elder Kalu Chiowa, traveled on foot with us from Ebem Ohafia back to our village. As per our routine, my father took me to "Bar David Oke." Later, Mother prepared a special meal and invited neighbors to help celebrate my success at the BVS selection.

After the celebration, Father told me he had not wanted me to transfer to Achara and Obinto for my Standards V and VI programs, because even if I achieved the highest scores in either school, they would not have recommended me, a non-native, to represent them at the BVS. In addition, if I had applied to any of them for admission, they would have gladly granted it to me only because my school fees would have helped them financially to maintain their school. Father said that ever since Umuama started serving as a feeder school to the two schools, they had never recommended any students from our village to study at the Boys Vocational School. Thus, without attending it, my educational career might have ended at the primary school level since he lacked the wherewithal to sponsor my education in any of the secondary schools they offered me admission. My father was right in his assessment. I thanked him for always thinking ahead about my academic progress.

Chapter 6

Beyond the Village

As the day of my departure from the village to Ididep drew near, I was apprehensive. How well would I fit into the new school environment? Would our teachers teach some subjects in English and others in Ibibio, the native language? Would we have adequate protection from the people whom our Igbo people rumored to be cannibals? If we traveled to fetch firewood from the forest as we did at home, would they capture and kill us? How would my mother endure or survive if such an atrocity befell her beloved son? Should I discuss such fearful thoughts with my father? No, he may not understand, for he might think that I am a coward. In addition, if I made bold to ask, he would only look at me sternly and ask, "*O giran bu onye jehin ule akwukwo ahu*? Will you be the only one going to attend the school?" followed by, "*Ele omuiyi mere di ndu I mealu nno.* Make sure you do whatever others do to survive."

And, somehow, that imagined conversation gave me the spiritual boost I needed to face whatever unforeseen dangers might come my way. Yes, that and the strong and ever-abiding belief that Jesus would protect me from all alarms and dangers. I considered it, therefore, unnecessary to discuss my fears with my father. Besides, as the son of Ogbaa *nwa* Ikpo, everybody expected me show courage, though I was only twelve. I did not want anybody, especially my father, to see me as a coward.

With my initial anxieties now behind me, I was ready to travel outside of my village to begin the next level of my training as a Young Pupil Teacher (PYT). The night before my departure, I visited my elder sister, Mgbore, and her daughter, Enyia. Brother Ikpo, who was working as a stenographer in Enugu, had sent Father money to cover my tuition and fees. He also sent Father money, which I delivered, to purchase wedding presents for Sister Nwannennaya, who was getting married the following week. That night, my friends met me and Sister Nwannennaya to express their good wishes and bid me farewell.

The next morning, Mother appeared apprehensive, quiet. She sent word to Sister Mgbore to come with her daughter for a final family prayer before my departure.

"Why are you so sad, Nne? Don't you want me to go?" I asked.

"No. Not that, son. It's just that I have the feeling that you may not meet all of us alive when you return." She shook her head.

"You scare me, Nne. I can cancel my travel and stay back with you in the village, if it is what you want."

"No, no. You must go. We'll be alright."

"Are you sure you really want me to go?"

"Yes, I'm sure. You have to go."

Soon, Sister Mgbore and her daughter, Enyia, joined the rest of us. Father led us in prayers then everybody hugged me. Sister Mgbore held me tightly and wept on my shoulders.

"I will miss you, Kalu. Very much."

I, too, wept. She had always especially loved me, always proud to have me as her little brother from the day I was born. Now we were separating, not knowing where or when we would meet again.

Then the truck came and a crowd of family and friends walked me toward it. A boy named Eni Udo carried my small luggage until Father and I boarded. Mother, Sister Mgbore, and Enyia watched, sorrow in their eyes as they waved at us driving off for Itu en route to the BVS campus at Ididep. I watched them through the window until they disappeared in the dust.

It was harmattan season again, January 1958. When we arrived in Itu, Father introduced me to his old friend, Mr. David from Nkporo in Old Bende Division in Eastern Nigeria, who took us to his downtown apartment for a brief snack and later to his store in Itu Market. Before leaving, David asked us to visit him in both places whenever we came from school to buy groceries and other school supplies during the weekends. Then Father loaded school supplies, groceries, and beverages onto the truck, prayed for my safety, and sent me on to Eke Uwakwe.

Ididep, a small, sleepy Ibibio town, was twelve miles away from Itu. It became a weekly routine for us BVS students to trek the distance on Friday evenings, sleep over at David's house, rise on Saturday mornings, buy groceries and other items we'd need for the week, and carry them on our heads back to school in the afternoons. As soon as we would arrive back at the dormitory, we'd cook enough yam pottage and soup to last a whole week. We'd warm and store them securely in our chop boxes after each meal. Ironically, the experience I had cooking for Teacher Ikoro in the dormitory at Umuama helped me a lot. Moreover, I liked the cheap, fresh fish we bought from Itu, a riverside town, although not the twelve-mile trek from my school to it.

Life at the vocational school was both exciting and challenging. For the first time in my life, I wore shoes. I was excited to try on the white canvas shoes Father had picked out. They felt too tight for my feet at the store, but the sales clerk said they would stretch out if I continued to wear them. I looked to Father for confirmation. He nodded, yes, and smiled.

I was also excited about living in an Ibibio community where students would be required to speak English any time they were on campus. The policy gave me the opportunity to study and speak English more often than I did at Umuama, where we spoke English in school and Igbo at home. My early childhood education, which was initially bilingual, had become monolingual during the school terms, except when we either went to church or to the demonstration school downtown. I spoke English better than most of my classmates at the vocational school and attributed my success to the assistance I received from my father, Brother Ikpo, and my teachers in primary school.

The curricular offerings in the school were similar to those taught in primary school, except that the level of the materials was more demanding. The major difference, however, was that in addition to the post-primary school courses, teachers offered School Method courses to introduce us to primary school pedagogy. We went to a nearby demonstration school twice a week to teach under observation, our teachers critiquing our performance after we returned to campus.

The first time the pupils addressed me as "sir," I felt proud. Moreover, they always politely called me Mr. Ogbaa. *Wow!* I thought. *Only certified teachers were entitled to being addressed as Mister.* Then it hit me. I was on my way to becoming an educated man with a prospective respectable, good job.

At the end of my second week in school, I wrote letters to Brother Ikpo and Father to thank them for sponsoring my education at the school. I asked Father, specifically, to tell my mother and Sister Mgbore all about my new life away from home, because I knew they were worried and wondered how I was coping. The replies I later received from them, letting me know that all was well, especially my mother, made me happy. Mother and I were both quickly learning to cope in life without each other, despite our sad and painful separation.

Then, four days before our second term break, I came down with a terrible fever. They treated me at the school clinic and discharged me home for the break. I asked Eke Uwakwe to take me home, but he refused, saying that he was going to spend the break with his uncles at Ikot Ekpene. I begged him, thinking I was going to die. Still, he refused. But another Ibibio classmate agreed to take me to the motor park and helped me on a truck that took me to David's house. There, I slept overnight, and in a dream, I saw somebody coming to kill me. I ran, faster and faster as he continued to chase me. And, then, I was flying. I looked down just in time to see him aim his bow and arrow. I turned and flew up further. Then I felt an arrow pierce my back, and I fell. I woke up screaming, my body sweaty, trembling. David heard me and quickly ran to my assistance.

"Calm down. Calm down. It's only a dream."

"I'm dying. Help me," I said. "I don't want to die. Help me." My teeth chattered as I looked at the clock. It was 8:30 p.m.

David felt my head. "You're suffering from *iba*, acute malaria." He left and quickly returned with quinine tablets and water.

After taking the medicine, I lay back on the bed and slept in snatches, the nightmares continuing the rest of the night. The next morning, David gave me another treatment after breakfast and asked me to rest before travelling home. At noon, he asked a cyclist to take me to Arochukwu. From there I would board a truck to take me the rest of the way.

Torrential rain poured down that afternoon as we rode through the streets, which worsened my condition. The cyclist was so afraid that I might die that he abandoned me in the Government Headquarters, Arochukwu, and fled without collecting the transport fare. I managed to ask around and find Corporal Alicho Awah, a man from our village. I staggered into his house and walked straight to the hearth to warm myself even before telling him what was wrong. His wife crossed the living room and felt my head, then winced.

"What's wrong, Mama Bridget?" Corporal Awah asked.

"He is delirious. He must be suffering from acute malaria."

"Have you eaten anything this afternoon, young man?" Corporal Awah asked.

"No sir. But I'm not hungry," I mumbled.

"Mama Bridget. Go prepare food for him."

"Don't worry. You'll be alright," he assured me.

"Yes, sir," I said and collapsed.

I felt better when I awoke the next morning.

"Where am I, sir?" I asked the man leaning over me.

"Oh! Son. You were very sick all through the night. But Mama Bridget fed you hot soup and applied cold compresses all over your body to cool you. Don't worry; we'll soon take you home to our village."

Then another man from our village, Umachi Kalu Ogoro, moved across the room to my bed.

"Good morning, sir. How is home?"

"Oh, all is well. Don't worry. I'll take you home myself after talking with Corporal Awah." He looked away as if he were hiding something.

"Is something wrong with my people?"

"No, no. It's just that you are so sick. We'll all take care of you when we get home."

"Thank you, sir. I appreciate that."

"Thank God, Umachi is here to take you home after you have eaten breakfast. I would have done so myself if he wasn't here," Corporal Awah said.

"Oh, thank you both. I can't wait to get home and see my family."

"Yes. You'll see everyone. And you'll be fine," Umachi said finally.

As soon as Umachi and I arrived in our compound, a crowd of agnate family members ran toward me. Some of them were crying and saying how sorry they were.

"Sorry for what?" I wondered. "What? Because of my illness?" I looked around, confused.

Soon, Father came running, picked me up and hurried to his house, Mother following close behind, her eyes swollen and red. I began to worry at their strange behavior.

"Oh! God. What's wrong? Tell me. Is someone dead?"

"Don't worry. All is well." Tears rolled down Father's cheeks.

Then Mother screamed and fell to the floor where she rolled and shouted, "Mgbore! Mgbore! Mgbore! Why me, and why now, God?"

I ran to her, sobbing and lifting her up from the floor, gently sat her down on a mud bed. I told her not to worry because I was still alive to take good care of her. Gradually, she looked up. Our eyes met. Then she screamed, writhing uncontrollably, and collapsed on my lap. I gently massaged her back and let her rest for a while.

Father came immediately to us, speaking words of comfort from the Bible, but I didn't hear much. My mind was burdened with so much grief and sorrow. My body started shaking. I looked up.

"Where are you, Sister Mgbore? Brother Kalu is here to see you. Mother is crying to see you. Where are you?" I asked aloud. I started to stand and search for Mgbore, and then realized Mother was still resting on my lap. Mother raised herself and we embraced. As we sobbed together, the entire family joined in the chorus of blues.

Later, Father took me to an inner room and told me Sister Mgbore had died delivering her baby son. There were complications and the midwives could not stop the bleeding. Sister Mgbore and her baby son died at 8:30 p.m. (the exact time and day of my terrible nightmare). I returned to Mother's hut to console her. Then, I asked Father to take me to Sister Mgbore's grave. When I arrived, other villagers gathered to console me and together we prayed for the repose of the souls of my sister and my nephew. Afterwards, I returned to my mother's home and stayed with her the rest of the night. I promised her that as long as I lived, she would not lack for anything. But first, I had to finish my training at Ididep to fulfill my obligations to her and others dear to my heart.

After I returned to school, I was unusually quiet. Everybody, including my teachers, began asking what was wrong. But I was unable to share my loss, because I was unable to deal with it fully myself. My friend, Eke Uwakwe, however, had received the news of Sister Mgbore's death while he was at Ikot Ekpene, and one day soon after my arrival, Mr. Edeme invited me to his office and talked to me.

"How are you, Kalu?"

"I am well, sir. Thank you."

"I was told that your sister died during the holidays."

"Yes, she died, sir, but that was shortly before I went home for the holidays."

"Oh, I'm sorry to hear that. It must have been difficult for you and your family to bear."

"Yes, it was, especially for my mother. She needed me during the burial of my sister."

"Well, even though you weren't there, I'm sure she appreciated your coming home to console her after the funeral."

"Yes, she did. We both consoled each other, even though the pain is still there."

"Well, I'm happy you came back to finish your studies so you can finally go home after graduation to help everybody in your family."

"Yes, I told them that. Although it was difficult to leave my mother at home, I had to because she will need me to make money after I graduate and help her."

"I admire your courage, Kalu. I hope that you will continue to work as hard as you used to, so you can continue to maintain the top position in your class. I pray that God continues to strengthen and bless you in Jesus' name."

"Thank you, sir, for your good wishes and prayers. I will work as hard as I used to, knowing fully well now what is at stake."

After I thanked him for his fatherly concern, I left his office and thereafter was able to continue my coursework, although my heart never really got over the loss of Sister Mgbore.

But my sorrow over my mother, whom I could not console while at school, continued to eat me up inside every day. Nevertheless, my promise to help her the rest of her days drove me to study even harder. I finished at the top of my class in our final exams. Mr. Edeme was so pleased that he called me to his office and congratulated me. He had known I was smart, but he was surprised that in spite of my sister's death I could have beaten all my classmates in the last two terms. In addition, I had achieved the highest academic record that year and all the other years the school existed before government transformed it into a tertiary institution after the civil war. Consequently, he wrote a glowing recommendation letter to Mr. Agwu Kalu Ogwe, the supervising teacher of the Arochukwu/Ohafia school district and formally requested that the CSM Synod send me there for a posting at the district's school. The Synod granted his request.

In January 1959, Mr. Agwu Kalu Ogwe assigned me to teach in my former school, CSM Primary School, Umuama Ihe. My old headmaster, Mr. Frank Nwankwo Okereke (FNO), was still in charge of the school. He now welcomed me back as a member of his teaching staff, assigning me to teach Infant 1 class where his youngest son Okoro was studying.

Before my first day in school, I wasn't sure of how the pupils would receive me. To my surprise, students in the Infant 1 class were enthusiastic and happy, a few even telling others that I was their relation. At the first staff meeting, the headmaster introduced me as the newest addition to the faculty and informed all the "C" teachers that we would be required to attend preparation classes for entrance exams into Grade III Teacher Training College at the end of our second year of service. Thereafter, he gave each of us the class schedule and ended the staff meeting. Overnight, I had become a young adult in charge of my own class, qualified to earn a salary like the adult teachers of the school.

By the second term, Headmaster FNO reassigned me to his daughter Lovena's Standard II class. Impressed by my teaching, the following year he sent me to teach his son Alex's Standard III class. It seems I had become his favorite young teacher and consequently enjoyed his strong patronage.

My parents were equally happy to have their son serving in their village school. After church services on Sundays, they often stopped by my new house for lunch and conversation. Mother embarrassed me greatly when she called me "sir," addressing me respectfully in the manner of our locals. I protested and struck a deal that she could call me Teacher Kalu, but not sir.

After my return from Ididep, I also saw my village from a different perspective, that of a more mature and confident thirteen-year-old who had traveled outside of its confines and been given an education that had broadened and expanded my view of the outside world. Now, more than ever, I admired people's close relationships in our community and enjoyed their good food as well as their rituals, ceremonies, and festivals. I admired the good effort each age group made with counterpart age groups to bring developments to the community. I admired the strivings of the rich people to help the weak and the poor, sharing in the universal ethos of the Igbo of Southeast Nigeria. I admired the religious and pious nature of every villager since he or she belonged to one of the three Christian denominations—the RCM, the CSM, and the Unity Study Group (the Igbo traditional religion, *Igo Mmuo*). I admired the healthy competition in both academics and sports between the Catholic and Protestant school students, especially since we, the "Scottish boys," used to trounce the "Catholic boys" in those competitions. As a young and energetic teacher, I was determined to help our pupils to uphold the rich tradition of the school in both areas of competition. Soon, they appointed me assistant choirmaster and games master.

Apart from playing my role as a classroom teacher, I was responsible for dispatching messages to members of the PTA of which my father was either the secretary or chairperson, alternating the role every other year with Mr. Dickson Okoro Kalu of Amammiri, who was the father of James Okoro. James and I became good friends because of the roles each of our fathers played in the association. He always accompanied his father to the meetings just as did I. He was older by two years, and one year ahead of me in school. However, because I repeated Standard V while he was attending Standard VI at Achara, he later maintained a two-class gap between us. Unfortunately, in 1955, his father died, and he failed his Standard VI exams. His maternal uncle, Kalu Ikeogu, withdrew him from school to live with him at Ikot Ekpene. We had both been heart-broken because of our separation. I remember we met in Church when he came home that Christmas Holiday in 1956. After the morning service, I hugged him warmly.

"You look very good, James. Why didn't you write me all these months?"

"I thought of you every day, but I was so busily engaged in selling Uncle Kalu Ikeogu's goods in the market that I didn't have time to write."

"Tell me, James, are you going back with him to Ikot Ekpene?"

"I don't want to go back, but I don't know if he'll let me stay home to continue my education."

"Please persuade him to let you stay so that you and I can study with each other in the same class. The government has just authorized our school to offer the Standard VI program, which we all were praying for."

"Is that so? I didn't know that. I'll tell my uncle about it when I get home later today."

"Do you want me to come with you to tell him?"

"No, my mother and I will tell him. I'm sure he'll understand."

All through that night, I thought about my reunion with my bosom friend, James. Early the next morning, I ran to my father to ask if he could go to Amammiri and persuade James's uncle, Kalu Ikeogu, to let my friend return to our school. I had hoped that since Father was close friends with James's father before he died, his uncle might heed Father's input.

"When did James return from Ikot Ekpene?" Father asked.

"I don't know exactly, but I met him in church yesterday."

"Do you think he wants to come back to school after failing Standard VI?"

"Oh, yes! I'm very sure. I know he failed because of his father's death that year."

"You're right. James was very close to his father, and his father's death must have affected him very much."

"Are you then going to talk to Kalu Ikeogu on his behalf?"

"Yes, I will. For I know how close you two have been since childhood."

"Thank you very much, Father. You've made my day."

I ran to tell Mother about James's return and Father's willingness to persuade his uncle to allow him to come back to school.

"Are you sure that James would be happy to come back to school after his father's death? Who will help him cope with school work without his father's help?"

"Oh, I'll help him with his homework. And his mother and uncle will pay for his tuition and fees, school uniform, and other things he needs for school. Above all, our renewed friendship will help him a lot. And Father will be there for both of us."

"Yes, that's a good idea. Her mother and I will provide the food that both of you will need in the dormitory."

"Thank you, Mother. I knew you'd understand."

I thanked God for giving me the greatest Christmas gift that one can ask for. When James and I met in church the next Sunday, he told me that Father had persuaded his uncle to let him return to school. Father had assured his uncle of James's protection in school, in spite of his father's absence.

That year, James and I lived like twins in the dormitory. We studied and shared all aspects of our life together, within and outside of the school premises. But my father's presence always reminded him of his own father's absence. In addition, his absence from school the whole of 1956 did not help him cope with the tedium of work in his final year of primary school education. In the end, he failed Standard VI exams again, despite all the help I gave him with his homework. I tried to help him think less often of his father so that he could concentrate on his academics, which was the only way he could succeed in getting a future job to help his widowed mother. But it was of no avail. Later, he and I had talked shortly before I left in January 1958, to study at the BVS. I gave him my class notes and he promised to work hard to qualify for admission into the school. He kept the promise, and was eventually admitted to the BVS in January 1959, my first year of teaching at Umuama.

After my first year, they assigned James to teach with me. That was 1960. What a wonderful way to begin a new year with a joyous second reunion! As the most recent junior staff, however, James did not get accommodations on the school premises. Every day, he had to walk to school from his village. Early one morning, after seeing him run to school in a torrential rainfall, I asked him to live with me in the one bedroom mud-and-thatch house where I lived. Without hesitation, he agreed. I informed the headmaster who didn't have any objections over the arrangement. He was well aware how close James and I were in his primary school classes and was happy to consent.

But not everyone in my village supported the arrangement because they feared someone from his village would poison me. Umuchiakuma and Amammiri had had constant land disputes since 1936. I knew James wouldn't poison me, but I wasn't so sure of some of the others from his village. So I decided to ask James if he would agree to use common utensils, the same drinking pot, and to cooking our meals and storing them in one chop box, which meant we would always eat together. James knew why I made the suggestions and agreed. When I questioned Father about it, he permitted me to carry out the arrangement, though he never believed anybody would poison me. From that point on, the friendship between our two families grew stronger, and our mothers would visit one another for lunch with friends after almost every Sunday service.

In the meantime, my education continued. I passed the entrance exams to the two-year Grade III Teachers College where I would train from January 1, 1961 through December 31, 1962. All the candidates from Arochukwu/Ohafia School District gathered at Ebem Ohafia in December 1960 to check the postings, curious to know who would be number one. The leading candidate from Ohafia, Ukoha thought that he was going to be the one. If so, he expected to study at the TTC in Ohafia, which was in his home clan. But when they posted the official list outside Mr. Ogwe's office, he discovered that I had the highest scores in the system. Our supervising teacher, Mr. Ogwe, was proud enough to recommend me after the Synod representative, Mr. Otisi, asked him to pick the number one candidate to study at the Teacher Training College (TTC). My other friends, Eke Uwakwe, who transferred from Obinto to Umuama in his second year, came fifth on the list and was posted, along with another colleague, Ekpe Ekpe Okorafor, to Macgregor College, Afikpo. The second person on the list, Ukoha Kalu Ukoha from Ohafia, was posted to the TTC at Uyo. James took and passed the exams in December 1961. They posted him to my college in January 1962. We continued our friendship there and, as an upper classman, I gave him all the assistance he needed to do well in his first year.

In 1961, I began my two-year Grade III Teachers' training at the Teacher's College, Ania Ohafia. As with the Boys Vocational School, we trained for teaching elementary level Arithmetic, English, Bible Knowledge, Nature Study, Gardening, General Knowledge, and Physical Education from Infant 1 through Standard IV. In addition, we took courses in School Methods and Child Psychology, complemented with weekly teaching practices in a demonstration school at Akanu Ohafia. For recreation, we played soccer and wrestled in the late afternoons, held prayer and Bible study meetings in the evenings, and then went back to our studies in the evening.

As an all-male Presbyterian institution, our teachers did not allow students to bring female visitors on campus, but we could visit people wherever and whenever we wanted on weekends. However, attendance to church worship on Sundays was mandatory, and our two soccer teams competed with each other from time to time on weekdays. In addition, we played soccer matches with area elementary school teachers and students, or with other teacher training college teams. I enjoyed our soccer matches, playing number seven, the center forward position, an experience that helped me to coach soccer in the schools I taught after graduation. In addition, I competed in track and field, sprinting and relay, long jump and pole vault. I also received several book awards during my two years at Ania, and dabbled in sports commentating (using the moniker Uncle K, after Kalu Nsi, a famous anchorperson of the Nigerian Broadcasting Corporation, Enugu).

In academics, I studied hard enough to earn top positions in all the exams we took in the two years our training. The faculty members were happy to see my admission exam results confirmed through my performance while at the college. I also made several new friends, including my classmates, Onuoha Eme from Okagwe Ohafia, and Ukobasi Okereke from Abakaliki. In addition, James and I rekindled our friendship after his admission in 1961. I was happy to protect him from the hazing of upperclassmen. We were both posted back to our home school, Umuama Presbyterian School, after our respective graduations in 1962 and 1963. And since then, to this day, James and I have maintained our close friendship.

In January 1963, when I returned to teach Grade III in Umuama, Mr. Okereke again appointed me choirmaster and games master for the school in addition to my regular teaching assignments. We won several choir competitions among Presbyterian schools and sporting games between both Presbyterian and Catholic schools in Ihechiowa clan, in addition to winning awards in Arochukwu district sports competitions. I was pleased to serve under Mr. Okereke, the headmaster I had known since my elementary school years. So when they transferred him to another school in December 1964, I was sad. His replacement, Mr. Thomas Okoro Dike, did not like me as much as Mr. Okereke, so in April, 1965, I asked the supervising teacher, Mr. Ogwe, to transfer me out of Umuama. He granted my request and transferred me to Ihe Central School, Obinto.

But I was bored teaching at Obinto, and decided not to go back to college for a Grade II teachers' certificate training. Instead, I took private correspondence courses with Rapid Results College in London, which would prepare me to take General Certificate of Education (GCE) exams, which the University of London conducted. Passing the exams would enable me to gain admission into a university, or work in the civil service. Further, I was not getting along with my new headmaster, Mr. Nnechi Ota. He did not approve of my friendship with one of the female teachers in the school and asked the supervising teacher to transfer her. Consequently, I too applied for transfer from the school, and was posted to Eleoha Ihe Primary School in January 1966. I had taken several GCE exams between the last week of December 1965 and the first week in January 1966, passing one advanced level exam and four at the ordinary level.

At my new posting, Mr. Okereke was serving then as the headmaster, and he quickly appointed me to serve once again as a school choirmaster. The students and parents liked the reorganization of the choir. Using new hymnals I purchased, we won several competitions among Presbyterian school choirs in the clan. I also assisted the games master, Mr. Oji Anya, a relative of mine. But I had hardly completed the first four months in the school when Mr. Nnechi Ota wrote a scathing report against the female teacher and me at his school, and requested the Synod to post me out of Calabar Presbytery. I was not given the opportunity to defend myself against the allegation, and in spite of my manager's protest, the Synod posted me to Abakaliki Presbytery where the school manager sent me to teach at the Presbyterian Primary School, Kpirikpiri, in May 1966.

Ironically, the transfer was actually a blessing, because the school was less than 60 minutes' drive to Enugu, where my brother Ikpo lived and worked. Besides, as the capital of Eastern Nigeria, Enugu had the best libraries in the region, where I frequently visited to prepare for my GCE exams. Between late December 1966, and early January 1967, I took several more GCE exams. I also took an entrance exam into the Advanced Teacher Training College, ATTC, Owerri, and passed. I was thus ready to begin my studies there in January 1967. Furthermore, I met an American Peace Corps volunteer serving in a government department near my school in Abakaliki. Through him, I learned about American universities, and he helped me to apply for and gain admission to Boston College, Massachusetts. Indeed, I had worked hard enough on my preparations that I qualified for admission into universities both in Nigeria and abroad. It was a good year, and another win on the match that would take me closer to my ultimate match.

Chapter 7

War Days in Biafra

1966 was the most cruel and bloody year in Nigerian national history. A group of Nigerian Army Majors plotted and carried out the first coup in Nigeria on January 15, assassinating the country's political leaders, especially those from the Northern region. Following the coup, some high military officers from the Northern region led soldiers and civilians, enraged over the insult, on a rampage destroying the lives and properties of thousands of Eastern Nigerian peoples, especially the Igbo, who were living in the Northern region. The organizers and rioters justified their actions by claiming that Igbo military officers led the coup. As evidence to support their claim, they pointed to several powerful sociopolitical, religious, and military leaders from the North whom the Nigerian Army Majors had assassinated, such as Alhaji Sir Ahmadu Bello, Premier of Northern Nigeria and the Sardauna of Sokoto; Alhaji Sir Abubakar Tafawa Balewa, the Prime Minister of Nigeria; and Brigadier Zakari Maimalari.

Furthermore, senior military officers of Northern Nigeria then systematically carried out what they called counter-coups on May 29, July 29, and September 29, 1966, again killing thousands of Eastern military officers and civilians, especially the Igbo ethnic peoples, including women and children, publically raping women and schoolchildren, disemboweling pregnant women, and decapitating old, infirm men. Those who escaped the killings flooded back into their homeland, Eastern Nigeria, creating refugee problems too large and too complex for the government to handle with any level of practical efficiency. However, with the help of families and friends, the refugees resettled in their hometowns and villages, while the military governor, Col. Chukwuemeka (Emeka) Odumegwu Ojukwu, continued to negotiate privately, oftentimes unsuccessfully, with the federal military government officials in Lagos. A cloud of uncertainty hung over the nation through the rest of the year.

Despite such crushing political and military devastation, however, educational institutions in the region continued to function without disruptions. The regional government continued its effort to rehabilitate the refugees up through the last two months of the year. In addition, peace talks, which leaders from both sides of the conflict hoped would bring a permanent solution to the crises, were scheduled to take place in Ghana in the coming months. In this atmosphere of hope and optimism for a possible peaceful resolution of the conflicts, I registered at the Advanced Teacher Training College, Owerri, in January 1967.

When I arrived on campus, I met Ukoha Kalu Ukoha, my number one competitor for Grade III Teacher Training College entrance exams in 1961. We both had been admitted to ATTC, Owerri to study as English/French majors—Ukoha with a Grade II teachers' certificate, and I with GCE papers from the University of London. Over time, we became close friends, studying together and sharing the dream of completing our education at the ATTC and thereafter proceeding to work on a university degree. It never occurred to us then, however, that we might not even complete a full year of studies at the institution, even though signs of imminent trouble loomed all around us. Maybe we were too naïve or overly optimistic, believing that the two warring governments—federal and regional—could settle their differences and bring peace and stability to Nigeria as one united country.

Unfortunately, it turned out that the wounds inflicted on the Nigerians' souls were too fresh and deep for a lasting peace. Thus, the worst day in our national history was yet to come: the actions the federal military government took against Eastern Nigerians forced our local government to consider making Eastern Nigeria an independent republic.

But before the formal proclamation of the new Republic of Biafra was issued by Governor Ojukwu, the ethnic peoples of the region had received reliable information that the federal government was preparing to attack our region for seceding from the federation. We firmly believed, then, that only through secession could we save ourselves from more widespread pogroms which Northern soldiers and civilians perpetrated against our people during the Northern riots. The slaughter of our Igbo people had continued unabated in Lagos, Western Nigeria, and Midwestern Nigeria in their so-called counter-coups.

Despite all the entreaties to stop the continuing slaughter of Eastern Nigerians made by our leaders to the Supreme Military Council of the Hausa/Fulani-led junta in Lagos, the government seemed either cruelly insensitive to our dilemma or blatantly incapable of stopping the carnage. In fact, the federal government's attitude toward the continued mass slaughter of our people made us believe, more than ever, that if our government could not somehow stop the Northerners, they would wipe the Igbo race out of existence in Nigeria.

Therefore, as a personal security measure, Governor Ojukwu did not attend national security meetings the federal army arranged, neither in Lagos, nor elsewhere in Nigeria. Instead, he sent his senior government representatives who attended the last scheduled peace talks in Lagos and Enugu, the Midwest Regional city of Benin. In addition, Governor Ojukwu and a contingent of Eastern Nigerian military and civilian leaders attended another peace talk meeting with federal government officials, in Ethiopia, a leading member country of the Organization for African Unity (OAU). Unfortunately, both of these peace meetings failed to produce an accord. Thus, a cloud of uncertainty continued to hang over our crises-ridden nation.

Nevertheless, in late December 1966, the federal government in Lagos and the Eastern Regional government in Enugu made contacts with influential OAU officials to hold peace talks outside Nigeria as a means to end the impenetrable impasse in the relationship between Lagos and Enugu. Eventually, both governments agreed to attend the meeting in Ghana.

The meeting took place on January 4 and 5, 1967 in Aburi, Ghana. After two-day deliberations, both parties arrived at a number of agreements, dubbed the "Aburi Accord," which, if fully implemented, would have united Eastern Nigerians with the other regions of the country. When the delegates returned home, however, federal government authorities reneged on the Aburi Accord. Because of the ominous security reports the returning Governor Ojukwu and his delegation gave to the Eastern Nigeria Consultative Assembly in Enugu, it became pointedly clear that the federal Nigerian leaders were neither sincere nor serious in proposing and pursuing any peaceful means of resolving the differences between the two governments. Instead, they would threaten to use their federal might and machinations to force our region back to the Nigerian federation.

Furthermore, our senior military and political leaders believed that it was no longer safe for Governor Ojukwu or members of his government to engage in further peace talks with the Nigerian military authorities. Therefore, instead of continuing to wait for federal subventions that might never come from Lagos to ease the financial burdens of Eastern Nigerians, Enugu concentrated all its efforts into good governance of the region, particularly addressing the problem of the teeming refugees now flooding the area from other regions of Nigeria. But as the federal government slowly choked off money to the region, the suffering of our people increased. Ironically, the Nigerians' actions only inspired the citizenry to make more internal efforts to survive—including efforts that involved everybody thinking seriously and creatively about practical ways of supporting the government in its determination to make the region internally independent at the economic, defense, and security levels. Moreover, it became clear to all socially conscious people that the survival of the people rested on the people. They had to achieve it by any means available to them, including engaging in some form of armed struggle.

Consequently, the federal military government responded by blockading Eastern Nigeria by land, sea, and air—determined to choke off our region economically, and then attack us militarily.

The Eastern Nigeria Consultative Assembly reacted by authorizing Governor Ojukwu to declare the region the Republic of Biafra, which he eventually did on May 30, 1967. Thereafter, the Governor embarked on a meet-the-people tour of all the provinces of the new country, and sent a group of senior military officers to prepare the students of each of the two tertiary institutions, the University of Nigeria, Nsukka, and the Advanced Teachers Training College, Owerri, politically, psychologically, and militarily in case Nigeria attacked our young republic.

The students applauded Governor Ojukwu for his courage, shouting: "On Aburi we stand!" while those of us majoring in French shouted: "*Sur Aburi nous sommes de buts!*" We also asked the visiting officers to train and arm us with guns so we could avenge the deaths of our friends and family while simultaneously fighting to protect and defend the Republic of Biafra. They trained us with clubs, machetes, and a few guns, giving us rigorous training in physical exercises, use of small arms, war tactics and maneuvers, and lessons on civil defense.

On a bright and sunny afternoon, thirty-six days after Governor Ojukwu had declared Biafra's independence, Ukoha and I sat reading in the library. Suddenly, the sound of gunfire broke through the silence of the book stacks.

"Did you hear that?" Ukoha whispered.

"Yes. I hear it. It sounds like Christmas fireworks," I said.

"No. It's more than fireworks. It sounds like gunshots."

"Then, let's go outside and see what is happening." I stood and walked toward the doors.

"Yes. Let's go. I hope Nigeria has not decided to attack us." Ukoha followed closely behind.

"I don't think so," I called back over my shoulder. "Governor Ojukwu would never let them."

"How is he going to stop them if they decide to attack?" Ukoha asked.

"I don't know. Time will tell." But I was worried as I opened the door.

Then, two deafening bomb explosions shook the air from the direction of the Owerri market square. Gunshots rang out from our Biafran law enforcement officers who had fired at the Nigerian bombers fleeing the market. The bomb blasts had killed dozens of people as they stampeded to take cover. Thatched sheds burned. Charred bodies, and pools of blood puddled in the market streets.

The sirens' shrill whine pierced the air and the pandemonium reigned over all the Owerri campus and town. People passing by wondered aloud: "Has Colonel Yakubu Gowon started to implement his promised police action against Eastern Nigeria, or has he declared an all-out war on us?" College administrators quickly summoned students, faculty, and staff to the Auditorium and asked us to be vigilant and to listen to the Voice of Biafra news station and read bulletins on campus for further briefings by the administration. A few days later, we learned that the Nigeria-Biafra War had already begun in border towns. The administration immediately ordered all the students home.

I had just returned from college when Agwu Ogbaa came to fetch me from Chief Amos Ota Mmagu's house.

"Good morning, sir." Agwu is my younger half-brother. Before the war, he lived with me as a houseboy at Eloha Ihe Primary School and at the Presbyterian Primary School, Kpirikpiri in Abakaliki, where I taught classes until I went to study at the ATTC. "A group meeting in the *Awada nde ezi anyi* (compound community hall) asked me to fetch you," he said.

I quickly prepared to leave. "Do you know the others called to the meeting?"

"I saw Eke Kalu, Eke Uwakwe, Joseph Kalu Imaga (JKIMA), Martin Okoro, Ogbonnaya Kalu Ulu, and a few other teachers and secondary school students. They said they wanted to discuss the war."

I threw on a coat and we made a dash back to the hall. But I stopped him so he and I could go there together. He was too young to participate in the meeting scheduled for *men*, but he could attend as my assistant.

Several people arose as we entered to welcome me back to the village and exchange pleasantries.

"When did you come back, KO?" JKIMA asked me.

"I got back four days ago. But I was busy looking for a place where I could live until the end of the war. I found a room in Chief Amos Ota Mmagu's house. But I pray for the war to end soon so I can go back to school. How have you been? Where are you staying?" I asked JKIMA.

"I came back a week ago. I'm staying with my brother Okoro Imaga in our compound. Like you, I hope and pray for the war's end so we can all return to our places of employment and education," he replied.

We then found seats together and after a few minutes, the chair called the meeting to order.

Everyone took turns in relating their experiences with the crises before and after the outbreak of armed hostilities. Many were interested in hearing about my college experiences since we were one of two tertiary institutions in Biafra where exhaustive discussions had helped to develop the strategies of approaches to the military, security, and refugee issues now facing our young country. I related all the information I could concerning our future, particularly emphasizing the importance of creating a strong civil defense and the need for us to schedule other plenary sessions to form various committees to organize defense and security of our villagers and clansmen. Moreover, I collaborated with others to prepare our people psychologically, emotionally, and tactically about how to approach the war.

Initially, I served in the newly formed Akanu Ibiam National Ambulance (an indigenous equivalent of the Red Cross Society), which accompanied soldiers and troops in border towns of Ipene and Agbanwan. Later, I worked in civil defense alongside colleagues from other academic institutions, civil servants, and businesspersons who returned from various regions of Nigeria, many with deep physical and emotional wounds from exposure to mass beatings and killings (decapitations, rapes, disembowelments of pregnant women), some of which they either witnessed from a hiding place or experienced directly in Northern Nigeria.

I also helped to organize and educate our people on the importance of vigilance at all times. Every villager and clansman had to contribute money, food, vehicles, clothes, and other materials to support our troops on the warfronts. Their initial response was tremendous since the Northern riots and mass killings that took place during the 1966 coups and counter-coups affected virtually every Igbo family. A group of educated men in the clan, including myself, called together our young primary school teachers, university and secondary school students, as well as civil servants to organize "Ihe Youth Association (IYA)." IYA's primary objective was to promote the secondary and university education of all sons and daughters of the clan, because Ihechiowa, the largest clan in Arochukwu District, had produced only a few university graduates compared to those produced by the smaller neighboring clans of Arochukwu and Ututu. Consequently, one of the greatest ironies of the Nigeria-Biafra War is that it drove native Ihechiowa indigenes home from other parts of the country and thus made it possible for the youth to meet regularly and have serious discussions on issues of higher education.

But as the war situation deteriorated, members of IYA shifted our focus to helping local authorities to set up and run civil defense committees. The committees included the land army, the combing organizations, and the vigilante groups (*nde nche*) that would ensure that Nigerian enemies did not infiltrate our clan, which shared borders with villages in the old Calabar Province of Nigeria. IYA also served as a liaison between the clan and the army. However, some Ohafia people suspected one ethnic minority group, the Ibibio-speaking Biakpan people (who shared borders with Ohafia and Ihechiowa clans), of engaging in acts of sabotage against Biafra. Therefore, from time to time men from Asaga Ohafia would comb Biakpan villages in search of such saboteurs and the Nigerian enemy. Periodically, we received reports that Asaga people tortured and killed their Biakpan counterparts, a sad consequence of such bloody conflicts that still haunts me to this day.

One night, hundreds of Biakpans secretly left their homes to take refuge in Achara Ihechiowa, with whom they had blood covenant. Upon learning of the exodus, the Asaga villagers sent soldiers to Achara with orders to arrest *Eze Ogo* Achara (the village head) for collaborating with the Biafran saboteurs. After arresting and detaining the

Achara village head in Ohafia, the IYA executive members, including myself, sent an ultimatum for the immediate release and return of the *Eze Ogo* Achara. Colonel Uwakwe, commander of the Upper Itu Sector, defused the tension between the two villages by agreeing to act as intermediary and ordered his soldiers to release and return *Eze Ogo* Achara. He was returned immediately. Since Ihechiowa was a central agricultural center for the region, supplying his army with important food staples, he wanted the IYA to stay happy.

In early August 1967, representatives of the Biafran Armed Forces began to recruit troops from the Arochukwu District. I organized prospective recruits from Ihechiowa clan. I had previously applied for admission into the newly created Biafran Officers Training School (BOTS) in Orlu. But before my interview, I experienced a traumatic fall from a bicycle accident in which I broke my two arms, bent one of my left, upper-front teeth, split my upper lip, and severely bruised my face—injuries that made it impossible for me to serve as a combat soldier. I was thoroughly disappointed, and so was my father. But by late October, when I had healed a bit, I decided to get involved in non-combat support, including supplying food to the S&T Directorate based at the army depot in Obinto.

In April 1968, I was at market buying the food for the S&T when soldiers took me into custody and hauled me to the Upper Itu Sector Headquarters at Ndi Uduma Awoke for conscription into the army. There I met Commander Uwakwe and his civilian assistant, Lt. A. C. C. Azodo. Lieutenant Azodo recognized me as his student from ATTC. We shook hands and took me to the commander where they both interviewed me for conscription. The Commander ordered me to become his food supply officer for his office. I received a new pass to replace the one issued by the S&T. Then I was driven home with orders to be prepared each Orie day for one of his Army Jeeps to pick me up and gather supplies for his headquarters.

Buying food supplies from Ukwa (now in Akwa Ibom State) gave me a great opportunity to intermingle with the Ukwa people and gather useful intelligence for the army. Initially, I carried out such intelligence gathering with much discretion. Later, as I gained more allies, I was able to do so in the company of the Upper Itu Sector Headquarters soldiers. In the company of returning Biafran soldiers and members of the Biafran Organization of Freedom Fighters (BOFF), I continued to gather useful intelligence, which enabled our people to prevent random killings, rape, arson, and looting that jubilant Efik/Ibibio soldiers were committing against us as they passed through Ihechiowa villages returning to their home state in southeast Nigeria. I played the dual role for the army until the war ended in that sector on January 12, 1970.

During the war, I experienced the greatest spiritual awakening of my life. One day, a man approaching the checkpoint at the Umuchiakuma/Achara Junction, accosted me.

"Hello there! Are you Mr. Kalu Ogbaa?"

"Yes, I am. Who are you?"

"I am Brother Amaramiro, Alex Amaramiro. Can we talk privately?"

"Why should we?" I was skeptical and suspicious of this stranger.

"Because what I'm going to tell you is private and important to both of us."

I studied him for a moment. He was serious. "Sure." I pointed. "Let's step over under that mango tree."

Amaramiro introduced himself as the director of the refugee camp in our village and a native of Arochukwu town. He was interested in opening a branch of the first Pentecostal Church in West Africa in our village, and wanted me to assist him. I listened carefully, then looked him in the eyes and asked why he believed I was the right person (I had been a secret member of the Holy Order for four years, but only members of my family knew about it since I was a primary school teacher with the Presbyterian school and did not want to get fired). I worshiped openly in the Presbyterian Church but secretly worshipped at home as a Pentecostal Cherubim and Seraphim member (except during the holidays, when I worshiped openly in Enugu, about 150 miles away from school).

During our discussion, Amaramiro said that he did his homework before approaching me and had made inquiries, which led him to the family of a senior elder of the Order, Rabbi Jonah Harbor, who lived and worshiped in Enugu. His mother was a member of the Presbyterian Church and strong sympathizer of the Order. He had made his decision to approach me at her suggestion. In addition, Amaramiro said he would begin the formation of the branch by converting refugees in his camp, beginning their worship in the house of Chief Oleh Okoko. He had enough relief materials from World Council of Churches and Caritas International to begin the conversion. He needed me to start looking for a plot of land where we could erect a mud-and-thatch church. He and a group of elders from his hometown of Arochukwu would pay for the initial expenses to help us establish the branch.

I saw he was sincere in asking me to join him to do God's work. I told him that I would seriously think about what he had just told me and give him a response soon.

"May God bless you, my brother." He took my hand and shook it generously.

I was greatly moved by his demeanor, humility, and candor. I went back to work at the checkpoint, and at the end of the day, I took a quick shower, ate my dinner, and went directly to my small altar to pray and thank God for His protection against the air raids that the Nigerian Air Force had been intensely carrying out over our Biafran towns and villages. As I meditated, I drifted back to the conversation with Amaramiro. All of a sudden, I flashed back to the evening of a hazy day in October 1964, when Brother Ikpo rushed me to the Eternal Sacred Order of Cherubim and Seraphim church in Enugu for urgent healing prayers.

Earlier that day, a naturopathic doctor, Thomas Ndolo, had given me an herbal concoction to evacuate what he called "abdominal impurities," which he believed had been causing the acute pains I had been suffering for a time. I had already consulted many conventional doctors at the General Hospital at Arochukwu and Enugu, and a Specialist Hospital, and no one could find the cause of my symptoms. Dr. Ndolo was my last hope and for finding a cure to my mysterious condition.

But twenty minutes after I took the concoction, I began to have a violent intestinal reaction, including cramps and diarrhea that continued for so long that I became faint and exhausted. Fearing I might die, I shouted for help until Ikpo rushed in and took me to his parlor. At that moment, Rabbi Jonah Harbor dropped in to visit before heading to his evening prayers at the Cherubim and Seraphim. After seeing my helpless condition, he ordered my brother to rush me to the church for prayers. Ikpo rushed me immediately to the church, and Rabbi Harbor beckoned two Army of Salvation members to take me to a corner and pray over me. He then informed Supervising Apostle Umezinwa of my condition and the apostle instructed the congregation to form a circle around me for spiritual threshing. They sprinkled holy water all over my body and asked me to drink of the cup. I drank, and motioned for more, which they gave until I drank my fill.

Then the congregation began shouting prayers over me, so loud, so alluring that I involuntarily began to shout "Amen" and "Amen" at the end of each sentence until I regained my energy and felt healed. Then a bell rang and the loud congregational prayers ceased. Each member went back to their seats and sat down. Suddenly a young Yoruba member, possessed, it seemed, by the Holy Spirit, leaped out of his seat and spoke. Rabbi Harbor asked me to continue kneeling and listen while the spirit-possessed man prophesied to me:

Before God and man [and the congregation said Amen]: My brother, you should rejoice exceedingly in the Lord. Yes, in the eyes of men, they brought you here to receive treatment for a disease, which is unknown to medical doctors. That is why none of them has been able to diagnose and treat it effectively. However, to the Saints above, your illness is a means through which our merciful God wanted you to come join the Saints below to worship, honor, and serve Him. You are His elect. You must be baptized by immersion so you can take your preordained position in the Holy Order. You have such a bright future that the enemy has been trying to destroy you right from birth to no avail. You have had two major accidents in the past that could have taken your life. Rejoice because the Lord has saved you from suffering un-timely death because He surrounded you with His guardian angels...

Suddenly, another member jumped up and shouted with uplifted hands, "Hallelujah, Iye. Hosanna, Amen!" Then the entire congregation rose to their feet and shouted a victory chorus three times, and sat down again. Then the young prophet continued:

I saw you walking on a wide coal-tarred road with burning torches lined up on both of its sides. You appeared very happy and joyous. All of a sudden, I saw two outstretched black hands attempting to quench the torches, but each time they tried, an angel burned them with fire. Eventually, the enemy withdrew from the road and disappeared into the dark. God is saying to you, "Fear not, for I am with you all the time and all the way."...

Loud shouts of "Hallelujah, Iye, Hosanna, Amen!" from the congregation filled the air.

> *I saw you in spirit making effort to enter the university, but you were afraid and unhappy that you might not make it because of your illness. Be not afraid, for the Lord says you will not only attend a university in this country, but also other universities overseas. When all these things shall come to pass, do not feel too big to worship God in this Holy Order, for He has already ordained you in spirit as one of His powerful apostles. In fact, you will lead others to establish some branches of the Holy Order in your life. My brother, our mighty God has blessed you; praise Him forevermore! The vision went off my sight, before God and man!*

After delivering God's message, the man fell to the floor unconscious. Several senior elders surrounded him and began praying, sprinkling him and me with holy water, and then offering it for him to drink. As soon as he was revived, he got up and walked back to his seat. Responding to my healing experience and the seer's revival, the congregation burst into singing a hortatory song, clapping hands and dancing in praise of the Almighty Jehovah, their God of victory:

> *Stand up Army of Salvation*
> *Praise the name of Jesus Christ*
> *For the great day you've seen today*
> *Is for Michael our captain*
>
> *Holy Michael our captain*
> *Holy Michael our captain*
> *Guide us to the end of our life*
> *Conquer Lucifer for us.*
>
> *Jesus Holy Son of our Father*
> *We will ever praise Thy name*
> *Michael has conquered the Satan*
> *All Satanic war vanquished.*

At the end of the service, the elders took me to their private vestry and asked me to purchase a white flowing prayer gown and to come every evening to their church to prepare my spirit for full-immersion baptism. I was so impressed by the content of the prophecy and by my recovery that I decided there and then to purchase the gown and receive the baptism at the earliest opportunity. One week later,

Supervising Apostle Umezinwa took me and six other new converts to a designated lake in the city and baptized us. Each of us received the power of the Holy Spirit, and I was ready to follow Jesus Christ as my Lord and Savior with the help of the Holy Order.

Amaramiro came to the checkpoint the next day. He knew I would be there because I volunteered to work there daily alongside the civil defense workers and soldiers. I had an answer ready for him, because on the night he had asked me to help him, I had knelt down at my altar and prayed for God to guide me in making the right decision. I began the prayers with a song I usually sang whenever I sought the face of God on important issues:

Lead me Lord; lead me in Thy righteousness
Make Thy way plain before my face
For it is Thou oh Lord, oh Lord Thou only
That maketh me dwell in safety

As I prayed for God to guide me to make the right decision, I first thanked Him for his blessings. I also asked myself serious questions to ensure that the decision came from my soul.

Could it be that God sent Amaramiro to offer me the opportunity to fulfill an aspect of the prophecy given to me at 14, Ilukwe Street, Asata in Enugu on the fateful day, when they rushed me to the Holy Order for instant healing in October 1964?

Could it be that the hour had come when I must serve my God openly in the Holy Order?

Could it be that the hour had come when I must act in obedience to what Jesus said in John 4: 24, "God is a Spirit: and they that worship him must worship *him* in spirit and in truth"?

Could it be that God had chosen this time to use me as a vessel through which He would save the lives of many people spiritually and materially, especially the refugees in our village?

Could it be that if I served God in this capacity the fear of losing my teaching job and membership in the Presbyterian Church would all go away?

Could it be that the branch of the Holy Order we built would be here *eternally* in my village for me and other members to worship whenever we chose to do so without any fears?

Could it be that God wanted to use me as a useful hand to build a branch of his Holy Order, where people could freely receive healing and grace as I once did in Enugu?

After the meditation, I knew I was ready to give Amaramiro an answer that would make him happy. The Holy Spirit had persuaded me to embark on such a service to God and man. There was no turning back. Finally, I knelt down and prayerfully sang the following song:

All to Jesus I surrender
All to Him I freely give
I will ever love and trust Him
In His presence daily live

   I surrender all
   I surrender all
   All to Thee my blessed Savior
   I surrender all

All to Jesus I surrender
Lord, I give myself to Thee
Fill me with Thy love and power
Let Thy blessing rest on me

The next day, when Amaramiro came to the checkpoint, I was ready. "Good day, Brother Amaramiro. I believe you're coming to see me."

"Good day, Brother Ogbaa. Yes! I came to see you, but how did you know that I was coming specifically to see you and not just passing by?" He smiled.

"Because I see it written all over your face. You want an answer to the question you asked me yesterday. Let's go under the mango tree and talk."

As we sat on a log under the tree, I told him that I was willing and ready to assist him whatever way I could to build the house of prayer. In the discussion that followed between us, I narrated to him how I converted to the Holy Order in 1964 and had been worshiping secretly in the Holy Order because I was afraid of losing my teaching job under the Presbyterian school authorities. I told him how uncomfortable and hypocritical I felt worshiping in both churches. I told him how long I had been praying for God to give me the grace, strength, and opportunity to worship Him in spirit and in truth without losing my teaching job. I told him how I felt like an ingrate for failing to requite the healing grace of God through serving Him fervently and in the open. I told him how, after meditating on the request he made of me last night, I had decided to serve God and man boldly by partaking in the building of a branch of the Holy Order in my own hometown.

Brother Amaramiro jumped up. "Hallelujah, Iye. Hosanna, Amen," he shouted, and gave me a big bear hug. He then shared his own story with me. He too had been an ardent member of the Presbyterian Church but recently converted to the Holy Order. He assured me, however, that after his conversion, he experienced a kind of joy he'd never felt before. And that's what had driven him to build a branch of the Holy Order here, where he could openly worship God anytime he wanted.

After, we held hands and prayed together, asking God to assist us in working his purposes through us. At the end of the prayer, I heard a voice. "Why don't you ask your people to donate this very land on which you are standing and praying?" I turned and looked around. There was no one. "Who said that?" I asked Amaramiro.

He turned. "Who said what?"

At that moment, I knew it was the voice of God. I told Amaramiro what I heard.

"God is here to bless us." He shook his head. Then we sang Number 54, a familiar song from the Order's hymnal that echoed what he had said. We sang joyously, smiling and clapping hands together like long-lost brothers recently reunited.

When I arrived home that evening, I went to my landlord, Chief Amos Ota Mmagu, and sought his advice about how we could acquire the land. I knew from the history of the village that at the turn of the twentieth century, representatives of the Church of Scotland Mission (CSM) came through Ohafia to establish a church. When they had originally settled and begun to proselytize our people, they had condemned all aspects of our traditional religion, customs, and culture, calling them the practices of heathens. Consequently, our people had driven them out of the land with deadly stinging bees. They had hastily withdrawn to Obinto, which later became the headquarters of the CSM in Ihechiowa. Thereafter, the land became a playground where villagers practiced wrestling and other sports, and masqueraded in sacred garb during annual and seasonal festivals of the village. Chief Mmagu, a highly influential chief in the village, knew that if I were involved, the Church could not be bad for our people. So he helped us acquire the land to build the church.

Amaramiro brought elders from the church of Arochukwu, including Rabbi Orji Akweke, Leader Ebeniro, Aladura Akpo, and one Lady Leader whose name I cannot now recall, to consecrate the land and the foundation trenches before we began building. The elders returned and consecrated it again once the building was completed. And they came thereafter almost every weekend to conduct Saturday midnight prayers and Sunday services with us until the war ended.

Soon, native members of the Holy Order returned from Eastern Nigeria, people such as Kalu Okoro and Bassey Okwuagwu from Amamiri, Achi Ukonu, Lawson Uche Arunsi, Nne Jonah Harbor, and Lily Ikpo Ogbaa from Umuchiakuma, and two other members from Achara and Okpo, who formed the pioneer members of the Umuchiakuma branch. The elders from Arochukwu appointed Amaramiro the elder in charge, and me his second-in-command. We worked closely together to ensure that the church membership grew. In less than one year, our membership grew to 250, and we established two other branches in Umuye and Achara in Ihechiowa clan.

God used Amaramiro and me to provide not only spiritual leadership, but also the material needs of the church. Amaramiro used relief materials from his refugee camp to help not only the refugees, but also the poor, the sick, and the needy that depended on such relief materials for survival. I employed refugees as regular carriers of the food supplies I was buying for the army from Ukwa and Ihechiowa area markets. In addition to paying the refugees for their services, I occasionally donated yams and *garri* to them. The more I did, the more I prospered. So much so, I was inspired to buy virtually all the church benches, a table, and two bells for the church. Moreover, all our members did their best to provide food and money for the church to care for the poor and needy, as well as the refugees. In fact, our church was the only one, among the four churches, that did not depend on external aid for its survival. We lived the lives of First Century Christians.

During the final throes of the war, between January 8 and 12, 1970, the Nigerian troops, who were advancing from the Cross River axis of the Upper Itu Sector into mainland Biafra, attacked Arochukwu District with heavy weapons. The stunningly deafening explosions sent everybody packing in our village to take refuge in distant thick forests and ancient caves. As the troops came closer and closer, our civil defense committees quickly met and planned safe evacuation of people away from enemy mortar bombs, rockets, and shelling. Until those deadly days in January, the war had not had a great impact on Ihechiowa. No land battles had been fought in their region. Nevertheless, the constant air raids and bombs the Nigerian Air Force threw at the region, while never killing many people, had caused deep psychological and emotional injuries to everyone.

The biggest reason the enemy had not fought ground battles in our region was because our troops had laid mines along the Cross River shorelines in anticipation that Nigerian troops would attempt crossing the river to overrun the sector. Moreover, because the shorelines were important entry points between South Eastern State of Nigeria and the Republic of Biafra, troops from both countries fortified them heavily on both sides. Hence, the pandemonium that followed the Nigerian troops' sudden and surprising incursion into the sector became too unnerving for our soldiers and civil defense units to handle. But our saving grace was that the roads leading to those hidden caves and tangled forests, where we planned to take refuge, were narrow, rocky, winding, and unusable by motorists, in addition to being unknown by non-natives. And even if the enemy troops were led on foot by saboteurs to our hideouts, they might not have been willing to risk their lives engaging us in hand-to-hand combat, for they were aware that many of our men had been trained in martial art and guerilla warfare.

As our villagers prepared to leave their homes, we instructed them to take only their most valuable possessions: money, jewelry, clothes, and important documents. But some ignored the instructions, taking many trips from their homes to the designated safe-haven, collecting as much food and livestock as they could before the Nigerian vandals reached the village.

I checked on arrangements my father had made to take his second wife, Orieji, and her children to safety. I also checked on my brother Ikpo and his family before I left. Then I took Mother, Charity Elezuo (the refugee woman who always went with me to buy food supplies for the S&T Directorate), and her four children to a spot in the safe-haven, where we took refuge until it became safe for all of us to go back to the village.

On January 11, 1970, our Biafran soldiers brought war casualties, armament, and medical supplies from battlefields to our town hall. While they stockpiled the arms and ammunition there, they kept severely wounded soldiers in my mother's nearby mud-and-thatch house awaiting a military ambulance to carry them to safety. Unfortunately, enemy soldiers from Cross River axis discovered the arms—including the dreaded homemade *ogbunigwe* (the mass destroyer). From a safe distance, they fired rockets on the arms and set the whole village ablaze. We could see the raging fire from four miles away.

When we returned home following the announcement of the official end of the war on January 16, Mother and I found twelve skulls and the ashes of dead soldiers on an empty spot that used to be her kitchen. I consoled her, and with the help of others, dug a shallow grave, said a short prayer, and interred their *freed* remains. They became part of the numerous unknown soldiers, whose loved ones continued to cling hopelessly to the dream that they would somehow, someday, return. Thank God that Mother is no longer alive to wonder who they were; and thank God that so many relatives of those unknown Biafran braves now rest in peace, themselves!

Overall, my memories of war-torn Biafra primarily arise from my work in civil defense for our clan. I served as a volunteer in Akanu Ibiam National Ambulance during the early days. I bought food supplies for the army through the S&T Directorate. I gathered intelligence for the army. I served God and man through the Eternal Sacred Oder of Cherubim and Seraphim. I learned to trust God in whatever circumstances I found myself. And it is that faith which has helped me to endure the most heartbreaking moments in my life since the war. As I go through the trials and temptations of life in peacetime, the great wartime spiritual awakening I experienced will continue to serve as an enduring anchor of my life. Until I am called back to meet Jesus Christ, my Lord and Savior, I pray for all my loved ones, who already rest there in perfect peace. Oh, what a joy that meeting will be!

But that time is not yet. For, indeed, there are many people in my family and in the world, who still need my services on earth. With God's help, I intend to serve them faithfully in any way I can, for I believe God spared my life during and after the bloody war to fulfill many unknown sacred obligations. In the words of Robert Frost:

> *But I have promises to keep,*
> *And miles to go before I sleep.*
> *And miles to go before I sleep.*

Chapter 8

Postwar Reconstruction

At the end of the war, the Federal Military Government (FMG) ceded the Republic of Biafra to Nigeria and renamed it East Central State, the former title given it by the Gowon administration prior to the war. While the other two sister states—South Eastern State and Rivers State—resumed normal everyday activities, especially schooling, the FMG did not allow our state government to reopen its pre-war schools and tertiary institutions, citing security concerns. They feared that the self-exiled Biafran strongman, General Ojukwu, was planning a postwar Biafran government in exile and that he might use senior administrators and professors in our academic institutions to execute his plans at home in Nigeria. Moreover, the Nigerian military leaders accused him and the university professors of planning the secession of Eastern Nigeria on the UNN campus before the war. In addition, they alleged that UNN intellectuals invented and mass-produced the homemade arms, which Biafran troops used in waging the war. Consequently, the FMG summoned those who served as officers in Biafran Armed Forces to Owerri where they were detained, interrogated, debriefed and, later, released.

Our campus in Nsukka remained closed ten months after the war ended until October 1970. On the other hand, the FMG permitted all primary and secondary schools, teacher training colleges, and the ATTC to reopen in April. Apparently, the Nigerian military authorities did not consider these teachers and administrators as dangerous as those from the UNN Campus.

While the schools and colleges remained closed, I continued to buy food supplies. Only now, I purchased the supplies for civilians instead of the now defunct S&T Directorate. There was widespread hunger and disease, especially in Kwashiorkor in East Central State. The war prevented farmers in this war-torn area from producing enough food. I therefore purchased mass quantities at vastly reduced costs to help the families who needed food for their survival. I was able to make a slight profit and saved as much of it as I could to help pay tuition and fees at the UNN, when the military authorized its reopening and I gained admission to study in it.

Another immediate difficulty presented to us at the end of the war was the total devaluation of Biafran currency. The Gowon administration declared the Biafran currency illegal tender in Nigeria, and decreed that anyone with bank accounts in Biafran currency exchange whatever balance they had on each of their accounts. Each person received £20 Nigerian pounds for their complete balances. By chance, I was one of the first to find out about the new Nigerian currency notes. While buying food supplies from Obinto Market, I met a Nigerian military officer of Yoruba in charge of the military post based in our clan.

"Come here, young man," the officer ordered.

"Good morning, officer." I stepped his way.

"What's your name?"

"Kalu Ogbaa. And yours?"

"I am Lt. Olu Adebayo." He got up from his seat and shook hands with me.

"Please, sit." He motioned to a chair. "Let's chat." He watched me closely as I moved to the seat. He was up to something.

"Thank you very much." I studied his face.

He knew from my proficient use of English that I was a well-educated man. And because he chose his words carefully and spoke politely and respectfully, I assumed that he believed I was an ex-Biafran military officer. On my part, I respected him as a military officer who had a job to do. Nevertheless, I refused to address him as "sir." He wasn't older than I was, and therefore did not deserve that kind of respect from me. Besides, I suspected that he thought I was superior to him in age, military rank, and educational attainment since he began his interrogation in a well-calculated friendly tone.

"In what sector of the war did you serve in the secessionist army?"

"Do you mean in the Biafran Armed Forces?" I retorted.

"Yes. If you like to call East Central State Biafra...."

"Yes. I lived in the Republic of Biafra during the war. Now that the war is over, I live in East Central State."

"Okay. But you have not told me the sectors in which you fought the war."

"What makes you think that I was a soldier?"

"You look every inch an officer. And we know that every able-bodied man or woman like you fought in your defunct country."

"Your assumption is partly correct and partly wrong."

"Oh? How so?" He leaned back, eyebrows raised.

"Your assumption is right in that every Biafran fought the war in one form or another. That was why we regarded ourselves as citizen soldiers. But I can tell you that not every able-bodied person served their country in uniform."

"So what specific roles did you play?"

"Oh, I played many roles. Just like many other Biafrans for our people's collective survival. But not in uniform." I tried to use "Biafra" or "Biafran" in all my answers (which every Nigerian soldier hated to hear) in order to frustrate him into revealing his true intentions. But he remained cool as he continued to interrogate me.

"But you must have belonged to a paramilitary organization, like the BOFF, the Militia, or the Boy Scout Society?" he mused.

"You know that the Boy Scout Society is not a paramilitary organization."

"But some of the Boy Scouts assisted your troops in one form or another at the war front." He straightened, a bit frustrated.

I knew he was insinuating that I must have engaged in gathering useful intelligence for the military without wearing a uniform.

"No, I did not belong to any of those organizations. I was just a bloody civilian."

"Then how did you get the scars on your face and arms?" He looked intently into my face searching for me to tell a lie.

"Well, Officer Adebayo, if that is the evidence you have for suspecting me to be a Biafran military officer, you are wrong. For, there are many other Biafrans, including women and children, with deeper wounds and scars than mine, inflicted on them by Nigerian soldiers and civilians during the Western Nigerian riots in 1965, the Northern riots in 1966, the army coups and countercoups in 1966, and during the war that began in 1967. Like me, most of those people did not go to the battlefields to fight when their fellow Nigerians attacked and wounded or even killed some of them. The only crime I know they must have committed against their fellow Nigerians to deserve being marked for death or any of the heinous atrocities they suffered was that they belonged to the wrong ethnic group: the Igbo. For many of us, the physical war has ended, but the psychological, emotional, and financial war is just beginning. Hence we wonder, 'Who would come to our rescue?'"

My long pent-up emotions spilled out in a flood of indignity. I suddenly realized that I was almost shouting at one of the enemy soldiers. So I abruptly stopped talking and took a breath. All the while, Officer Adebayo had remained unruffled. He paused a moment before continuing his interrogation

"How did you get your own wounds?" His voice sounded almost compassionate.

"From a bicycle fall in a near-death accident. But God was merciful. I survived. That is why I couldn't enlist into the Biafran Officers Training School (BOTS) where I had applied to train as a combatant army officer prior to the accident." I finished and watched his reaction.

"I'm sorry to hear. Were you ever called to serve after that?" he persisted.

"No. But my colleagues told the army what happened to me. And when I was later conscripted to serve while buying food for the army, they interviewed me, inspected my wounds, which were not yet completely healed at the time, and let me go."

"If I asked you to buy food for our army unit here, would you do it?"

"Sure. Provided you would pay me well. But not in Biafran currency notes," I said, and smiled.

At that, we both relaxed a little and ended the interrogation making general observations on the state of postwar Nigeria. Thereafter, I told him that I had some personal belongings I wanted to sell and wondered if he was interested. I needed money to continue buying and selling food. He offered to take me home, so we took his army jeep, accompanied by his two bodyguards, to see the items. He bought the tape recorder I used in studying French at the ATTC before the war plus a few other items for which he paid me £15 in new Nigerian currency notes. After he left for Obinto, several curious villagers came to find out why the soldiers paid me a visit. I showed them the new money the officer paid me for my items, after which some of them expressed interest in selling some of their own belongings if the opportunity came again to earn the new Nigerian money and replace the obsolete Biafran currency. We were all desperate for a better exchange rate.

At the time of the exchange, I had saved £335,000 in Biafran currency toward my university education. Of that amount, I saved £430 in old Nigerian currency in the Enugu branch before the war and the rest in Biafran currency, which I had saved in the Arochukwu branch during the war. In accordance with the decree, I received £20 in Nigerian currency from each of the two branches of the bank. In addition, I had £1,250 Biafran currency in cash at home, and our church had £200 in Biafran currency in cash, which we had to exchange for the new Nigerian money. With the help of a member of our church, I was able to combine the two amounts into one account and exchanged it for £20 Nigerian currency before the exchange deadline. The church and I received £10 each. Overall, I received only £50 in new Nigerian currency for all the money I had saved.

In the end, with £65 in new Nigerian currency in my possession, I went to A. W. Ibe Stores in Enugu, the capital of East Central State, and bought stockfish, other leftover war relief materials, and cigarettes to sell within and around Ihechiowa clan. In addition, I bought dried fish and other seafood in large quantities from Abakaliki to add to the stock I bought from Enugu and carried the goods on my head, selling them on foot in the three major markets in our clan: Umuchiakuma Market on Afor, Achara Market on Eke, and Obinto Market on Orie days. I also sold goods daily at my home village whenever friends and neighbors needed them.

When the Ututu/Ihe High School finally reopened in April, the principal invited me to teach English Language and Literature. I welcomed the invitation since it gave me the opportunity to earn and save more money for my prospective university tuition and fees. I walked four miles each day to school with the students from the twin villages of Umuchiakuma and Amammiri. A month after my engagement, the principal invited me to his office and informed me that the government instructed him to rehire only teachers who served in the school before the war. He would pay each of them with a bale of stockfish and a blanket until the state received some subvention from Lagos to pay workers' salaries in Nigerian currency. He regretted that the board of education did not approve his plea to hire me officially or at least pay me for the one month I had served and that he was letting me go without any form of remuneration. I thanked him for inviting me there in the first place and assured him that I bore him no grudge. After clearing my cubicle, I left the school and walked home, highly disappointed.

Despite the beliefs of detractors who misjudged why I was neither continuing my education at the ATTC or holding my short-lived job at the Ututu/Ihe High School, I was determined to prove to them that the two institutions were beneath my academic qualifications. I decided to do whatever was necessary to gain admission into the UNN, one of the two most prestigious universities in Nigeria. I explained to Father why I was neither studying at the ATTC nor teaching in the high school. As expected, he believed me since I was his most trusted son and had always brought honor to his family.

With his blessing, I continued my trek to Obinto with the high school students, but now I once again carried goods on my head to sell on Orie Market days. Some of the students sneered and laughed at me. And my younger brother, Agwu Ogbaa, felt so embarrassed that he asked me for an explanation. I showed him my GCE papers and explained the situation, which satisfied him. And I continued to buy and sell food over the months, remembering what I'd read about the American meaning of the dignity of labor, which complemented my spiritual belief that God would surely give me the grace to enter the university, eventually. I fasted and prayed before buying and selling the food, and made more money. Sometimes I even forgot the indignity of the Ututu/Ihe High School.

But the real test of my faith came in September 1970, when the Admissions Office at the University of Nigeria, Nsukka, posted the names of those they offered admission, and mine was not there. Kalu Okoro, the man who went through the list, gave me the sad news, and I told Brother Ikpo about it. Instead of sympathizing with me, Ikpo became angry, saying that I brought my own undoing upon myself for arrogantly refusing to go back to the ATTC, where applicants were bribing officials to admit them. He was also afraid that I might not be able to sponsor myself at the university, even if I eventually received admission. I was greatly disappointed in him since I had shown him my certificates in April, when others, except Father, doubted that I could get admission into any university. I stormed out of his house in a rage and headed to the Cherubim and Seraphim Church to pray. At the end of my prayers, Brother Achi Ukonu prophesied that the disappointment I was experiencing happened because of human error. Nevertheless, it was a test of my faith in God. He advised me to go to Nsukka and sort things out in person, for God had already given me victory in spirit. Buoyed by the spiritual revelation, I rose up, shouting "Hallelujah, Iye. Hosanna, Amen," and kept up my faith with three days of fasting and prayers.

I traveled to Nsukka and checked the list. I confirmed the information Kalu Okoro had given me, then spoke to Mr. Onyekwere, from Umuahia, an assistant registrar in the Admissions Office. He asked me to give him my full personal information. He left his desk, and five minutes later, he came back and informed me that I was number five on the list of those recommended for admission into the English department. He didn't know why my name was omitted from the list of those admitted. Then he suggested I find a professor on campus to help me obtain the information I needed from the head of the English department. I thanked him for all his help, and assured him that even though I didn't know anybody on campus, God would surely provide a person through whom my name would be restored in the list of admitted candidates.

After leaving the Admissions Office, I went straight to Kalu Okoro from my village and told him what I had discovered. At the time, he was serving as chauffeur to Professor Eme Awah, the dean of the College of Social Sciences. I asked him to introduce me to his boss whose immediate help I needed. He agreed. Once introduced to the dean, Professor Awah, I narrated my story and without hesitation, he wrote a note of recommendation that I took to the head of the English department. After reading the note, he pulled out a file from his drawer and studied it. Then he asked me to follow him to the Admissions Office where he asked me to wait outside while he talked with the registrar. In a few minutes, he came out and apologized for omitting my name, and handed me an official letter of admission.

I thanked him for rectifying the situation and for his kindness. Then Kalu Okoro and I went back to his boss's office and I thanked him as well. I left the dean's office, and immediately found a quiet corner to kneel down, and thanked God. I then thanked Kalu Okoro for being the vessel through which God worked his purpose out for me. He drove me to the Motor Park in downtown Nsukka, where I took a cab that brought me home via Enugu and Umuahia towns.

Immediately after I arrived in my village, I went straight to our church and broke the happy news to Brother Achi Ukonu and the other members conducting evening prayers. Then I ran to Father's house and told him all about my trip, showing him my letter of admission. He laughed and gave me a big hug, asking me to kneel down for him to pray to our gracious God, for not allowing our enemies to laugh at us. He then invited the elders of our agnate family to pour libations to our ancestors. Everyone in attendance expressed their joy, saying that they knew I would always be a great achiever for Nde Ikpo agnate family and Nde Ngwo compound. After thanking them, I left for dinner at my mother's house before finally returning to my apartment room where I went straight to my altar and once again offered a heart-felt thanksgiving prayer to God before slipping into a long, blissful sleep.

Three days later, Brother Ikpo came to see me in the late afternoon at Chief Mmagu's house. Normally, I would be the one to go to his house for any family discussions. This time was different. Other members of our family had told him about my admission into the UNN, but because I did not go to him, he recalled our earlier altercation and decided to come to me instead.
"Good afternoon, KO, and congratulations on ..."
"On what?" I cut him short.
"I heard you've been admitted into the University of Nigeria, Nsukka."
"With what qualifications, if I may ask?"
"I never doubted your qualifications, KO. It's just that I feared that the family could not sponsor the cost of university...."
"Did I ask you for money before you talked to me the way you did? Why didn't you discuss the situation with me first before jumping into conclusion like the rest of our villagers, strangers who didn't know that I had passed the GCE exams at both the advanced and ordinary levels? Thank you for stopping by. But please, leave me alone to deal with my personal problems," I told him.
"I apologize for not discussing the matter with you as I should have. But now that you've been offered the admission, we still have to discuss your sponsorship as a family." He lowered his eyes as he turned to leave.
"No, wait! Before you go, you should know that I can't accept your apology without accompanying it with a pot of palm wine." I smiled.
He turned. "Why do you sell me so cheap? I thought you should have asked for a cow since *E gburu m ochu megide gi,* I committed manslaughter against you."
"Come," I said. We embraced and shook hands. All was forgiven. We walked together to Father's house to discuss how I was going to apply for a loan scholarship from the village. Father said he would sell all the yams in his barn or place them as collateral if necessary in support of any loans I would need for my university education. He

also promised not to let me down as he did in 1956 when he could not sponsor my prospective secondary school education because of his illness. I thanked him and informed him that I would qualify for the loan since I was one of six people who inspired our elders to institute the loan scholarship program in our village.

The history of our village loan scholarship scheme began in 1964 when Agwu Uche gained admission to study at the UNN and he needed financial assistance. Unable to pay all of his tuition and fees, he approached his mentor, Imaga Oleh, for help. Instead of giving him money, Imaga Oleh took him and his friend Amah Ola of Okpo Ihechiowa, with a small bottle of foreign gin, to the chief of the Nde Ngwo compound, Kalu Okoro, to get advice about how to approach the Eziukwu bloc about his university sponsorship. Chief Okoro sent for me to witness the meeting, as was custom whenever people discussed educational issues in our compound. When I arrived, I suggested that we discuss the matter at the home of *Eze Ezi*, the chief of the compound over our bloc.

When we arrived, *Eze Ezi* invited us into his house and brought out some kola nuts from his goatskin bag and a pot of palm wine to pour libations to the dead-living ancestors whose presence were needed in our deliberations. Then, Chief Okoro presented the gin to the *Eze Ezi* and told him why we came. In a proverb-laden response, he thanked us for coming to him but added that he alone could not handle the matter.

"*Agwu otu onye furu bu eke* (a snake that one man sees is always the deadliest)," he said. "I'm afraid that I see with the eyes of one who has been bitten too many times. The entire village will need to discuss a matter such as this. We will need to bring together the other compound chiefs and elders to discuss this in *Awada* Nde Ngwo (Nde Ngwo compound hall) because *nkwa nada ososo eji mma n'ihu ete ya* (the talking drum that sounds urgent requires dancing to its rhythm with unsheathed machetes)." Then he sent a town crier out to summon all the male villagers in the twelve compounds for an urgent meeting in our compound hall.

Before the meeting began, Imaga Oleh asked me to bring some stationery to the hall to record the proceedings. To start the meeting formally, the *Eze Ezi* Nde Ngwo gave more kola nuts and a pot of palm wine to Chief Kalu Okoro to present them to the *Eze Ogo* Umuchiakuma, who, in turn, ordered a young page to break a kola nut and fill his *iko* (a gourd cup) with the palm wine. With a piece of the kola nut and a cup of the palm wine, the *Eze Ogo* offered an incantatory prayer and poured libations to the ancestors. Thereafter, everyone else was served pieces of the kola nut and cups of the palm wine and gin, beginning with the *Ndi Ichie* (the elderly traditional rulers) and proceeding to the youngest. Once the ritual was complete, the *Eze Ogo* asked the *Eze Ezi* to explain why such a meeting was called. *Eze Ezi* turned to Chief Kalu Okoro.

"Odum, *mma mma n!*" the Chief bellowed his greeting.

"*Yaa!*" the people answered.

"*Mma mma nu!*"

"*Yaa!*"

"*Mma mma nuwo!*"

"*Yaa wooo!*"

"*Imaga Oleh, nwa ada anyi* (tell us why you brought us here)," Chief Okoro said, feigning ignorance of the object of the meeting. For, as the elders say, "*Eze nanu oka ugbo rabuo*, a chief hears a petition twice."

Imaga Oleh stood, looked round, paused, and bowed to the chiefs and elders, before speaking.

"Odum, *mma mma nu!*"

"*Yaa!*"

"*Mma mma nu!*"

"*Yaa!*"

"*Mma mma nuwo!*"

"*Yaa wooo!*"

Then he paused again and apologized, thanking everybody for the sudden summons and said, "*Awo anaghi agba oso ehihie naefu* (a toad does not run in daylight without a cause)."

"*Obu ezi okwu* (it is true)," the people affirmed.

"I come humbly to you all on behalf of my friend and your son, Teacher Agwu Uche, to ask for a favor that will be of great benefit to all of us in the long run. He has just gained admission to study at the University of Nigeria, Nsukka, which is the first of its kind for our people. But he doesn't have the money to pay for all of his tuition and fees and buy the stationery he needs. That is why we have come to ask for assistance from the village. I thank you all for honoring our sudden invitation." He looked at them all, briefly, then sat.

"*Eze Ogo*," Chief Okoro called. "*Ji mbe din, awa ya ole?* (How do we deal with this matter?)"

"*Mma mma nuwo!*" the *Eze Ogo* called to the people.

"*Yaa!*" they answered.

"*Onye nwere ezi echiche ya tui ya ugbuo* (Whosoever has a good idea should contribute it now)," I said.

There was a long pause. Everyone waited to see who would be the first to speak and set the tone of the deliberation.

Kalu Oleh of Nde Ndu compound, a political rival of Imaga Oleh of Nde Ihuoma, rose up and paid his respects to the *Ndi Ichie* before speaking.

"What kind of assistance are you asking us to give?" he asked.

"Money, of course!" Imaga Oleh blurted.

"How much are you asking from us?" Kalu Oleh pressed.

Imaga Oleh asked for permission to consult with Agwu Uche. When he announced the amount, about £500 per academic year, many were surprised by what seemed to them an expensive proposition.

"Where and how are we going to get that kind of money?" Kalu Oleh inquired further. "And are you asking us to give it as a loan or gift?"

"Well, it is up to the people to decide," Imaga Oleh replied.

Then the *Eze Ogo* interrupted them and asked others to voice their opinions. After several heated exchanges, the village decided to grant Agwu Uche the money as a loan, given piecemeal at the beginning of each semester until he graduated. At any rate, he must start paying it back as soon as he found a job. That way, the village could to extend similar loans to other Umuchiakuma children when they applied for loans to study at the university level.

Then I asked the meeting to specify if they would give the loan to other students who wanted to study in both Nigerian and foreign universities. Imaga Oleh suggested that the village should give loans only to those studying in Nigerian or other West African universities since the village might not be able afford the cost of sponsoring students in Europe or America. The meeting unanimously accepted the suggestion, and adopted it as a condition for granting the loan to future applicants. I recorded the decision the people made to establish the loan scholarship scheme and read it back to them for the record.

Finally, the *Eze Ogo* instructed Ukeranoo to devise a means for levying and collecting the money from all able-bodied men and women in the compounds and blocs of the village. In addition, he gave them a deadline to accomplish the task. After the *Eze Ogo*'s final instructions, Imaga Oleh and Agwu Uche shook hands with everyone who attended the meeting, and entertained them with locally brewed gin *kaikai*, fried meat, and palm wine they had bought from Bar David Oke for granting the loan to Agwu Uche for his university education at Nsukka.

In September 1970, when I got the chance to apply for the loan scholarship, I asked Chief Mmagu and two other elders, Corporal Awah and Kalu Agwu Alicho, to lead me to *Awada* Nde Ngwo where I formally asked the village for a loan to help me study at the UNN. My mentor, Kalu Oleh, had gone back to his station at Aba. So I was forced to defend my application without one of my most staunch supporters. In his absence, Imaga Oleh dominated the discussion of my loan application.

"Teacher Kalu Ogbaa, did you in all honesty ask these respected men to bring you here to ask the village for a loan to study at Nsukka?" Imaga Oleh asked.

Chief Mmagu immediately jumped to my aid. "Imaga Oleh, what kind of question is that? Do you mean all three of us are so gullible that we would bring Teacher Kalu here without any genuine basis for doing so?" he fumed.

"With all due respect, Chief Amos, I don't doubt any of you three. It's Teacher Kalu Ogbaa that I doubt."

The room erupted in boos. Several elders asked Imaga Oleh to sit down. They knew he was only insulting me because of the rivalry between him and my mentor Kalu Oleh.

"Why do you doubt him, Imaga Oleh?" Chief Mmagu pressed.

"Because he left the ATTC at the outbreak of the war, but when the war ended, while other students immediately returned to school, he didn't. Second, he was fired after teaching for only a month at Ututu/Ihe High School. And since then, he has been carrying *okporoko* (stockfish) to sell on his head, going from market to market like *Nde Awusa* (nomadic Hausas). If he is not qualified to continue his studies at the ATTC or to teach at Ututu/Ihe High School, how can we be sure he is qualified to study in a prestigious university like Nsukka?"

At that point, I asked the elders for permission to answer his charges. They nodded their assent. And I made the following short plea:

> *Nde ogo anyi: Ewu r'okuko nuru kwa ya r'onu m ugbuo* (My people: Let the goat and the chicken hear it loud and clear from me now). While it is true that I did not go back to the ATTC to continue my studies, and that they fired from my teaching

appointment at the Ututu/Ihe High School, it was certainly not true that I left both institutions for lack of adequate qualifications to continue in both places. I had passed my GCE papers in March 1967. I therefore stayed home in anticipation of getting admission into the UNN. By then, I had also been admitted to study at Boston College in the United States, and Fourah Bay College in Sierra Leone. But without financial aid, I was not to accept the offers. I knew the village would not give me a loan to study in Boston, but I was optimistic about getting a loan for the West African Fourah Bay College. But when I broached my intentions to Kalu Oleh, he advised against it because Martin Okoro from Ekelogo was also applying. He argued that since Agwu Uche, the first recipient of the loan, came from my Ezukwu bloc, I should not compete for it with Martin Okoro unless I wanted to create disunity in our village. I took his wise counsel and stopped applying. In addition, there was still time for me to begin my studies at the UNN during the 1967 fall semester. Thereafter, the Nigeria-Biafra War broke out on June 6, 1967, and put my academic ambition on hold until this year, 1970.

Then I presented my certificates and the admission letter from Nsukka to prove to Imaga Oleh and other detractors that I was qualified to study at a university instead of continuing my studies at the ATTC.

Some of the more educated people inspected the documents and congratulated me for my achievements. Still, they were unable to persuade Imaga Oleh to let go of his enmity for my mentor Kalu Oleh. Finally, the elders decided to postpone the meeting and continue the next day.

When word got out that the village had not given me the loan, the Eziukwu bloc people were so outraged that they decided to give me some financial assistance on their own. Agwu Uche, Emmanuel Ekpesu Kalu, Kalu Ojiuko, and three others contributed £4 each to seed the loan. Then three elders took me to the village and called on all Ezukwu people to contribute as much money as they could to enable their "son" to attend the university. Their efforts yielded £165. I signed an agreement to pay it back as a loan as soon as I graduated from the university and got a job, which was a similar agreement, in spirit, to the original agreement I would have signed with the village. I was humbled and grateful for what Ezukwu people did for me. The efforts of the bloc were able to pull together what normally would have taken an entire village to do. I was more proud than ever of my community, which only spurred me to succeed at the highest level at university.

When I arrived in the University of Nigeria in October 1970, the sad face and cruel vagaries of war were all around. I saw roofless buildings with wall charred from bombings. I saw grassless lawns, firebombed and burned. I saw scared trenches. I saw libraries whose shelves, connecting wood panels, and books that enemy soldiers had removed and burned to warm their cold bodies. I saw skeletons and rotting remains of Igbo people piled up at street corners, still awaiting evacuation by street sweepers. I saw vultures making acrobatic dives, then scurrying away shyly at the sight of anxious, milling students and parents who watched them scavenge the dead bodies of humans and animals. I saw smoldering bonfires of debris, spiraling grey smoke kissing the yellow skyline of Nsukka country.

But I also saw the face and soul of a humbled people whose human spirit refused to die in face of crippling abject poverty and brutalized human psyche. I saw the face of a new generation, anxious but resolute, ready to work hard to realize their hopes and the dreams of the founding fathers of their great institution. I saw the face of young, proud Lions of the first indigenous university of an old British colonial country they loved though they themselves were yet unloved. I saw curious young minds that rose up, phoenix-like, from the ashes of burned towns and villages of their beloved Igbo country and stood tall to face uncertain days of their new beginning. I saw the soul of postwar Igbo professors who served with the same commitment as military officers during the war, equally ready and committed now to direct and protect their postwar students as they engaged in academic battles on campus against all odds. I saw a new generation of administrators and faculty anxious to rebuild all aspects of the community of their beloved university in order to actualize the motto of the institution: "To restore the dignity of man."

Oh! What better time to do so than now, when the Igbo man had just lost a physical war and stood on the brink of losing his primordial ethnic supremacy and pride in Nigeria? The eyes of the whole Igbo race and the entire Nigerian nation were upon us all—faculty, administration, and students—to see what we could achieve out of nothingness and hurt.

With that view in mind, I walked to the Registrar's office and checked in. After taking my photo and preparing my identification card, they assigned me to Okeke Hall, Room 207. Once there, I discovered I was to share the room with two other Igbo roommates. The room, built to accommodate two undergraduates or one graduate student before the war, was a bit too small for three. Nevertheless, we were all grateful that we survived the war and were given the opportunity to study at the university when other fellow Igbo people had been killed or maimed or were roaming the streets, homeless.

One of my roommates, Bernard, a junior, took half of the room space and left the remaining half for me, a sophomore, and Boniface, a freshman. We respected the decision the upperclassman, Bernard, made and got along well. In return, he served as a useful resource to us. Since there was no campus orientation, we depended on such help, along with the official information posted on university bulletin boards.

During our first postwar semester, we studied in classrooms whose roofs had been completely blown off or had bullet holes through which the sunbeams and raindrops fell on our heads. Yet we were happy and determined to come back to school after three years of fighting in battlefields. Students found cement blocks to sit on, or space along the classroom walls to lean while taking notes. Same for the refectories where we ate our meals, until a few private philanthropists, like Governor Samuel Ogbomudia of Bendel State, paid to repair some of the buildings. By the end of our first year, the state and federal governments had reconstructed most of the buildings, but not the libraries. However, many of the essential books we needed could be purchased from area markets. (Ironically, today in Nigeria students cannot find books they need even when they have the money. The current scarcity of books in Nigeria emanates from poor government trade policies and inadequate foreign exchange, making it difficult for booksellers to purchase enough books for students and their professors. However, those who have family and friends abroad can often purchase some of their book supplies from foreign countries.)

During the 1971/72 academic session, serving as president of the English Association at Nsukka, I was able to acquire some books and videos on American literature from the United States Information Service (USIS) in Lagos, and others on English literature from British Council representatives. With those books and other volumes donated by Igbo professors residing in the United States, we were able to rebuild our English department library.

And at the advice of the chair of our English department, Dr. M. J. C. Echeruo, a graduate of Cornell University in the United States, I resurrected the publication of our English student journal, *The Muse*, and appointed Chukwuma Azuonye its first postwar editor.

The Federal Military Government (FMG) had permitted the UNN administration to reopen the institution on the condition that they would give admission to candidates from the other eleven erstwhile states of Nigeria, whether or not they satisfied the high admission standards required of all candidates to meet. However, many of the candidates from Northern Nigeria could not achieve even such lowered standards. Still, the FMG insisted that the students must be admitted. And since the students' state governments awarded them scholarships, our university administrators (driven not only by the law, but also by financial considerations) complied with the FMG's directive. Some of the non-Igbo students stayed longer than they should have, in some cases more than four years if they came through entrance exam, or three years by direct entry. Later, Igbo students discovered that some of the non-Igbo students overstaying their time were actually paid secret agents from the State Security Service (SSS). Those of us in leadership positions often advised our fellow Igbo students to be careful about what they said to non-Igbo students, for we did not know who was who, *ama ndi anaeze*.

For the young scholars at the university, however, there were other dangers. Except for a few good lectures like Emmanuel Obiechina, Romanus Egudu, and Kalu Uka, I would have learned little more than how highly impressed the other English professors were with themselves, spending most of their classroom time showing off their "vast knowledge" of all things literate. Most of the lecturers in the English department at Nsukka tried their utmost to live up to their titles as opposed to instructing. Students were expected to sit quietly, take notes, memorize the notes, and regurgitate them verbatim during exams.

Once I read Paulo Freire's essay, "The 'Banking' Concept of Education," I fully realized the poverty of our Nsukka teachers' pedagogical approach. Nsukka professors used what Freire called the "banking" method of teaching, in which education suffers from narration sickness. Narration (with the teacher as narrator) leads the students to memorize the narrated content, turning them into "containers," into "receptacles" to be "filled" by the teacher. Using this approach, teachers are judged by how completely they fill the receptacles. And students are judged based on how meekly they (receptacles) allow their teachers to fill them with information. Education thus becomes an act of depositing, in which the students are the depositories and the teacher is the depositor. Instead of communicating, the teacher issues communiqués and makes deposits, which the students patiently receive, memorize, and repeat.[1]

But Freire proposed another approach to teaching, the "problem-posing" method, asserting that "problem-posing" education better responds to the essence of consciousness—*intentionality*—and thus rejects communiqués and instead embodies real communication which is a complex interaction between the sender and receiver.

But at Nsukka, even the most erudite professors used the "banking" method. And some lecturers were more interested in doing research and attending conferences for promotions than in settling down to instruct the students. To make up for lost time from attending conferences or working on their own research, they would call us to their office and lecture us about the same material already contained in textbooks. Nevertheless, like most of the other students in my class, I put forth much effort to memorize their lecture notes in order to pass the exams.

I did well in most of the courses until my final semester, when I suffered from infective hepatitis and thus became too sick to cram a lot of information for later regurgitation. Dr. Echeruo advised me not to take the final exams, but I rejected his advice and took them because I didn't want to repeat the semester. I wanted to graduate with my classmates. Consequently, I failed his course, which I later retook and passed. But I graduated with a GPA that was lower than what I had hoped. However, when I finally came to the United States four years later to attend graduate school, I was able to redeem myself to Dr. Echeruo and my other Nigerian lecturers and classmates. Once there, I was happy to find that professors employed "problem-posing" methods in teaching students in all their courses.

Despite such a disappointing English studies experience, I was grateful for two particular incidents that happened at Nsukka, which laid a solid foundation for my future academic and professional develop-

---

1. See Bartholomae, David, and Anthony Petrosky, editors. *Ways of Reading: An Anthology for Writers*, Eighth Edition. Boston, MA: Bedford/St. Martin's, 2008: 243–56.

ment. The first was my election as president of the English Association, serving under the tutelage of Dr. Echeruo, the chair of our department. The other was meeting Professor Chinua Achebe in person, who was working as director of the African Studies Institute.

Dr. Echeruo served as my guide, helping me to organize an international conference on literature on our campus for the English Association that attracted literary scholars and writers from all over Nigeria, Great Britain, and the United States, as well as representatives of the British Council and United States Information Service in Lagos. Among the conferees from the U.S. and U.K. were Professor Bernth Lindfors and Mr. Obi Egbuna. As the two argued their divergent positions regarding African literature back and forth, it seemed at times that they were going to start another Nigerian civil war. Egbuna, a London-based activist Igbo writer, physically threatened Lindfors whom he thought was imposing his White colonialist interpretation of African literature on Africans even there in Igbo heartland. But Lindfors stood his ground, saying that good interpretations of any literary writing didn't necessarily depend on one's skin color. At one point, I was so upset over Obi Egbuna's disrespectful demeanor that I shouted him down and reminded him of a well-known Igbo apothegm: "*Obiara nke onye abiagbula ya, mgbe o nala nkpukpu apula ya* (May no guest bring problems to his host so he doesn't suffer hunchback on his way back home)."

But what intrigued me most about the whole affair was that after the debate, the conferees ate and drank together, chatting and poking fun at one another. In addition, many of the Nigerian writers were willing to have interviews with Lindfors concerning their works. He later published the interviews in a book, titled *Dem Say: Interviews with Eight Nigerian Writers*.

The second greatest achievement for me while at UNN was meeting Chinua Achebe for the first time, an incident that seemed almost God-ordained later in my career. At Nsukka, the most important African novel was Achebe's *Things Fall Apart*. Who could better teach it to us than the man who wrote it himself? Why did the school not use Achebe as one of the lecturers to serve in the English department? These questions, among others, bothered me so much that I finally paid him a visit.

"Good afternoon, sir. My name is Kalu Ogbaa. I came to ask you a few questions, which are very important to me and the English Association I lead as its president."

"*Biko nodu ani* (Please, sit down), Kalu," he kindly said.

I sat down humbled and elated that this man, who *owned* the English language, stooped to speak humbly to me in our native Igbo language. I immediately drew the sharp contrast between his attitude and the other elitist lecturers on the campus. I sat down and began a candid conversation with him in Igbo (except those ideas I could only express in English).

We talked about a few passages I did not fully understand in *Things Fall Apart*, and in the process, I learned that he saw the novel as means to bring sociopolitical changes in any given society or country. After working up some nerve, I finally asked him why he was not teaching in our English department. He looked straight at me and smiled.

"Do you really want to know?"

"Yes. Absolutely, sir!"

He chuckled to hide his disappointment with the university administration over the matter. "You should pose that question to the chair of your department and the vice chancellor." He patted my leg. "Now why don't we leave the matter there?"

I humbly thanked him and left his office a better man.

Later, I approached Dr. Emmanuel Obiechina, one of my favorite lecturers, and asked him why Achebe was not lecturing in our department. Obiechina himself was bothered about the issue. He had already raised it with the university authorities, but they refused to change their policy, saying only that only terminal degreed professor should serve as lecturers. Achebe, a renowned creative writer and teacher, was not good enough to teach African literature in his home university. However, three years after my visit with him, a famous New England state university in America, the University of Massachusetts at Amherst, appointed Achebe a full professor of English. Soon afterwards, UNN changed their policy and offered him full professorship in the university, backdating the rank to 1970, when they first hired him to serve. Thus, his case became the Biblical stone builders had first rejected, which later became the chief cornerstone. Since then, the literary world has acknowledged Achebe as founder of the modern African novel. *Things Fall Apart* is the most widely read African novel in the world, and every Igbo writer or professor claims him as his or her big uncle.

As we approached our graduation in June 1973, the head of the FMG, General Yakubu Gowon, created the National Youth Service Corps (NYSC) program by decree, compelling graduates of all Nigerian universities to render a one-year service to the country with a paltry monthly allowance. In addition, graduates were not allowed to serve in his or her state of origin. The NYSC directorate had its headquarters in Lagos, and its first appointed director was a senior Northern Nigerian military officer. Although the NYSC was patriotic in principle (in that it was intended to promote national unity through the services of the university graduates from all the states in the country), in practice it was a clever way for Northern Nigerian military and political leaders to exploit the talents of Southern Nigerian university graduates. That was why they posted all the pioneer NYSC members from the South to the North.

I received my orientation training in Ilorin, and served at Idah (in Kwara State, now Benue State) from July 1, 1973 to June 30, 1974. The compulsory service was particularly unfair in that NYSC members who borrowed money to train without government subsidies or scholarship awards could not begin to pay back those loans until they had completed their one-year service obligation, while those who had received government scholarship or bursary awards need not worry. So those who'd studied on loans fell a year behind before they could look for jobs to enable them start paying back the loans to their creditors.

Although I borrowed £165 pounds from my village to attend college, I was lucky and happy to have also been awarded a federal bursary after my first year, which I continued to enjoy until I graduated. So I was not one of those who complained bitterly about the unfairness of the NYSC program, for I somehow knew that I was morally, if not patriotically, indebted to the federal government. Moreover, the lessons of life I learned while serving on the program were enormous and everlasting.

I began my career at the Holy Rosary College, Idah. One week before classes began, I arrived at the school where Sister Principal welcomed me enthusiastically. She regretted that she had no accommodation for me, but helped me to find a private accommodation in one Anthony's house. I also found a suitable eatery at Alhaji Abu Abaji's place downtown. He had two daughters and a younger son. The older daughter, Rhekia, was a third year student at the college, so she and her parents were excited to serve me food in their outdoor shed and tell me a little bit about the college each time I stopped to eat. On the third day, the Alhaji ordered his wife and the younger daughter, Kulu, to serve me food in their home as a show of respect for Rhekia's prospective teacher.

For the first time in my life, I lived in close contact with a Moslem family. I learned much about their religious culture during my first week at Idah. They prayed five times a day, facing Mecca, piously washing their faces, hands, and feet before praying. They loved me, their new neighbor, as themselves, and showed respect and genuine love to every person they met, regardless of age, gender or religion. Their women, however, were often servile, submitting their will almost entirely to the men and following the practice of *hijab*, taking great care to cover almost their entire bodies as a means to preserve their virtuousness.

On the other hand, the Alhaji was just as curious to learn about my Christian faith as I was about his Moslem faith. I spent long hours at the Alhaji's place, since I was not yet teaching, and Rhekia brought some of her schoolmates to visit, giving me a head start in understanding my prospective students.

The city of Idah represented what an ideal Nigerian society should be: there were as many Muslims as there were Christians. The Muslims attended the Catholic primary school, the Holy Rosary College for girls in the day, and mosques every evening, on Fridays, and during Ramadan. The Reverend Sisters cooperated by making allowances for the Moslem students' prayer times. In addition, parents allowed their Moslem daughters to take Christian Religion as one of their curricular offerings in the college, and their Christian neighbors never bullied or socially dominated them. Above all, although Idah was an Igala land, some of their enlightened men were married to Igbo women. As a result, their young children spoke Igala, English, and Igbo. So when they met me, especially Rose Okwunya whose father was Igala and her mother Igbo, they accepted me as their Igbo uncle. Through them, I quickly picked up phrases in Igala (especially curse words and those used to express greetings and pleasantries). In essence, as a microcosmic society, the town of Idah exhibited the type of mutual coexistence, tolerance, and acceptance of otherness among people of divergent ethnic, linguistic, and religious backgrounds, which Nigeria as a macrocosmic society has been lacking since its creation on January 1, 1914. Since its inception, Nigerians have witnessed persistent war, and, consequently, have continued to experience persistent religious bigotry and political instability.

When the classes began, the Sister Principal asked me to teach English Language and Literature to students in forms III and IV. But the Bishop had also authorized the school to change from a teacher training college into a secondary school. Therefore, one of my first tasks was to modify the curriculum of the two courses to satisfy secondary school requirements. The regular Math and History teachers (both Igbo men) and the other NYSC member and I (another Igbo man) were the senior teaching staff members. We shaped the new curricular offerings in the school without much input from the three junior Igala teachers. And since they had only high school and teacher training certificates, they were unqualified to develop the curriculum, even in the courses we gave them to teach.

Consequently, tensions began to arise between Igbo and Igala teachers. In time, they influenced students to demonstrate against us. And in spite of the Sister Principal's appeal for them to disband, the students refused to stop their demonstration. When I attempted to talk to their leaders, one of the junior teachers cursed me in Igala language. So I slapped him.

At that point, the other teachers got scared and quickly ran to the school office, and the students retreated to their dormitory. I went to the Sister Principal's office and told her what had happened and threatened to leave the college immediately. I would go to Ilorin and ask for deployment to another town in the state. Sister Principal pleaded with me to calm down while she sent for the Sole Administrator of Idah and the Attah of Igala. Both men came to the school Assembly Hall and sternly scolded the students and Igala teachers for insulting Igbo teachers and disobeying the principal's orders. In addition, the Attah gave them an oral history on how Igbo Catholics from Onitsha diocese helped white Catholic missionaries to establish the churches and schools they now enjoyed. Finally, he asked them to render unqualified apologies to us and the principal. They did, and thereafter, the school was calm. Additionally, the teacher who had used the ethnic slur against me came to the office and apologized privately to me. I forgave him.

After I lived outside the campus for a month, the Sister Principal gave me a big two-bedroom house on campus, rent-free. In return, she asked me to supervise the girls during their nightly studies, in the classrooms, and on every other weekend.

One Saturday evening, a man stumbled onto the quad of the campus, drunk, and began sexually harassing several girls. Scared, the girls ran to me for protection. He was a drug addict, I found out later. And when I asked him to leave the school premises, he turned and swung at me. I parried off his intended blow and firmly gripped his left hand, then, once again, I asked him to leave. But he refused again and slapped me on the ribs with his right hand. I punched him several times on his side. He continued to fight back until I punched him in the stomach, and he finally fell. Some girls had run to find Sister Principal and some other teachers to help to take him off the campus. When we finally got him clear of the campus, the girls cheered and told me how he had been harassing them for weeks without anyone stopping him. He'd gotten away with his crimes because his rich father bribed the police to release him from detention each time he was arrested. But after that incident, he never came on campus again to harass our female students.

In the third week of June 1974, when the other NYSC member and I were getting ready to leave the college at the end of the month, the Sister Principal invited me to her office and offered me a two-month temporary job. She wanted me to conduct an entrance exam for the proposed Girls Secondary School, which would replace the Holy Rosary College. I was to work with two regular teachers of the college. They would set and mark their papers, but I was to coordinate the conduct of the exam and the interview, and recommend the successful candidates for admission as the first batch of students of the new school. She offered to pay me a higher amount than the monthly allowance the government paid me as an NYSC member. I felt honored as the one chosen to carry out the assignment.

When word got out that I was going to conduct the entrance exam, parents and guardians of the prospective candidates began to invite me to social occasions. I turned the invitations down to avoid possible conflict of interest problems. In fact, two rich Alhajis came to my house and offered me bribes, which I rejected, explaining to them that it was both immoral and criminal to accept their bribes and gently assured them that all the girls would have their fair chances at the exam. Nevertheless, another group sent the most powerful man in town, the Sole Administrator, to influence me. He refused to help them because he knew from experience that I would not do them the favor they were asking: he had already twice tried to bribe me to ask some of the girls to visit him during the weekends, and failed. I was so angry that I had threatened to report him to both the Sister Principal and the Bishop. At that, he had knelt down and begged me to forgive him. Thereafter, we became social friends. Perhaps the Sister Principal knew about the incident, hence she trusted that I would conduct the exams fairly.

I finally left Idah in August, 1974, with many fond memories. At the end of the NYSC year, all serving members in Kwara State went back to the state capital at Ilorin for official discharge and issued discharge certificates. Before then, however, employers of labor interviewed us for appointments in all the states of Nigeria. I landed seven jobs — namely, working in the Nigerian Broadcasting Corporation (NBC) in Lagos, Ilorin, and Enugu; in the Eastern Nigeria Broadcasting Service (ENBS) Enugu; and as an education officer in Lagos, Ilorin, and Enugu.

I did not take any of the offers since I received another, better paying lectureship in English at the ATTC, Owerri. By October 7, 1974, when I joined its faculty, they had upgraded the college and renamed it Alvan Ikoku College of Education (AICE) under its first provost, Professor Ukeje. Thus, when they write the history of the first Nigerian college of education, my name will be among its first faculty members.

My appointment at the AICE, Owerri, marked the end of the life I led through the postwar reconstruction era and the beginning of a more positive life I hoped to lead in postwar Nigeria. I had saved a good amount of money from the monthly NYSC allowances I had received while at Idah. Moreover, I had saved all the salary that the Sister Principal paid me for two months after my NYSC service period. With a little money in my pocket, a university degree, and a letter of appointment in my possession, I went home, free at last to see my people — especially my father, who expected no less achievement than what I had shown him. And I wrestled once again with my need for his approval against my growing desire to find my own voice and position in a world that more and more seemed to need a voice, such as mine, I hoped, that might help to close the divide of grievances between East and West, Black and White, Muslim and Christian. I thanked God for leading me through the metaphoric desert journey. And now, it was time for me to go forth into my new world to face new responsibilities and challenges, in His protective hands.

Chapter 9

Starting a Career and a Family

In 1974, I began my college/university teaching career at Alvan Ikoku College of Education (AICE), Owerri. The chair of the English department, Mr. Azu Irondi, had occupied the same chair when I briefly attended the college in spring 1967, then administered by UNESCO as the Advanced Teacher Training College (ATTC). European teachers and administrators had left the college shortly before the outbreak of the Nigeria-Biafra War, and never returned after it ended. On the other hand, the entire indigenous Igbo personnel returned to their old positions and departments under a new administration headed by a provost, who hired new lecturers with higher degrees to head most of the academic departments. Irondi was excited to hire me as an assistant lecturer and treated me as a younger brother. He encouraged me to work hard to earn his trust and high regard for me. I assured him that I would always carry out my responsibilities diligently, both within and outside the English department. I was confident that he would eventually discover my underlying desire and sturdy work ethic, and thereby become satisfied and happy that he hired me.

I arrived on the college campus the week after classes had begun. Mr. Irondi, therefore, asked me to conduct tutorials in African novels and poetry, a blessing in disguise as it prepared me for my future teaching duties at Ohio State University in the U.S. The assignment was also fulfilling since most of the other lecturers in the department were not familiar with African literary texts, apparently because they attended college when African literature had not been taught in Nigeria's premier university, Ibadan University. Therefore, I was in a position to reach students through literature written by their own native, continental writers. They were particularly excited and enthusiastic to discover the great contributions made by their comrades. They were also happy to work with a teacher whose teaching methodology included real problem-posing communication.

In many of their other classes, the lecturers were still using the "banking method," dictating their lesson notes to students in large classes and expecting them to memorize and regurgitate the material during quizzes and exams. Consequently, students who couldn't take notes accurately often misunderstood the course content. And as I tutored the students, I discovered that, oftentimes, their lecturers didn't explain clearly enough the assigned poems or chapters of novels. I often had to re-teach the material. Over time, students in my tutorial classes began to do better in African literature courses than their counterparts in other tutorial classes. As a result, several even decided to leave their assigned classes to attend mine.

One morning, one of the lecturers came unannounced into my classroom and scolded the students who left his tutorial class, telling them that I was only an assistant lecturer assigned to conduct tutorials for lecturers like him. He also reminded the students that he had the authority to pass or fail them, not me. Then the students began booing him as he stormed out of the class. I immediately asked them to stop, and then we continued our discussion.

I was offended by the lecturer's interruption, but did not want to show it visibly for the students. Instead, I was further motivated to study the texts even more closely so I could explicate them better for the students. The more I studied, the better of a teacher I became. Consequently, more and more students began attending my tutorial classes, in spite of the warnings from the offended lecturer.

Contrary to this one lecturer, however, another lecturer, Mr. Cosmas Uzomah, candidly confided in me that he was not familiar with African poetry and encouraged me to tutor as many students from his classes as needed to enable them to understand the texts better. I thanked him for his candor and appreciation for what I did. He was never condescending to me for being his junior colleague, as were some, and over time we became close friends.

In addition to tutoring African literature, I served as the student academic and social advisor. While serving in that capacity, I founded a student English association, based on my experience as erstwhile president of the English Association at Nsukka, and guided students to elect an executive committee and suggested activities that would make their organization meaningful. We began to hold organized debates, performed cultural dances on campus, and publically presented films based on British and American literatures. In addition, I also spearheaded the publication of a new student journal, *The AICE Tablet*, serving as the first editorial board advisor. Through my active participation on such extra-curricular activities, my good name and reputation grew among the student population.

Before I found an apartment downtown in Owerri, I commuted to campus from Arugo High School, where I lived with a clansman, Mr. Kalu Alfred, a tutor at Arugo High. Occasionally, he and I discussed activities on our college campuses and the progress I was making. But just as important, he was also interested in my matrimonial aspirations. I was twenty-eight years old, and one evening, after dinner, he raised the point.

"I hear you are the most eligible bachelor on campus." Alfred smiled.

"Oh yeah, who told you that?" I was a bit embarrassed, but happy to hear.

"Don't tell me you're not attracted to any of those lovely 'chicks' on your campus."

"Yes. Of course I like 'chicks.' But only when they have been killed and roasted. Not when they're roaming wild. For you never know who owns them. I'm no chicken thief."

"Come on. *Nna ogbo m*; you know what I'm talking about."

"I do." I was a bit uncomfortable discussing women this way, but I knew he was well-intentioned by his inquisition.

"But I haven't yet seen any girl on campus I'd like to marry," I continued. "I've been looking only in my village. The two or three girls I approached were ready to get serious with me, but their people objected, saying that both sides of my family die too young."

"Does that mean you'll never get married?" Alfred was serious, now.

"No. It doesn't mean that. But when you're given such news as a young man, you get a little discouraged, if not totally disappointed, like a curse placed on your family."

"Have you approached other girls outside your village?"

"No. I haven't. The truth is that I want to marry a girl who has a secondary school education, not just one who attended teacher training college or has passed Standard VI."

"Why is secondary school education so important to you?"

"Well, as you know, you and I attended university with Grade III teachers' certificates and GCE from London University without studying math and science subjects. That's a major deficiency in our education. It is, at least, to me."

"So what do you want to do about it?"

"I want to marry a girl with a math and science background so that when we have children, I'll teach English, literature, and other humanities to them, and she would be able to complement my effort with teaching math and science to them."

He chuckled. "Have you started looking for 'Miss Right' yet?"

"No, I haven't. But it won't be long before I start."

"You better. Otherwise I'll throw you out of my house." He laughed, patting my on the shoulder.

"Come on, now." I shrugged. "Admit it. You don't really want me to bring lovely women to your house. You're already jealous of me, *okokporo* (the most eligible bachelor)," I jabbed.

"Are you kidding? Can any of your ladies compare with my beauty queen, Rose?"

"We shall see." I winked.

"We'll see, indeed. We'll see!"

On that note, we finished what began as ordinary banter between friends, and ended as a very serious matter to me. I slept little that night. Attempts I had made during the war to engage a girl for marriage came rushing back vividly. I recalled one girl I asked to marry whose sister and brother in-law had refused to consent. And another, whose father had asked me to take her to Abiriba for registration in a secondary school which indicated, I thought at the time, that he approved of me. But after she accepted my proposal, her father refused to give his approval. Another man asked that I prepare his daughter for secondary school education and marry her after her graduation. I accepted his proposal and studied with her throughout the war. But after the war ended, the girl's mother rejected the pact I made with her husband, even after my father had given the traditional wine and *anu anwu* (antelope meat) to the family to validate the girl's official betrothal to me.

According to the mother, after twenty years of marriage, the war caused too many tensions in her own marriage. "I married *di lukwu-lukwu*, a difficult, struggling husband," she said. "I don't want my daughter to marry *di lukwu-lukwu*." After so many rejections, I was discouraged from proposing marriage to other girls from my village.

My unsuccessful marriage proposals so upset my father's second wife, Orieji, that she decided to question the parents of the three girls to find out why they refused my proposals. Their consensus was that although they knew I was a bright, well-educated young man, they firmly believed that my family's history of younger mortality made such a proposal less than ideal for their daughters. But Orieji believed that they actually more disliked my family's material poverty than the superstitious belief in our purported premature deaths.

My detractors felt vindicated for rejecting my marriage proposals based on my family's material poverty when I gained admission to study at the University of Nigeria, Nsukka, and none of my family members had the wherewithal to sponsor me. My maternal uncle, Ulu Kalu Ulu, who could have helped to sponsor me, died suddenly of acute malaria on July 21, 1970. And previously, our agnate family had buried four of their members who had died within the first year of the war. Consequently, I began to worry over such things, which drove me constantly to the church to seek comfort and understanding.

The morning after my conversation with Kalu Alfred, I recalled one inspirational verse in the Bible as I meditated over my life situation:

> One *thing* have I desired of the Lord, and that will I seek after; that I may dwell in the house of the Lord all the days of my life, to behold the beauty of the Lord, and to inquire in his temple (Psalm 27:4).

I prayed and asked God to protect me from all alarms, dangers, and un-timely death, and to guide me to find a girl of my dream. At the end of the prayers, I heard the echo of Kalu Alfred's voice asking, "Have you approached other girls outside your village?" I decided to keep my eyes open for young women on campus. Hope, once again, sprang in my heart.

The same day, after conducting my tutorial classes, a girl named Clara came to my office and asked me to explicate a poem we had gone through in class. That was not the first time she had sought my help, but it was the first time I noticed how beautiful she was. After explicating the poem, she expressed confidence in producing a good paper, smiled broadly and thanked me. I asked her to let me know how she did after the paper had been graded and given back to her.

A few days after, Clara returned and showed me the "A" she made on the paper.

"Good morning sir; I came to show you the grade I made." She smiled.

"Good morning, Madam," I said, using the address we used for married women in our country.

"I'm not married, Sir." She smiled, a bit embarrassed.
"I'm sorry for that assumption. What's your name again?" I teased.
"My name is Clara Nwankwo." She smiled more openly. "I thought I already told you."
"Please." I motioned. "Sit down. Where are you from?"
"Ufuma, in Orumba District."
"I'm from Ihechiowa, in Arochukwu District."
"Oh. I know where that is."
"Are you serious?"
"Yes. I am serious, sir!"

Could this be the woman? I wondered. "Who took you to our jungle?" I joked.

"Please. Don't say that about your own home. I passed through Ihechiowa while visiting my friend, Nnennaya Ajah, at Ututu."

"Oh, I know the Ajah family at Ututu. But how did you come to know Nnennaya Ajah?"

"She's my best high school friend. We knew one another from our primary school days to Girls High School, Awkunanaw, in Enugu. I even lived briefly with her family during my high school days."

"Are you still friends?"

"Oh yes. Very much so! And how did you come to know the family?"

"Nnennaya's father, Mr. Kalu Ajah, helped my brother Ikpo to find a job in Eastern Nigeria Information Service (ENIS) at Enugu in 1958. He has been our family friend since then."

"Yes, they all are good friends of mine."

"Well, Miss Nwankwo, you and I now have mutual family friends. Please, feel free to stop by the office whenever you can so we can study more poems together and chat about the Ajahs again."

"I'll do so sir. And thanks again for all your help with the poem."

I watched as Clara left my office then closed my office door, knelt down, and prayed that if it were God's will, let her become my future wife. For the next week, she didn't come back. And each time I asked her questions in the classroom, she lowered her eyes when she answered. My interest in her grew more intense each days as I fasted and prayed, seeking God's guidance and help on the matter.

Later, I told Kalu Alfred about my conversation with Clara and about my strong feelings toward her, and asked him to advise me how to approach Clara and declare my intentions toward her since his wife came from Nimo in Awka, a village near Clara's. Alfred asked me to tell Clara about him and his wife, and then invite her to visit me in their home, where I was temporarily residing at the time.

When I invited Clara to my off-campus residence, she expressed reluctance, saying that she knew neither Alfred's family nor me well enough to visit. I told her I understood and that maybe over time she would feel comfortable enough. Thereafter, we talked occasionally in my office until we became familiar enough with each other that I was encouraged to invite her again in early November, 1974. She agreed.

I drove my new Renault 12TL to campus in Alfred's company to collect her from the dormitory. When she saw Alfred, she agreed to go with us to his home in Arugo High School. After dinner, Clara and I talked privately in his parlor for a long time. Over time, I learned almost everything I needed to know about her and the family to propose marriage. I also shared everything she wanted to know about me, and my family. In the end, we were both happy with what we learned.

During that first conversation, the most important thing Clara told me was that if both of my parents were not alive, she would not consider marrying me. She was happy to discover they were both well. Then I told her about my church and found that she was not only familiar with it, but also connected to it. And when I told her why the girls I had earlier proposed marriage to in my village were dissuaded, she said if we ever got married and I died suddenly, she would be unhappy but proud to be my widow. She added that both of us should pray always against our un-timely death or that of our prospective family members, for her mother also died young. That was why she wanted to marry a man with both parents so that she could again have both a mother and a father. "Your parents," Clara said, "shall be my parents. Your church shall be my church. And your God shall be my God."

I was grateful for her faithfulness and belief in our living and righteous God. The only impediment she feared was her father, who might not permit her to marry a man outside her village in Ufuma. I told her that if I was not able to persuade her father to allow me marry her, then I did not deserve her as my wife.

"If you can persuade my father, I will marry you," she said.

When I jumped up and swept her off her feet to hug her, she swung her purse, hitting me hard on top of my head. I gently put her down on a chair, apologized and explained how excited and joyful I was about her willingness to marry me. Yet, despite my apologies, Clara was determined to return immediately to her dormitory. I knelt down and begged her to forgive me, which she finally did. After we were married, I discovered her reaction was based on the facts that she had not known any man before me, and I had greatly insulted her integrity.

Clara and I continued to meet in my office until the college rented an apartment opposite Uzomah's downtown Owerri, where she and I talked freely and more frequently. Finally, I formally proposed marriage to her. She agreed and we both knelt down in my altar and prayed God to touch her father's heart to grant our request. I then sent her to Ufuma to tell her father about the proposal. She came back with a positive massage: Bring me to her village in two weeks' time for a personal conversation with her father.

Why in two weeks' time? I wondered. Then it dawned on me that in Igboland, a father does not say "yes" or "no" to such a life-changing request until he has thoroughly investigated the background of his daughter's suitor. Hence, my prospective father in-law, Deacon Joshua Nwankwo, wrote Clara's cousin, Christian Nwankwo, who was by then working at Aba, telling him to ask Nnennaya Ajah's father to find out everything about my family and me. Especially if we were *osu*. When Mr. Ajah was contacted, he told Christian that he knew my family well and that we were not *osu*. Christian also contacted his business associates from my village, Kalu Oleh and Imaga Oleh, to find out more about me. In the end, Clara's father was highly impressed by what they told him about me and my family.

At long last, Clara and I visited her people on an appointed day in early January, 1975. When we arrived, I was the center of attention. After exchanging pleasantries, I requested Deacon Nwankwo to lead us in prayers. He seemed impressed by my first move. Little did he know that I, too, had done my homework about him and knew he would be honored by my prayer request since I'd learned he was an Anglican Church deacon in their village, Afo Ufuma.

After the prayer, he asked his son, Christopher, to summon his aunt, uncle, and other agnate family members to come and receive me. By the time Christopher returned, Clara's stepmother and the other women of the household had set the table. Deacon Nwanko led us in prayers before and after the meal. Then we were served wine, *abacha ncha* (dried fish and tapioca pudding), and other local delicacies. Clara's father again seemed impressed that I did not imbibe in the wine. Toward the end of the meal and entertainment, I ceremonially offered to them palm wine, kola nuts, and brandy and introduced the object of my visit. I openly requested their daughter's hand in marriage, and while the merriment continued, my prospective father in-law drew me aside and interrogated me thoroughly on why I wanted to marry his daughter and when I was going to wed her if he granted my request.

I answered his questions satisfactorily and told him about my ambition to go to graduate school in the U.S. with Clara as my wife if he permitted us to marry. He was satisfied with my answers and agreed to allow the marriage to go ahead. He then admonished me to love and cherish Clara, his most beloved child, as he loved and cherished her deceased mother throughout her life. I hugged and thanked him for granting my request. Then he gave me a list of all the things I had to purchase and bring along with a bride price to the traditional marriage and asked me to give it to my father. He did not want us to embarrass his family when we came to perform the marriage ceremony in their village. I thanked him again, and we rejoined others to continue the merriment.

Deacon Nwankwo then announced to everyone that after hearing all that I said, he had given me a message to give to my father, implying that he had given his permission to my proposal of marriage to his daughter. Before we left the village, Clara talked privately with her father, while the women teased her for rejecting marriage proposals from both a handsome man in her village with whom she grew up, and with another who had a medical degree. The women wondered what she found in this outsider, who was darker-skinned than the two others. Clara told them that, in time, they would discover for themselves why her choice was wise. We thanked everybody and drove away, happy that the stage was set for us to become man and wife at last.

On April 25, 1975, Clara and I were traditionally married. I was accompanied to Ufuma by Cosmas Uzomah, Kalu Ajah, Kalu Alfred, Lawrence Oleh, and Brother Ikpo. When we returned to Owerri, Clara and I went to the Eternal Sacred Order of Cherubim and Seraphim Church for the blessing of our marriage and to the Municipal Court to register the marriage officially. Uzomah served as our witness. I thus became a married man, ready to begin a family with Clara Kalu Ogbaa, née Clara Onyejiaka Nwankwo. The marriage brought the happiest moment in my life, relieving my fears of a premature death and material poverty, which other people had foreseen in my future.

One week after our marriage, I took Clara to our home in Umuchiakuma to meet my parents. Father was overjoyed to see her. He drew her to his bosom and gave her a big hug.

"Come, *Ada m* (my daughter). You come to replace my long-lost daughter, Mgbore. I hope you live long for me and for my family. *Chukwu gozie gi* (May God bless you)."

Instantly, the women expressed their joy with loud ululation, which brought many villagers to our compound to meet Clara, the new addition to the family, many commenting on her stunning beauty. So much so that the following day, the man whose wife had refused to allow me marry their daughter brought her to our house.

"Young Ogbaa," he said. "Here's your fiancée. You should not take another wife."

"Thank you, sir." I answered. "But as you can see, I am officially married to another girl." I pointed to Clara. "She is right here with me." I winked at Clara.

"But your father had offered me the traditional wine and meat for my daughter's betrothal to you, which I gladly accepted. I was waiting for your family to pay her bride price to us when you were ready to marry her."

"Yes, it's true that you did all that. But it's also true that your wife prevented me from marrying your daughter. I cannot begin now to tell you how I felt when she treated me like riffraff after I had been with your family for three years. Your daughter knows how much I wanted to marry her, but because I was not a rich man, your wife did not consider me good enough for her. Please, let go, sir. For I've found and married a girl who, along with her family, don't mind my apparent poverty and, perhaps, untimely death."

It pained me to say these things in his daughter's presence, for she was not the one who rejected the marriage proposal. But Clara, the consummate hostess, offered kola nuts and soft drinks to them as a humble gesture of conciliation. As they left our house, I felt sorry for them, and I would have been embarrassed if I had not told Clara about the girl beforehand.

From the first day Clara came into our family, Father received her wholeheartedly as he would have his own daughter, always calling her by the name Ada. Oh, how she loved Father dearly like her own father until his death! I often wondered who among our villagers could have believed that I would marry a woman after my heart— one who wasn't afraid to face my imagined sudden death and poverty.

Clara gave the lie to all those fears, and at age sixty-six, I still stand on the promises of my Lord and Savior, always praising Him dearly for the shower of blessings He has poured on my life.

During the 1975/76 academic year, Dr. Ernest N. Emenyonu, arriving back from the U.S., replaced Mr. Irondi as the chair of our English department. I was officially assigned to teach a course in African poetry and one in the British novel, as well as assisting Dr. Emenyonu in teaching the African novel. I was happy finally to have full control over the content and pedagogy of my own courses. And although I was no longer officially required to tutor students, I continued to work privately with several whenever my official assignments allowed. Some of the female students who were angry that Clara had "stolen" me away from them occasionally verbally attacked her. But such juvenile jealous behavior didn't stop her from loving me dearly.

Dr. Emenyonu traveled frequently to conferences, and on those occasions, I taught his classes. Consequently, he developed great admiration for me as a trustworthy man and budding scholar, enough so that he asked me to proofread the typescript of his book, *The Rise of the Igbo Novel* (Oxford UP, 1978). I gladly gave him any personal assistance for which he asked, hoping that such dedication would secure his help applying for admissions and financial aid in American universities, or at least secure a strong recommendation for sponsorship by our college.

One evening, I delivered a report to Dr. Emenyonu on the materials I had purchased for a bungalow he was building. When I arrived at his home, I found his guest, Professor Emmanuel Okechukwu Odita, alone in the house. I asked Professor Odita to let him know that I'd stopped by and turned to leave when he stopped me.

"How are you today, young man?" He motioned me to sit.

"I'm fine. Thank you, sir." I sat down.

"Ernest tells me how useful you've been in assisting him in the classroom, and that you've started proofreading the typescript of his book. That's very kind of you."

"I try my best to assist him in any way I can, sir. He is my boss."

"Very well. But what are your ambitions as an assistant lecturer in your college?"

"My ambition is to apply for graduate studies, both in Nigeria and the United States. I gained admission with teaching assistantship in the African Area Studies program at UCLA in June 1973. Unfortunately, I could not take the offer because the Gowon administration forced all graduates of Nigerian universities to serve in the newly established NYSC program. At the end of my service, they renewed my admission offer from UCLA without the teaching assistantship. The chair who made the offer, Professor Obichere, said he hired another person to replace me when I failed to attend in fall 1973. I've since applied to Nsukka and Ibadan, but have not yet received admission or financial aid offers from them."

"In other words, you are still interested in studying in the United States if you are given the opportunity."

"Yes. Very much so, sir."

"Well, then. Let me give you the name and address of the director of the Black Studies program at Ohio State University. Apply to him for graduate studies admission and ask for a Teaching Associate award. Please, do not mention me to him, or anyone else as the person who directed you to apply." I carefully wrote down the information as he dictated it.

"Thank you very much, sir. I will write the letter tonight and mail it out first thing in the morning." I stood and shook hands with him.

"Thank you. And good luck," he said, smiling.

I excused myself and left to tell Clara about the happy incident. Unbeknownst to me at the time, Emmanuel Odita was a professor of Art History in Ohio State University (OSU) at Columbus on sabbatical in the Arts department at AICE, Owerri. Less than two months after my application to Professor William Nelson, Jr., I received two letters. One letter contained an offer of admission into the graduate program, and the other an offer of a teaching associate with a monthly stipend of $318 with all tuition and fees waived for the duration of my studies in the department. Both offers took effect in the fall quarter, 1976.

A mistake on my student visa application delayed my arrival to the United States and I wasn't able to enroll at OSU in time. However, unlike UCLA, OSU eventually renewed both the admission and teaching associate offers for winter quarter, 1977. Even though the delay was, at first, a great disappointment, God knew what He was doing. For during the very week I was to leave for the U.S. in late August 1976, Clara found out she was pregnant with our first baby. Thus, it was a blessing that I missed my trip to the USA and was able to stay in Nigeria to take care of her during the first trimester of her pregnancy.

Overall, the good and bad intellectual and social differences that I had with my senior colleagues in the English department at AICE, helped me to prepare for the racial and professional discriminations I would ultimately face in the U.S. I chose to play it cool the rest of my tenure at AICE for the sake of my Clara, whose academic fate was still in their hands. I stayed with her until December 30, 1976, when I left Nigeria for America. We were both happy that I was eventually going to begin the next phase of my academic pursuit. Our joy and love continued to grow stronger in spite of our physical separation. And we honored each other because of our strong faith in God who granted us the two most cherished blessings we had asked of Him: our happy marriage and my graduate studies in America. As I reflected on those first fruits of our young marriage, I often thought of Father's own marital successes—and failures. I knew that the discipline and honor for family Father had instilled in me were both virtues from which my family would benefit. I grappled, however, with his frequent lack of kind-hearted understanding for others' feelings, and hoped that I could resist that character flaw in myself and treat my wife and children with the kind of respect and consideration that he often seemed unable to cultivate, especially in times of familial distress. If I could, I knew that with God's help, all was going to be well with us, no matter where Clara and I landed.

My father, Mazi Stephen Ogbaa Ikpo

My mother, Mrs. Ogonnaya Ogbaa Ikpo

The author, Kalu Ogbaa

The author (behind his father), leaving home for BVS, Ididep, 1958

Kalu plays soccer (#7) for T.T.C., Ohafia, 1st XI team, 1961

Kalu (with Brother Ikpo) after graduating from T.T.C., Ohafia, 1962

Kalu at ATTC, Owerri, 1967

Kalu (L) with his roommates at the University of Nigeria, Nsukka, 1972

Kalu graduates from the University of Nigeria, Nsukka, 1973

Kalu and his wife Clara at AICE, Owerri, 1975

Kalu arrives at the Ohio State University, Columbus, 1977

Kalu graduates PhD in English from U.T.-Austin, Texas, 1981

Kalu going to teach at Imo State University, Okigwe, 1986

Kalu and his family after the funeral of his father, 1989

Kalu arrives at Southern Connecticut State University, 1992

Kalu and his wife Glory at Southern, 1997

Kalu wins "The 1999 Faculty Scholar Award" at Southern, 1999

Dr. Ikenna Ogbaa, MD, taken during his residency, 2004

My children with Clara (L-R): Kelechi, Chukwuemeka, Ikenna, Nneka, Ndubuisi, and Enyinna, during Dr. Ikenna's graduation, 2002

Michael Ogbaa and his family, 2012, (clockwise) Michael, Sandra, Daniel, Derek, Darren, and David Ogbaa

Kalu and his family, 2012, (clockwise) Adanne, Kalu, Glory, Uchenna, Ekeoma, and Kalu (KK) Ogbaa.

Part Three

My American Experience

Chapter 10

Coming to America for Graduate Studies

I left the Murtala Mohammad International Airport in Lagos, Nigeria, aboard a Pan-Am flight on December 31, 1976, and arrived in Port Columbus, Ohio, on January 1, 1977. It was cold: seven degrees below zero. During the first week, seven people froze to death.

As I walked from the tarmac to the airport reception room, my teeth chattered, my hands numbed, and a strong shiver ran up my spine as snowflakes cascaded to the icy ground. I wore a light grey silk French suit without a winter coat since it had been hot and humid when I left Lagos.

Fortunately, the host family Ohio State University sent to pick me up was already at the airport when I arrived. I bought a coat for $60 at an airport store I could have gotten for $25 at a second-hand store and heaved a sigh of relief as we slid into their heated car. We drove straight to the campus International Students Office where the director interviewed and assigned me a residential hall in Jones Tower. We drove immediately to the residential hall where a party welcoming new students was already under way. I settled into my new room on the twelfth floor, and thanked the host couple for their help and support as they left.

The severe weather on that first day foreshadowed the cold reception I would receive concerning the racial segregation, discrimination, and deprivation I would face as a double minority (black and foreign) living in America. But that would come later. For now, I prepared myself mentally and psychologically to face the challenges of realizing my dream of receiving a world-class education in United States universities. I truly believed that America would give me the greatest opportunity to succeed in life.

The following day, Nnadozie Nkpa and two other Nigerian graduate students dropped by to welcome me, a fellow Igbo man, to the university. I caught them up on news from home, and then we took a tour of the important campus landmarks, like the refectory, the library, and the Black Studies department while they filled me in on the important information, which would enable me to adjust quickly to my new home. I thanked God for protecting me all through my long journey from Nigeria to the U.S. and asked Him to continue guiding me in all my endeavors to acquire a higher education in a foreign land.

Early Monday, I prepared for my first day of classes, dressing in a nice suit and tie (as some professors in Nigeria usually did) to impress my U.S. faculty and students. Then I headed to the office of the department chair, Professor William E. Nelson, Jr., and introduced myself. He asked the department secretary, Ms. Penny, to assign me an office, introduce me to Professor Oscar Ronald Dathorne, my academic advisor and the professor to whom I would serve as an associate, and who would give me the necessary information about my dual roles in the department. I filled out some administrative forms, including an application for a social security number, and then Ms. Penny took me to Professor Dathorne's office.

During our first meeting, I got the impression that Professor Dathorne liked me. He too had lived in Nigeria, serving as a professor of English at a local university. He knew much about the Igbo and spoke to me using a Nigerian Pidgin English to make me feel at ease. He told me that although he had dual appointments in the English and Black Studies departments, I would serve as his teaching associate only in Black literature. Then he helped me select my semester coursework.

After registering, I observed Professor Dathorne teaching. He introduced me to the students as his teaching associate, who would teach his classes whenever he was away from campus. He also encouraged them to visit me whenever they needed help with their African literature courses. He'd hardly finished the introduction when several students began asking me questions about Africa. While most were impressed at my answers, some complained about my heavy Nigerian accent. I assured them they would get used to it in a couple of weeks, but in the meantime, they should raise their hands whenever they did not understand and I would spell it out on the chalkboard. I also joked that I did not quite understand their American accent either, but I was prepared to adjust my listening so that

I would understand it soon. They clapped at my not-so-subtle humorous reference to "otherness."

I was a bit surprised, nevertheless, that by the end of my first week of classes, I felt *colored* black by other people. Since I had never travelled outside Nigeria before, I had no experience of the effects of racism, or the notion that my black skin in any way connoted inferiority to whites. Even in Nigeria, where people fought the twin demons of discrimination and deprivations based on one's ethnicity, those did not affect me as an Igbo man, because the Igbo are one of three dominant ethnic groups in the country. But in America, where I was the only black male in the English classroom, along with two black female students, I automatically became a minority, feeling a little intimidated. Still, as I sat in the second row of the classroom surrounded by white students, I found it curious that the black students sat at the back row when there were vacant seats up front. And while I took an active part in our class discussions, none of the other blacks said a word, sitting silently and taking notes as other students confidently made their points. I also thought it curious that the professor did not seem to make any effort to engage these other blacks either by asking them questions prompting them for their opinions.

Immediately after the class ended, the two women, Jocelyn and Linda, rushed over to introduce themselves. Linda was just a slight shade lighter than I, but Jocelyn was so light that I would never have guessed she was black. They asked if I lived off campus. When I told them I had just moved into Jones Graduate Tower, Jocelyn smiled widely and told me she lived there too, and that Linda lived in the dormitory adjacent to ours.

When I asked why they segregated themselves from the rest of the students in the classroom, they laughed uneasily and said that while they could not easily explain the situation to me at that moment, they were sure that I would soon understand. Before we split up to head to our separate classes, Jocelyn took my room number and promised to visit me soon.

Later that evening, I heard a knock at my door and found Jocelyn standing in the hallway, smiling. After I asked her in, she told me that she came to say hello and answer some of the questions I had asked her and Linda earlier in the day. I was a little nervous, because before I left Nigeria, Father had warned me of *crazy* American women, especially since I was coming without my wife. I wondered if Jocelyn, coming at what seemed a late hour, was one of those *crazies*.

But Jocelyn was not. She told me about the racism currently practised in America and how the self-segregation I had witnessed in class was one of the ways that blacks dealt with it. She felt it was important that I know a bit of the cankerworm that might enable me, a foreign black man, to survive, both on and off the campus. I was surprised, but not naïve. I told Jocelyn I'd seen ethnic bigotry practiced in Nigeria. Some of my Igbo people were among those who perpetrated it, and consequently we as a people collectively suffered its evil effects more than we deserved during the Nigeria-Biafra War. Jocelyn encouraged me to visit her if I ever needed to talk. I thanked her and walked her to her room.

The first lecture for Professor Dathorne's class was on Chinua Achebe's novel, *Things Fall Apart*. Many students praised the strongman, Okonkwo, for standing up to the invading white men in Igboland. They asked good questions about the Igbo and other West African cultures, but I was saddened by the ignorance of some students about African issues. They had never been fully taught black history. For instance, they asked if my country was Africa, whether we had highways, culture and civilization, and if women were allowed to attend school in my country. I told them that my country was Nigeria, Africa was a continent made up of many countries, and that it was larger in size and population than continental Europe.

On the issue of highways, I joked: "No, we don't have highways. We hop from one tree top to another when we are going somewhere, and the American Embassy is situated on top of the tallest Iroko tree." The entire class burst into laughter. On the question of women attending school in Nigeria, I told them that they did, adding that although men dominated women in education, we had many highly educated women who became university professors, politicians, and writers, like Flora Nwapa, the author of the novels, *Efuru, Idu,* and *Never Again*.

I could understand why many of the students would be that ignorant of their black African heritage: while some of them weren't taught anything at all about Africa, what others knew about the continent came from Tarzan movies shot in Southern Africa and shown on American TV. After a time, the students began to see me as one of their distant cousins from Africa and felt free to ask me more probing questions about the continent, both openly in class and privately in my office. I enjoyed answering the questions, and connecting with them on a cultural and spiritual level.

At the end of the first week, Professor Dathorne formally introduced me to the rest of the faculty and graduate students of the Black Studies department, and I immediately saw the benefits of both instructing and studying courses in the Black Studies department. Both roles helped me to develop my race consciousness as a black man living in a white-dominated country.

Such course as Seminar in Black Literature, Major Black Authors, Black Revolutionary Aesthetics, Black Role Models, Mental Health in Black Communities, Citizen Participation, and Research in Black Studies increased my consciousness as a black man. They were based on global black experience, which involved the examination of the relationship between black peoples in continental Africa, Oceania, the Americas, and Europe on the one hand, and white people on the other. We also focused our attention on the discussion of the negative effects of colonialism, imperialism, and racism on black peoples, and the role of black revolutionary sociopolitical and civil rights leaders in all parts of the world working alongside black writers and activists to fight for the liberation and freedom of the various black peoples in the world. The history and writings of such civil rights leaders and renowned authors as Nelson Mandela, Dr. Martin Luther King Jr., Rosa Parks, General Chukwuemeka Odumegwu Ojukwu, Richard Wright, Langston Hughes, James Baldwin, Ralph Ellison, George Lamming, Wilson Harris, and Aime Cesair, for example, were the subjects of symposia, seminars, colloquia, and research. The courses prepared and enabled me to become more conscious of who I was as a black man. Also, I was ready to become a college professor, who would ultimately teach other people about the cultures and civilizations of blacks both in the U.S. and my native Nigeria. In addition, my Black Studies internship in a predominantly black East High School, Columbus, offered me an opportunity to further my black experience, at the fringes of the American society.

To further my understanding, I took four elective English courses at the Masters level, paying close attention to those that embodied the themes of racism, colonialism, and oppression, to complement what I was studying in the Black Studies program. One course, Twentieth-century British Fiction, taught by Professor Berger, introduced me to the novels of the Irish James Joyce, and Welsh novelist, Thomas Hardy in which I learned how both novelists dealt with the issue of Irish and Welsh nationalisms under British imperial control of their countries. I also took a course on William Butler Yeats' revolutionary poems ("The Stolen Child," "September 1913," "Easter 1916," "The Republic of Ireland," "The Lake Isle of Innisfree," "A Dream of Death," "The Magi," and "Crazy Jane Talks with the Bishop"), which also taught me how Yeats dealt with the same issue from a poet's point of view.

In essence, the English courses helped me to appreciate more the revolutionary writings of such African novelists as Chinua Achebe, Ngugi *wa* Thiong'o, Peter Abrahams, and Ferdinand Oyono, as well as the poetry of Wole Soyinka, Leopold Sedar Senghor, Dennis Brutus, and Okot p'Bitek. In other words, I enjoyed studying how the British and African writers used their works as a medium to expose the evil effects of white colonialism and imperialism on the colonized peoples. Through reading such authors' works, the oppressed peoples became aware of their oppression and enabled to find various ways of fighting their oppressors in order to reclaim their lost sovereignty. Ostensibly, that was why Western critics often characterize such black writings as protest or revolutionary works.

I began my graduate seminar courses in Black Studies at the same time my native Nigeria was hosting a global conference for action against the apartheid regime in South Africa, which was part of the second Black Festival of Art and Culture (FESTAC '77). The colorful events, broadcast from Lagos to the U.S., brought together black peoples in the Diaspora to rediscover their roots and reestablish ties with Mother Africa, and whetted my intellectual curiosity with regard to the place of the black man in any white-dominated society. The daily communiqués from FESTAC gave the black faculty and graduate students of the college many issues for discussion and debate, reminiscent of the black students from Africa and the Caribbean studying in France in the 1940s who had started a revolutionary movement known as Negritude, giving rise to global black writings in Africa, the Caribbean, and Oceana. The movement followed and complemented another black literary movement in the United States between 1919 and 1940 known as the Harlem Renaissance.

In both revolutionary movements, what began as a literary effort by a few students and writers ended up sparking a socio-literary and political program and agenda that eventually raised the position of black peoples everywhere in the world. As a Nigerian graduate student in America, I was proud that my home was host-country of a conference whose primary aim was to plan actions against the oppressive South African government apartheid system put in place to dominate, dehumanize, segregate, and discriminate against blacks in their own God-given land. Proud that the black intelligentsia at the conference was working to free blacks from tyranny and oppression, which my own Igbo people still craved, but had not received, from external forces during the Nigeria-Biafra War. Anything the FESTAC conferees planned to help free the oppressed people in South Africa had to be applauded by *all* oppressed people, everywhere in the world.

Consequently, the more I learned about the struggles and triumphs of the oppressed blacks in America, the more I was inspired to tell my colleagues the story of our Biafran struggles and unacknowledged triumphs. I knew that most of them did not know much about the achievements of the Biafran revolution because we had lost the war to Nigeria. Furthermore, aware that historians often tell the history of wars only from the victors' points of view, I felt obliged to tell the American blacks about our Biafran triumphs during those three grueling years. They included the ingenuity of our indigenous military and technological advancements, the stronger emerging Igbo ethnic unity and nationalism, and our indefatigable self-reliance and industriousness—all of which enabled us to withstand the brutality of three nations: Nigeria, Great Britain and the USSR. Despite the desperate roads we had traveled, most Biafrans had managed to survive the war, characterized by some as the bloodiest war the Igbo people have ever faced in their national history.

By the end of the winter quarter, I was elected to the executive committee of the Black Students Association, based on the active role I played in the association and the good grades I made in my courses. I also joined the National Black Students Association. Both organizations enabled me to represent our students in the faculty meetings and attend national conferences where I could see how other Black Studies programs in the country were handling some of the same issues facing black people around the world. And to educate myself further about black issues, I subscribed to black journals such as *Research in African Literatures, The New Negro, The Black Scholar, Ufahamu,* and *College Language Association Journal.* Reading the articles also inspired me to write and publish my own in American journals between 1978 and 1992.

Clara gave birth to our first child, Ikenna, on May 7, 1977. Six weeks later, I brought them over to the U.S. with the assistance of my good friends in Nigeria. I rented a two-bedroom apartment in the university's Cuyahoga Married Students Apartments, and Dr. Florence Odita, wife of Professor Odita, helped me to purchase used furniture, a color television, and other things that would help Clara feel at home.

Our reunion was glorious. Ikenna was a handsome, chubby, baby boy (handsome enough that *American Babies* magazine wanted to use his photo for a cover). But I objected on religious grounds (Clara was not happy). But I was, nevertheless, so fond of Ikenna and spent so many precious hours with him that I cut back on my studies. Consequently, I scored the only B+ grade in all my courses that semester (although the rest were A- and above). These were the best joys of fatherhood.

My additional expenses required that I carry a maximum course load each academic quarter to complete my Masters, which I did in only eleven months and received my diploma in December 1977. I had applied for admission and a teaching assistantship into the doctoral programs in English at the University of Texas in Austin (UT-Austin) and the University of California at Los Angeles (UCLA), and at OSU with a possible renewal of my appointment as a teaching associate.

UCLA gave me admission for the 1978 spring semester, but they didn't want to offer me a teaching assistantship until August, when I would have taken some graduate courses from their English department and would have had my grades evaluated for an award for the fall semester. Likewise, the English department at OSU gave me admission without renewing my teaching associate appointment. It was not their department policy to hire foreign graduate students as instructors. I was surprised they had not taken into consideration the graduate English courses I had taken and passed with high grades, my teaching associate position and the strong letters of recommendation written by three of their English professors. I was so disappointed that I accused them of denying my assistantship because I was black, then stormed out telling them to offer the assistantships to other "qualified" candidates.

Three days later, I received two letters from the English department at UT-Austin: an offer of admission into their doctoral program, and an appointment as an assistant instructor for fall 1978. Even better, it was a higher position than a graduate assistantship, paying $500 per month with all tuition and fees waived. I enthusiastically accepted both offers. Clara could not contain her joy when I showed her the letters, feeling the tight pinch of our budget as she was.

After taking my last exams in November 1977, I looked for a temporary job in downtown Columbus. The chair of our department, Professor William Nelson, Jr., wrote me a strong letter of recommendation. I applied at the Urban League, but when the white officer who interviewed me saw my credentials, he said I was overqualified for the available jobs. He also wondered why I wasted my time accumulating degrees that couldn't earn me a job. So we stayed in Columbus until I received my last paycheck in December, then moved to Austin.

Overall, I was pleased with the education I received from the Ohio State University. I worked so hard on my courses that I had no social life, always studying in the libraries on campus and late into the night at home. In the meantime, Clara and Ikenna attended church and other social gatherings with a close friend, Jackie. I graduated at the top of the dean's list of our graduating class and received national academic recognition becoming a member of the Honor Society of Phi Kappa Phi.

Austin was sunny and warm when we arrived, in the middle of winter. The city was beautiful, clean, quiet, and relatively small. Unlike Columbus, where we regularly experienced snow, ice and windstorms, the climate in Austin felt like the harmattan season. There was not one snowstorm during the entire four years of our stay. And I never wore that heavy winter coat I bought at the Columbus Airport in January 1977. Another warm discovery was the large number of Nigerian (indeed Igbo) families who lived in Austin and who gladly welcomed us on arrival (one of them even kindly offered us their home for two weeks until we rented our own apartment).

In spite of my relative physical and emotional ease regarding my new university home, one thing that intimidated me a bit was the large size of the university. Austin was the second most populous university campus in the U.S., with the campus spread out like a labyrinth around the city. But with the help of a great International Office, and my new Nigerian friends, I quickly learned to navigate it easily.

Before classes began, I went to the general office of the English department, in Parlin Hall, to register. The secretary, Kimberly, was friendly:

"Good morning, madam. My name is Kalu Ogbaa. I've come to register for the spring semester."

"Welcome to our department. We've been expecting you." She smiled.

"Thank you. I would've come sooner, but my family and I had to find an apartment to rent first."

"Yes, I understand. Have you found any yet?"

"Yes, we just moved into a one-bedroom apartment two days ago."

"That's good. Austin is a beautiful place to live in. I hope you and your family would like it here as many of us do."

"Oh we already like it here because of its warm weather, which is very unlike the one we've just come out of in Columbus, Ohio."

"Good for you. I've never been up North, but I hear that it's pretty cold during this time of the year."

"It's very much so. We had to move here because of your warm weather and reputedly excellent programs your English department offers."

"Thank you for your kind words about our city and department."

After our exchange of pleasantries, the secretary gave me the registration forms, showed me the graduate students' general office, the department library, and finally took me to the graduate advisor's office for my course registration. Before she left, she informed me that Professor Bernth Lindfors had asked of me and left his office and telephone numbers for me.

The graduate advisor interviewed me about my area of interest then helped me to choose my courses for the semester and encouraged me to see him during his office hours anytime I needed help on my courses. Later that morning, I went to Dr. Lindfors' office.

"Good morning, Professor Lindfors. I am Kalu Ogbaa. I hope you still remember me from Nigeria." I smiled.

"Oh, yes. I remember, even though you have grown since we met at Nsukka in 1972." He smiled back, nodding.

"I wanted to thank you for your assistance in getting me admitted into the doctoral program, and for the assistant instructorship award. You must have strongly supported my applications for both positions in the department."

"Thank you, Kalu. But your strong academic records and letters of recommendation spoke for you. Whatever I said to the committee was not as important as what they found in your records. Welcome to Austin."

Lindfors asked about my former Nsukka professors, my experiences at Ohio, and current socio-political and literary events in Nigeria. As a specialist in African literature, he was particularly interested in the emerging postwar literature in Nigeria. I found him the same old Lindfors that I met during the international conference organized at the University of Nigeria, Nsukka: charming, friendly, making his points with clarity, and enthusiastic about making the study of African literature a viable curricular offering in the English department. And I got the distinct impression that he had already planned for my academic development in his area of expertise. He gave me an open invitation to see him whenever I needed. I thanked him and left, very happy.

After paying my first semester's tuition and two months' rent for a one-bedroom apartment, I was broke. The accounts from my Barclays Bank in Nigeria were frozen. Ironically, the Nigerian government did so in obedience to the decision of the FESTAC 1977 conference to disinvest any monetary assets that Black countries had in Western countries, especially Great Britain (which supported the apartheid regime in South Africa). Consequently, $5,000 of my money was tied up while my family suffered, a casualty of the political warfare blacks in the Diaspora were waging against white South African government. But despite my financial hardship, I saw the justice in what my country Nigeria and other black countries were doing to end the oppression of South African blacks. Nevertheless, I had to do something to make money for the upkeep of my family.

I went downtown looking for jobs, however menial, and finally found a job at Red Tomato Restaurant that paid minimum wage, working as a dishwasher, standing for hours sandwiched between a steaming dishwashing machine and a red hot bread-baking oven. Both the Mexican American baker and I did our jobs standing on our feet all through our shifts. I had never done such arduous work before, but I was determined. The manager allowed us to eat one free meal per shift, but because the meals were prepared with pork and spaghetti, I could not eat them for religious reasons and went hungry most of the time. One day, when I took a cup of pop soda from the restaurant in place of the free meal, the manager ordered me to pay for it, not minding that the soda was cheaper than the meal I could have eaten if I chose to. I paid him on the spot. Nevertheless, as I punched in to work the next day, the manager asked me to punch out and go home, claiming that there were not enough customers to serve.

That evening, I wrote a letter to twenty churches in Austin, begging for alms to take care of my little baby Ikenna and Clara who was two months pregnant with our second baby. To ask her to go find a job while I studied in school was not an option since we had no money to babysit Ikenna. The following Monday, I went back to work at the Red Tomato. Once again, before I could punch in, the Mexican American worker told me that the manager wanted to see me in his office. When I met him, he said did not need my services any longer in the restaurant and gave me my first and last $50 paycheck. I thanked him and left immediately. I was mad and yet thankful to God that I had a little money in my pocket, which meant a lot to me.

As soon as I entered our apartment, I found Clara sobbing. I ran to the baby's crib to see if he was all right. He was, and when I told Clara why I came back early and showed the $50 check, she continued to sob. I held her tight and assured her that what we were going through then was a temporary setback, which I vowed we would overcome shortly with God's help. Then she showed me $200 from the members of one of the churches I wrote for charity. While she was still narrating how it happened, I heard a knock at the door. I opened the door and a tall man stood waiting.

"Hello, people. My name is Peter. May I come in?" the man said.

"Yes. Please, come in, Peter, and sit down," I invited him in and showed him to a chair.

"Are you Kalu Ogbaa?" He looked at a piece of paper he pulled out of his pocket.

"Yes, I am. And this is my wife Clara."

"That's good. And where is your baby, Ikenna?" he asked as he looked at the paper again.

"Oh. Let me show you. He is sleeping in the crib," I stood and showed him to the crib.

"Oh what a gorgeous baby!" He smiled down at Ikenna.

"Thank you very much."

"The reason I came is that our pastor read your letter and sent me to see the baby and buy him $80 worth of baby food and diapers. We do not want any child of God to starve. In addition, the pastor wants us to bring your family to our church, The World of Pentecost, for evening prayers on Saturday. One of our brothers will bring you."

Then he took me to a grocery store, bought some baby food and diapers for Ikenna, and brought me back home. I thanked Peter and asked him to convey our gratitude to the pastor and his congregation.

"Will do," he said, and drove off.

Clara continued to sob in gratitude over the $330 we received that day. When we arrived in the church the following Saturday, we were introduced to the pastor who interviewed us in his office. Then we joined the others in the chapel and worshipped with the other members. At the end of the service, the pastor asked my family to stand for introductions.

"Brethren in the Lord, it is my joy and privilege to introduce a new family visiting us tonight," the pastor began.

"Kalu Ogbaa is a graduate student at the University of Texas here in Austin. Because of some political circumstances, he could not withdraw money from his bank in his native Nigeria. In the meantime, his family needs our help so our little brother may not starve. So I want every member to reach into his or her pocket and get some money out to give to them," he continued.

As he spoke to the congregation, all eyes were riveted on Ikenna, Clara, and me. He asked us to sit down and then the ushers passed plates from pew to pew to collect alms for us. I felt humiliated. In the end, the collections were poured into one tray and handed over to the pastor. He prayed over it, gave it to Peter to bring to us, and asked me to stand up and receive it on behalf of my family. As Peter handed me the tray, my eyes glazed with tears. I couldn't clearly see his outstretched arms and missed the tray. Its contents clattered to the floor.

"Please, take it brother," the pastor said. "It is given to you by your fellow children of God." I wiped the tears from my eyes, received the alms, and thanked everybody for being so kind to my family.

The congregation prayed for us again, and the man who brought us to church drove us back to our apartment. When we counted the money, it came to a total of $365. All the blessings we received from all of God's children overwhelmed me, for within a week we had received $695, which enabled us to overcome our poverty for the moment. That evening, I felt too emotional to eat the dinner. While consoling me, Clara let me know why she'd been sobbing earlier that day. She knew how painful it had been for me to swallow my Igbo pride and write the letters begging for alms from strangers to save my family from starvation. But I assured her that it was not her fault that our money in Nigeria was frozen. We held hands and offered prayers of thanks to God who had been our helper, and after feeding Ikenna, we ate dinner together, went to bed, and slept peacefully.

A few weeks later, I landed a research assistant job at the Lyndon B. Johnson Library on campus, which paid me $214 a month, and the Internal Revenue Service sent me a tax refund of $80. I also received a stipend from Professor Ambrose Gordon for an impromptu lecture I gave in his course.

I was given the opportunity to present the lecture after Professor Gordon had chided us for not being prepared enough for his course on William Butler Yeats. The next day, I came to class ready to illustrate Yeats' theory of the moon as it applies to some of his poems and asked Professor Gordon if I might use the chalkboard. At the chalkboard, I drew a one-quarter moon, a half- moon, a three-quarter moon, and a full moon and used them to explain how each phase of the moon affected human behaviors, linking it to the meanings of the words "lunar" and "lunatic." The class was impressed enough by my presentation that they clapped. So was Professor Gordon. Two days later, I received a call from Professor Gordon.

"Hello, Kalu. This is Ambrose Gordon. How are you?"

"I'm doing well, sir. And how are you?"

"I'm okay. I'm calling to tell you that I was highly impressed by your presentation in class the other day."

"Thank you, sir, for allowing me to use the chalkboard to illustrate my points."

"Could you give me your full name, social security number, and mailing address? I have a present I want to mail out to you."

I gave him the information and thanked him again. Then we hung up.

Two days later, I received a check for $200, which he called a "Parlin Award," from the department. I was overjoyed. We need no longer worry about our bills or groceries for the next several months, and I could devote all my time to studying.

After my appointment as an assistant instructor took effect in the 1978 fall semester, Clara and I could attend classes with all of our tuition waived. The International Office also approved our application to rent a two-bedroom apartment in the University Married Students Housing complex, and we could leave Ikenna in a daycare center while we attended classes.

My major concentration was British Literature and my minor was American Literature. However, I was also required to take some Linguistics courses to complement the other areas of studies for the doctoral program. After reviewing my transcript, the graduate advisor credited me with most of the courses from OSU as out-of-department electives, which reduced my overall course load considerably. I found the courses as tough as those I took at OSU except for linguistics and medieval literature courses that I found a little tougher, but I passed them as well.

Of all the courses, I found "Theory and Practice of Literary Criticism" the most beneficial to my overall academic and professional development. Professor Kaufmann, who had a Masters in Physics and a Ph.D. in English, taught the course. Our first written assignment was a critical analysis of a poem. He instructed us to limit our answers to only one double-spaced page. I studied the poem very closely and wrote a response paper that I thought was very good. When he returned the assignment to us, my paper was mutilated with red ink. When he asked for our comments, I asked him why every sentence in my paper was marked red and whether I failed the paper. He smiled and asked me to check the back of the paper to see the grade I earned. To my surprise, it was an A-, despite the red marks. He then said that our ideas were good but most of our expressions were verbose. Moreover, he added that some of us in the literary field, unlike people in the sciences, tended to use more words than necessary in our writings. The distinction he made between literary and scientific writings in academe impressed me a lot.

Because of Professor Kaufmann's critical remarks, I became conscious of verbose constructs in my writings for the first time in my academic life. I worked harder on learning how to use suitcase or compendious words to express my ideas in my future assignments. Besides, I went regularly to his office for help on critical thinking and writing. I now count myself fortunate to have had him as a professor, for his instructions on writing helped me to improve my writing style in whatever I wrote and published within and outside the university.

After completing most of my course work, I began preparing for my English comprehensive exam. I knew that two of my fellow Nigerian students, who had come into the doctoral program before me, did not pass the exam the first time they took it, even though they both came with almost perfect records from their masters degrees. In fact, the department asked one of them to take more courses in English at the Masters level before they readmitted him to continue his doctoral studies. The other student retook the exam three more times before he passed.

Consequently, some of our professors had begun to form a low opinion of Nigerian students. Hence, I worked tirelessly to succeed and prove them wrong, despite the hurdles of preconceived prejudices that arose along my path to completion.

For example, when I approached my graduate advisor to sign off on the summer courses I needed to complete prior to the comprehensive exam, he required me to take a course that conflicted with my work schedule at the LBJ Library. He insisted that I take the course or he would not sign my registration form. I explained that I needed time to figure out how I could fit it into my schedule. If I quit my library job, I would lose the money I desperately needed to pay my bills. On the other hand, I knew it would be difficult, if not impossible, for me to pass the course while I worked in the library.

Back at home, I decided on a course of action that might allow me to complete my coursework in a reasonable fashion while keeping my job. The next day, I went to the advisor's office equipped with a hidden tape-recorder to discuss the registration issue with him again. I asked him to allow me to take another course I had chosen instead of his own, explaining once again about my job conflict. Once again, he refused, saying that he needed my registration so his class could meet the required number of students for the course. If I refused, he said he would not like it. I knew what he meant, and grudgingly signed up for his course. As I had feared, I missed some classes during the semester because of my job schedule, and he gave me a B- in the course.

I knew that, with such a low grade, our department would not let me take the comprehensive exam. So I reported the professor's actions to Professor Gordon, threatening to expose the graduate advisor for coercing me to take the course I did not want, and I played to him the conversation between us that I had recorded. Gordon was so angry that he immediately discussed the incident with the chair of the department who, in turn, discussed it with the committee responsible for administering the comprehensive exam. Consequently, the committee allowed me to take a variant of the course with another professor to avoid the shame the scandalous incident might bring to the department. I re-took the course and passed it with a higher grade.

When I finally took the comprehensive exam, I passed it on my first attempt. My success somewhat ended the myth that Nigerian students were incapable of passing the English comprehensive exams, and consequently the department allowed the Nigerian student whom they asked to take more courses at the Masters' level to continue with his doctoral studies. He passed the exam a year after I did.

At that juncture in my studies, funding was once again a problem. Clara had given birth to our second child, Ndubuisi, on August 23, 1978, and so I applied for postgraduate scholarship awards to my native Imo State Government and the Federal Government of Nigerian in fall 1979. Both governments approved my applications and announced their awards at the same time in *West African Magazine.* While the Imo State Government promptly sent me a check for $6,000 in the mail, the Federal Government sent their check for $10,000 through the Consulate General in New York. They withheld the funds and asked me to pick them up in New York so I could sign for it in person. When I arrived a few days later, they told me that somebody from our university had written them an anonymous letter, accusing me of applying for the graduate scholarship even though I was a professor of English. Hence, they had to return the check to Lagos, believing that I applied for the scholarship to defraud the federal government.

I was livid that they had not waited to hear from the accused person first before taking such extreme measure. I asked why they had returned the check without first interviewing me. Apparently, the anonymous writer had also given them information about me that enabled them to call for my university records, which confirmed that I taught courses at the school. In addition, they had looked at my transcript and seen that I made A's in most of my courses. Thus, they believed that my accuser was reliable. I explained that my appointment as an assistant instructor in the university was a form of internship training I had to undergo to acquire useful experiences I needed for teaching students in Nigerian universities and colleges after graduating. I also gave them examples of other Nigerian graduate students who received the scholarship awards while working for their doctorate degrees and serving as teaching assistants or assistant instructors.

After hearing my arguments and examining my documentary evidence, the officers apologized for acting without hearing first from me. Still, they insisted that they did so to prevent auditors from accusing them of collaborating with me to defraud the federal government. Eventually they gave me a letter, which I took to Lagos and reclaimed the returned check. In spite of the delay, however, the incident became a blessing in disguise because the scholarship money had greater value than it did a year before, in that one Nigerian Naira fetched two U.S. Dollars when I finally collected it in 1982 and started the construction of my new village home.

The graduate studies committee appointed Professor Lindfors as my dissertation director. In addition to directing my project, he played a big role in my academic and professional life by giving me rides all over the United States to academic conferences on African literature and cultural studies. In 1980, for instance, he and I attended an African Literature Association conference at the University of Florida in Gainesville, where I not only presented a paper on Chinua Achebe's novels but also interviewed the famous author. In January 1981, the interview was published as the lead article in *Research in African Literatures,* Vol. 12 # 1, which was devoted entirely to the published works of Chinua Achebe. Later, in 1997, Lindfors republished the interview as one of the chapters of his book, *Conversations with Chinua Achebe,* in the University of Mississippi Press.

Furthermore, Lindfors asked me to proofread the typescript of a book he and C. L. Innes edited in 1978, titled *Critical Perspectives on Chinua Achebe,* to ensure that they spelled the Igbo words and names in it accurately. For me, a budding Igbo scholar, to comment on the Igbo cultural exegesis they included in the critical study, was a great honor. And the work I did impressed Lindfors so much that he asked me to write reviews of a few other books for *World Literature Today.* After I'd reviewed a couple of books, the editor appointed me the reviewer of books on African and Caribbean issues. Both opportunities widened my knowledge of Achebe's works and my study of other Africana literary publications. From 1980 through 1986, I published ten solicited book reviews in some American and Canadian journals.

Periodically, the English department published the names of professors and graduate students and the titles of the papers they delivered or published in journals. In addition, assistant instructors, who taught "Rhetoric and Composition/Rhetoric and Literature" to freshman classes, were required to send in their students' essays for competition, publishing the names of the winners and their instructors in the English bulletin boards. My students' names and mine appeared frequently. The more I received those acknowledgments, the more I was encouraged to work harder as a means to strengthening my reputation as a budding scholar and prospective university professor.

In December 1980, I attended an MLA Annual Convention in Houston, Texas, where I presented a paper, "Death in African Literature: The Example of Chinua Achebe," in the graduate students caucus. The audience received the paper so well that two professors rushed to acquire it for publication. Since I did not want to disappoint either of them, I divided and modified the paper into two articles. I gave the one I titled "Death in African Literature: The Example of Achebe" (about the death of Ezeulu in *Arrow of God*) to Professor Douglas Killam of the University of Guelph in Canada. He published in *World Literature Written in English* (1981), and the other I titled "A Cultural Note on Okonkwo's Suicide" (about Okonkwo's death in *Things Fall Apart*) to Professor Anna Rutherford of the University of Aarhus in Denmark, which she published in *Kunapipi* (1981).

Furthermore, I had submitted my resume at the conference to some of the representatives of universities who reviewed them for initial interviews of candidates they could invite to their campuses for job interviews. I was happily surprised when an English professor from Ohio State University invited me to their booth for a chat after she sat through the presentation of my paper. When we talked, she indicated a strong desire to invite me to Columbus for an interview by their search committee. She indicated that they would hire me at the assistant professor level and named the minimum salary and other benefits, which I could negotiate upwards with the dean and the vice president for academic affairs. I thanked her for showing interest in my candidacy but declined the invitation. She asked why I would not consider it. I reminded her of the incident in which her school had refused to renew my teaching associate appointment in 1977 because I was a foreign black. I jokingly added that, as she could clearly see, my skin color had gotten darker than what it was when I was at Ohio because of the sun in Texas.

In addition to my scholarship training, my training in curriculum development was also strong and began when I took courses in the pedagogy of rhetoric and composition with two renowned modern rhetoricians: Professors James L. Kinneavy, author of *A Theory of Discourse* (1971) and John J. Ruszkiewicz, who later authored *Beyond Words* (2005). They taught us sound pedagogical theories and practices, how to develop good syllabi for the courses, visited our classes periodically as observers, and followed up those observations with weekly discussions of our classroom experiences. By the time I graduated, I had produced more than eighteen syllabi for the courses I taught.

Upon my graduation in May 1981, the English department hired me as a full time senior lecturer with the salary of an assistant professor to teach two of Lindfors's courses, who was away then on sabbatical leave in Africa. I was given the rank of lecturer because of the university policy that a graduate must work outside of the institution for four years before they could hire him or her to teach on tenure track. It came with a good salary and the opportunity to expand my teaching experience further while I looked for tenure-track positions at other universities. It also gave Clara time to finish her Master's degree.

During that academic year, Professor Michael Echeruo was on sabbatical at the University of Houston (UH), Texas. He regularly visited our university in Austin to make use of our Humanities Research Center (HRC). He was friends with Professor Robert Wren of UH and Professor Lindfors of UT. During those visits, he gained information about me from the English bulletin boards and discussed my progress as a doctoral candidate and assistant instructor with Lindfors. He also visited my family a few times. When the governor of the old Imo State, Chief Samuel O. Mbakwe, appointed him vice chancellor (president) to build the first state university in Nigeria, I was one of the first faculty members he recruited from the U.S. to help him carry out his task. From what he learned from Lindfors and our department information board, he knew I could develop a curriculum for students of English in the prospective Imo State University. Eventually, the curriculum development skills I learned from UT paid off at a time and place I had not expected.

Echeruo knew I had just started serving as a senior lecturer at UT in fall 1981, the same semester classes were supposed to start at the Imo State University; nevertheless, he offered me the position of Senior Lecturer II, starting immediately. I told him that while I would be delighted to accept the offer, I could not abandon my appointment and students at Austin in the middle of the semester. Still, he insisted that he would give me until the end of the semester to join his university in January 1982. We struck a deal. I would finish my fall semester teaching, and Clara could finish her Master's degree program, then we'd leave for home. I told our department chair about my decision to leave the country at the end of the semester so he could begin to look for my replacement.

Overall, the hand of God was in everything I did for the five years I studied and worked in the U.S. Before leaving Nigeria, I had focused on the sole aim of studying to earn an MA degree in Black Studies. Now that I had earned a Ph. D. in English, I had no second thought about leaving immediately to practice what I had learned in the service of my home country. The need was even greater since the two scholarship awards I received from Imo State and the Federal Government of Nigeria needed to be repaid, and I did not want to appear ungrateful to both governments. For my father once said to me: "Ingratitude is the greatest sin, yet it is common." God gave me the wonderful opportunities to acquire higher education and grow a family for a purpose. Hence, it was time for me to go forth and let my little light shine wherever I might be in my native Nigeria.

Chapter 11

Back Home with the Golden Fleece

The village was pitch dark, and our people had all gone to bed when we arrived. I barely recognized my brother's house except for the old familiar *okwukwa* tree on its frontage. Well, let me knock to see if I am right, I thought. After several knocks on the door, Brother Ikpo opened to see who had come at this late hour.
"Who is it?"
"It's me, Kalu Ogbaa. Your brother."
He rubbed his eyes with the back of his right palm, stepped out and peered into my face.
"Oh. My God!" He screamed so loudly that he woke the other family members.
"What is it, Ikpo? Are you injured?" The other members of the house rushed out of their beds.
"No. I'm not injured, but see who I found here." He pointed.
My niece, Ada, ran immediately to me. "Am I seeing Uncle Kalu and his family or their ghosts?" she asked. Then she embraced me so forcefully that I almost fell down.
"Please, come in my people," Brother Ikpo said to us.
His younger wife, Kathy, wanted to call everyone to celebrate. "Oh, let me go wake up Nne and tell her that Kalu and his family have just returned from America."
"How are you, Sister Clara? These must be Ikenna, my namesake Ndubuisi, and Emeka. Welcome, my brothers," Ikpo said, drawing each to his side.
We had hardly sat down in the house when more relatives rushed in to welcome us. The word must have quickly spread across the compound. They were all pleasantly surprised to see us, for we had not informed anyone in advance of our return. And even more surprised since I had left the village for the U.S. alone. When they saw that I

was accompanied by Clara and our three children, it was a most triumphant return and a joyous reunion for all my extended family members. While we were still standing, I looked at Ikpo.

"So, we still don't have electricity or running water anywhere in our village?"

"No, we don't, but I'll light the candles and kerosene lamps so we can see."

"Do you have some clean water I can give the children to drink?"

"Yes, we have some clean water my children fetched from *Akwuaka* spring—still as pure and clean as it was when you left. We continue to depend on it for our everyday use since the government failed to give us running water in spite of our entreaties."

Then Mother came in. Before I could greet her with "Nne, *i biale* (welcome mother)," she held the hurricane lamp high to our faces and peered into them closely. Satisfied that we were indeed her children, she hugged and rubbed each of us on the back, smiling broadly.

"Welcome, my children." Then, with open palms stretched skyward, she added, "*Ekele diri gi Obasi di r'elu,* (Praise be to you, the God on high)!"

My children were a bit confused by my people's strange behavior. They were also scared by the sound of bleating goats and sheep and clucking chickens they had never before seen in their young lives. And they understood neither the Igbo language everyone spoke nor the heavily Nigerian accented English my brother spoke. But, soon, they grew tired and fell asleep.

Then, accompanied by my nieces, Eliza and Oluchi, Sister Nwannennaya rushed in to see us. They began singing and dancing with loud ululation, echoing down the dark street and waking people in the adjoining compound of Chief Eke Ogbonnaya. Then they, too, joined the welcome. As everybody sang, clapped, and danced, more and more villagers stopped by to see what was going on. Ikpo's house bore an aura of great merriment.

When the neighbors finally left, my mother turned to me.

"Kalu *nwa m*. I'm not sure of what to serve the children for dinner. I have only yam *foofoo* and *egusi* soup available in the house."

"Please, give all of us, including the children, whatever is available."

We were too tired and hungry to wait for her to cook a new meal at that late hour, for we had traveled from the U.S. aboard a British Airways flight on Wednesday, December 30, 1981, through London and arrived in the Murtala Muhammad International Airport in Lagos, Nigeria, on Friday morning, January 1, 1982. From there, we had continued our return journey aboard a Nigerian Airways flight to the Port Harcourt International Airport, where we waited almost the whole day because transportation workers were celebrating New Year's Day. We finally boarded a minibus that took us safely home at 11:00 p.m. It was a long and tedious journey for everybody.

My mother quickly warmed the yam *foofoo* and *egusi* soup. Its sweet smell filled the air and caused our mouths to water. I immediately woke the children to join us.

"Nne, the soup is delicious." Clara said. "I know the meat is *anu nchi* (grass-cutter meat), cooked with *olugbu* vegetable, but what type of dried fish did you add to it?"

"Oh, *Nne ogbo nwa m* (mother of my son's namesake), do you mean to tell me that you've been so long away from Nigeria that you can't tell from its taste and feel that the fish is *ifi*?"

"Yes, Nne. It's been a long time since I last enjoyed your delicious meals. They all always tasted so good that I could not tell the difference between them. In fact, when we landed in Lagos very hungry, I began craving the meals you used to cook for the family," Clara teasingly flattered.

"Well, I hope you are not disappointed in eating this stale leftover meal," Mother said. "If I knew you were coming, I would have cooked something better. Now that all of you are home, I'll start tomorrow morning to cook you delicious meals, so you won't live so far away and so long a time from me again."

When she noticed that the boys and I were greedily lapping up the meal, she was surprised that *umu Amerika* (American children) could enjoy eating Igbo yam *foofoo* and *egusi* soup so much. Like my mother, other female relatives were happy to see our American-born children enjoying the meal and asked, "How did they learn to eat our kind of food? Do Americans grow yams and Igbo leafy vegetables like *ugu* and *olugbu* on their farms?"

"No," I said. "American farmers do not, but Clara and I substituted Igbo staple foodstuffs like *garri* and yam *foofoo* with mashed potatoes and cornmeal and prepared our soup with American-grown collard green and spinach to which we added West African-imported smoked fish and crawfish, which we bought from Africana grocery stores. We occasionally bought yams imported from Jamaica, which the children learned to eat with us, but they preferred eating American food like pizza, hamburgers, and French fries to our Igbo meals."

After the dinner, the children went back to sleep. Clara stayed up a little longer before she, too, went to bed. But I continued my conversations with Brother Ikpo and Mother until the early hours, when I finally went to bed. Before I laid myself down, however, I sent my nephews, Kalu and Nchor, to our ancestral home in the village to let my father know that we had just returned, and that I would come to see him first thing in the morning.

Around 9:00 a.m. the next day, Ndubuisi rushed into the bedroom shouting, "Daddy, daddy. Wake up. Grandpa is here to see you. Wake up!" I laughed as he tried to drag me out of bed. I got up and followed him, still in my pajamas and slippers, yawning. As soon as my father saw me, he quickened his steps to grab me and give me a big hug. When he came close to me, he paused, held me on my shoulders, and looked me full in the face.

"*Ikenga nna ya, o nwa bu anya gi* (Is this you in person)?"

"Yes, it's me, Nna. Have you met Clara and your three grandsons yet?"

"Oh, yes, I have met them! My namesake, Ikenna, is so handsome but a little shy; Ndubuisi is in every way like you in looks and aggressive behavior. He almost knocked me down when he attempted to drag me here to see you. But when I couldn't come with him, he decided to rush to you alone."

"That, indeed, is Ndubuisi. You read the two boys' different natures accurately."

Then we sat down and began to talk about everything we had missed discussing for the five years I was away.

"I hope, Nna, that you and Nne could understand why I was unable to send money to help you do your farm work as I used to while I was still in Nigeria. Clara and I struggled hard to pay for our university education and raise the little children. Through the mercy of God, however, the two universities in which I studied gave me part-time jobs, which went a long way to solve our financial problems. It was only during the last two years of our stay in America that I received scholarship awards from the federal and Imo state governments of Nigeria, which made our lives a little easier financially."

"*Ikenga nna ya*, please, stop," my father cut in. "I very well understand why you couldn't send us money from America. I read all the letters you sent us through your friends when they visited us in Nigeria. Did you forget explaining your hardships over there through those letters? Those people also told us how hard life was generally for every foreigner in that country. Please, note well that your mother and I are very proud of you for completing your education successfully and returning home immediately for our sake. We know you could have decided to stay back there like Peter Enyi of Amafia Ihechiowa, who never came home to visit his father before he died a lonely old man. But out of your love for us, you did not do that. On the other hand, we should be the ones to apologize for our inability to help you financially. But we prayed fervently every day to our Almighty God to protect and guide you in whatever you did all those years. Thank God, we are alive to see his blessings manifested in you and the whole family. As an example of those blessings, you left the country without a child, but now you have returned with three healthy and handsome sons."

While we were talking, a long line of villagers had lined up outside, waiting to say "*I luo lee, onye Amerika* (Welcome, American man)!" As soon as I saw them, I left my father, ran outside, and brought them into the house. While still exchanging pleasantries with the visitors, my nephews, Kalu and Sam, served them kola nuts, palm wine, and pop soda, which Clara and Brother Ikpo bought while I was still in bed.

In my absence, Clara took the conversation with my father in another room and served him a portion of the breakfast she had prepared for visiting relatives. She knew our custom of entertaining people on such an occasion well, and she carried it out without my asking. Later, Father told me that her quick mastery of things like that was one of the qualities that endeared her to him, and thus caused him to love her very dearly as "*Ada m* (my daughter)" when she first visited our village in 1975. As more and more visitors came, Clara sent for more kola nuts, palm wine, and soft drinks to entertain them. In addition, she went to the kitchen with my mother, my sister, and Brother Ikpo's wives and prepared lunch for everybody.

The entertainment and merriment continued until very late Saturday night, when I finally took a shower and went to bed. But busy as she was, Clara didn't seem tired of the hard work at all. Apparently, for the first time in all those years we lived in the U.S., no one except me had helped her taking care of the children and family chores. Now, however, Mother tended Chukwuemeka, who we named after Clara's uncle, Alfred Kalu Achi. And he thoroughly enjoyed Mother's company. And our other son, Ndubuisi, ran about chasing frogs and lizards with his first cousins who instantly loved him because he was their father's namesake. On the other hand, Ikenna allowed only my father, his namesake, to carry him for a brief moment before he ran back to Clara. Seeing how differently the children were behaving, an observant elder, Chief Eke Ogbonnaya, said of them, "*Otu nne, otutu chi-na-eke* (One mother, many creative spirits)," which was a fact that we their parents were noticing as they developed into vibrant young boys.

Early on Sunday morning, Brother Ikpo and Father formally asked, in the presence of our extended family, what I brought home from America.

"Do you mean whether I brought home the proverbial Golden Fleece?"

"Oh, yes. Precisely that!" Father said.

"Well, I earned a Master's degree in Black Studies from the Ohio State University at Columbus and a Ph. D. in English from the University of Texas at Austin. I also served as a teaching associate in Columbus and as an assistant instructor and senior lecturer in Austin."

"Does that mean we can now call you Dokita Kalu?"

"Yes, Nna. People call me Dr. Kalu Ogbaa, but I prefer that you call me Kalu."

"Come here, *Ikenga nna ya*, and shake my hand. From now henceforth, I will call you Dokita Kalu, for you have earned the honor." He shook hands with me and gave me a big hug.

"KO," Brother Ikpo called. "I'll always call you KO when we are alone. But like Father, I will always address you as Dr. Kalu Ogbaa in the presence of others. I'm very proud of what you've achieved for yourself and for our family as a whole."

Then he hugged me, tearfully. I, too, shed tears as I recalled our family's material poverty, which I hope we would begin to overcome once I start earning a salary from my teaching appointment at Imo State University.

"Before formally thanking both of you for expressing your appreciation for my achievements," I said. "Let me tell you about Clara's own academic achievements. She earned a BA in English and an MA in Library and Information Science from the same university in Austin. And she did all that in addition to giving birth to two children and taking care of all three with my assistance while we pursued our education."

"*Ada m ee*," my father called Clara. "You are a great woman, for you've practically demonstrated the saying that behind every great man, there is a great woman. I thank you equally for your great achievements. God bless you for being such a blessing to the Ogbaa family."

Clara curtsied. "*Kaawo, Nna, Chukwu nuru ekpele unu nile kpere nye ya maka anyi* (Thanks, Dad, for God heard all the prayers you all offered to him for our sake)."

Brother Ikpo then congratulated her. Then, led by Nne, all the other relatives stood, clapped, and danced to congratulate us. At last, Clara and I hugged everyone and shook their hands for coming to welcome us back from the U.S.

After our morning gathering, all the members of the family went to their various churches and gave thanks to God for our happy return. At the Eternal Sacred Order of Cherubim and Seraphim Church, members of our congregation stepped out of their pews in groups and sang, clapped, and danced in praise of our heavenly father for giving us the grace and blessings of a safe return journey, followed by great feasting, singing and dancing at the end of the services. Then the church members prayed to God that I commence my new employment in Nigeria happily and in safety.

When I arrived on the main campus of the Imo State University, I found that it was located on the former Catholic institution, Madonna Secondary School, Etiti, with a few new buildings sprinkled in-between brightly painted old ones. The atmosphere at the new university was eerily quiet, but alluringly dignified because it signified the beginning of the establishment of what would become historically the first state university in Nigeria, founded in a war-torn Igbo village. And such an establishment echoed the momentous establishment of the first indigenous Nigerian university at another Igbo village, at Nsukka.

The marked difference between the establishments of both universities, however, is that whereas the University of Nigeria was founded during peacetime and prosperity, the Imo State University was built ten years after the civil war in abject poverty and adversity. Therefore, no one doubted that the government of Imo State, the pioneer students and their parents, as well as the faculty and staff of the university would be required to make severe sacrifices for its development. Yet, in spite of such sacrifices, both universities would always attest to the enviable historic roles our Igbo people played in building these

Nigerian universities. As an Igboman, I was proud and ready to go to work.

Before doing anything else, I first reported for duty in the Office of the Vice Chancellor, Professor Michael Echeruo. When I entered the office, I saw his secretary's nametag on his table: "Mr. Okoli."

"Hello, Mr. Okoli, my name is Dr. Kalu Ogbaa. I've just come back from the U.S. and I'm here to report officially for duty. May I see the Vice Chancellor (VC), please?"

"Welcome back to Nigeria, Dr. Ogbaa. We've been expecting you. The VC is not yet in the office, sir. However, he instructed me to take you to Dr. Phanuel Egejuru in the English department when you arrived. So, may I take you to her now?"

"Yes, by all means, do. So, Dr. Egejuru is here on campus already?"

"Yes, she is here. She reported for duty in November. Do you know each other?"

"Yes, I knew her a few years back, in the U.S."

By the time that Mr. Okoli took me to see Egejuru, she was already in the classroom addressing the pioneer students. As soon as she saw me through the window, she stopped her lecture and dashed out of the room.

"Wow. You look groovy, Kalu! When did you get back?"

"Oh, I came back with my family this Friday. Thanks for the compliment. You look cute yourself."

"Where is your family now?"

"Clara and the boys are in the village. I thought I should report for duty and secure an accommodation before bringing them to campus."

"That's good. I'm happy you've come back to join us."

"Thanks. I can see Nigeria is treating you well, for you look happy and gorgeous."

"Thanks a lot. Now that you are home, I hope Nigeria will also treat you well."

Then she briefed me on how she and Dr. Afam Ebeogu, a colleague, had managed the students in my absence. She invited me to address the students who had been waiting anxiously for my arrival since school started back in November. Egejuru and I had known each other in the U.S. where we attended African Literature and African Studies Association conferences together. She had felt relieved that I had finally arrived to take over the courses she and Dr. Ebeogu had been teaching on my behalf. And since the vice chancellor informed them that I would be the program chair of the English department, they had awaited my coming to direct the curriculum development of the department.

However, such private faculty issues were unknown to the students. Consequently, as soon as Egejuru and I stepped into the classroom, the students began booing, hissing, and shouting, "*Ewu, ewu*: goat, goat," ostensibly in protest of the way she abruptly stopped her lecture to speak to a person who was unknown to them at the time. The more she tried to calm them down to introduce me, the noisier they became. Consequently, I whispered to her to allow me handle the situation.

I picked up a piece of chalk and wrote the word "literature" on the board. I then turned round and walked to one of the noisiest students.

"What's your name, sir?"

"Eddie."

"Eddie who?"

"Eddie Njemanze, sir."

"Could you, please, define the word I wrote on the board for the class?"

He stumbled and fumbled trying to define the word adequately. At that point, everyone else stopped talking, watched and waited for an answer he could not give. Then they all sat down quietly and began to pay attention.

I looked around. "Can any of you define the word for us?" No answer.

Then I proceeded to give them a working definition: "The finest writings (*belles lettres*) by a given *people* in a given *place* within a given *period* (usually measured in centuries)." I exemplified the definition using the distinctions of 20th Century African Literature, 19th Century American Literature, and 18th Century British Literature as examples. I also gave them the meaning of literary genres and told them that we were going to study them as courses in poetry, plays, and prose fiction.

After my brief lecture, I introduced myself to the students, told them why I was joining them late from the U.S., and encouraged them to take their studies seriously instead of behaving like *ndi ocho pasinja* (motor park touts). At the last, they all burst into laughter, clapped, and gave me a standing ovation. Then Eddie Njemanze shouted, "*Nkele wu ya o* (This is the real thing)!" provoking even more clapping and laughter.

I politely asked them to sit down and listen for further instructions from Dr. Egejuru who told them that they would be given regular class schedules now that I had come back to join the other lecturers. Then she dismissed them for lunch.

Eddie and a few other students followed me to the office, peppering me with questions about life in American universities, and expressing some eagerness to work hard on their studies. I was encouraged by their enthusiasm, which I hoped could make the process of building the new university a lot easier for both the faculty and students. After chatting with the lecturers, some students, and the dean of our college, Professor Iroh, I went back to see the vice chancellor, Professor Michael Echeruo, in his office.

"Hello, Mr. Okoli. Is the VC in now so I can see him?"

"Welcome back, Dr. Ogbaa. Yes, he is. Please, sit down while I go to let him know that you are here." He pointed me to one of his office chairs.

In a few minutes, Professor Echeruo emerged from his inner office. I stood up. "Good afternoon, sir."

He stretched his right hand. "Good afternoon, Kalu. So you finally made it, eh?"

"Yes, I did. Thank you, sir."

"Have you eaten lunch yet?"

"Yes, I have. Mr. Okoli took me to the University Cafeteria."

"Very good. And where are Clara and the boys?"

"I left them in the village while I reported for duty. I will go back to the village and collect them once I have been assigned a living accommodation."

"Have you met the dean and your colleagues in your department?"

"Yes. Dr. Egejuru introduced me to everybody as soon as I arrived."

"Very well. Let me take you to the University Guest House at Owerri, where you will be accommodated until you're assigned your own apartment. Except the university's principal officers, who've been given accommodation on campus, all faculty and staff members are quartered for now in Owerri from where they commute to work in Etiti."

"Thank you, sir."

He escorted me to his car and the chauffeur drove us to Owerri. As soon as we arrived at the Guest House, an attendant ushered me into a guest room upstairs and said I should come for dinner downstairs after unpacking and taking a shower, or that I could eat dinner before unpacking if I so chose. I decided to shower first, and after dinner, I quickly returned to sleep after a long day of travel and activities.

The following morning, I returned to Etiti and taught my first classes. Then I traveled back to Owerri, and signed for an apartment in one of the university-acquired properties at Ikenegbu Layout, a borough of Owerri metropolis. The rest of the week I taught classes, and on Friday, returned to my village and collected Clara, our children, my mother and one of my nieces who would serve as our children's nannies in Owerri.

"Ladies and gentlemen: In less than two months, the university will be formally inaugurated by our Imo State government and the university administrators," the VC began his announcement to faculty members in the University Auditorium. "As part of our preparations for the momentous occasion, I want us to elect the secretary of the University Congregation. To those who do not understand what a university congregation is, let me say it is an assembly, made up of the VC's cabinet, the teaching faculty, and graduate staff of the university, which meets from time to time to deliberate on any issues affecting the university. It is presided over by the VC or, in his absence, the deputy vice chancellor (DVC). The VC instructs and guides the secretary on when and where to call the meetings of the congregation, to solicit from members items to be included in the agenda, and to record the minutes of their deliberations. So, the first order of business is for us to elect the secretary of congregation today." He paused and looked around the room. "Well then, I now invite nominations of candidates for the office."

A man in the back raised his hand.

"Yes, Dr. Nwana."

"Sir, before we begin, how many nominations are we being asked to make?"

"Three."

"I nominate Dr. Ebeogu," Dr. Nwana said.

"Could you stand up for the people to see you, Dr. Ebeogu?"

"Yes sir," he said and stood up, turned around, and waived his right hand in the air.

"I nominate Dr. Okere," another person said.

Dr. Okere stood, smiling.

For about a minute or two, nobody else nominated a third candidate.

"Ladies and Gentlemen, we still need one more nomination before we begin casting our votes by secret ballots."

"I nominate Dr. Ogbaa," said Mr. Akaluso whom I did not know.

"Could you stand up for people to see you, Dr. Ogbaa?"

Someone sitting near me whispered, "Who is this guy?"

"Yes sir." I stood up and waived my hand in the air for them to recognize me.

"Oh. It is the new guy from the U.S.A., a lecturer in English department," whispered the same person.

I was surprised to see that I had garnered twice the combined number of votes cast for the others. Reacting to the results, the dean of College of Sciences, Professor Osuji jokingly remarked, "The difference is clear," alluding perhaps to my American university education and teaching experience.

"Now that we have elected the university congregation and its secretary," the VC said. "And now that the university senate is in place, and since the Imo State government has appointed the members of the governing council of the university, I believe we are ready to celebrate the official inauguration of our young university." Then he adjourned the meeting.

A few days later, I received a letter, announcing my appointment as chair of the university's security and protocols sub-committee in preparation for the impending official inauguration ceremony of the university. The VC directed me to work with the university chief security officer, Mr. Chikezie, and report the activities of the committee directly to the deputy vice chancellor (DVC), Professor Gabriel Umezurike, on behalf the VC, who lived in Owerri.

Two weeks before the inauguration ceremony, the DVC called a meeting of the security and protocols sub-committee to brief us on our duties. With the assistance of the principal accountant of the university, Mr. Akaluso, and the university engineer, Mr. Epoh, I worked out a budget for the outdoor festivities, setting up the chair and canvas canopies three days before the ceremony. After receiving a list of state dignitaries, university administrators, parents of the inaugural students chiefs, elders, and friends of the university from the administration, I assigned seating and coordinated with the chief security officer and his men to ensure that the occasion came off without a hitch.

On the eve of the ceremony while rehearsing the phases of the inauguration, the permanent secretary to the state government from Owerri stopped by to inspect the venue.

"Hello, Dr. Kalu Ogbaa, my name is Mr. Okezie. I'm the permanent secretary to the Imo State Government."

I shook his hand. "How are you, Mr. Okezie?"

"As you know, the official inauguration of the university is a very important ceremony to the state. I've been directed to come and see how the preparations for it are going."

"Thanks for coming," I said. "As you can see, we are ready with the fixtures. All that remains is labeling the various stations and seats for the government officials and dignitaries of the state, as well as for the university administrators, faculty, staff, students and their parents and guardians."

"Thank you." Mr. Okezie looked around. "But could you show me precisely where the governor, the deputy governor, the chief judge, commissioners, the permanent secretary, etc. of the state will be seated?"

"Here are the lists of state officials and dignitaries I received from the Office of the Vice Chancellor," I said and showed him the various platforms and booths with their labeled seats.

"Thank you, Dr. Ogbaa," he said, "But these affairs of state require some precise protocol, which may not be well-known to you." He then pointed out the protocol security requirements, then promptly turned and departed back to Owerri.

Crowds began to gather early from all parts of the country, especially Imo State, home of the university, and Lagos, the seat of the National Universities Commission (NUC), which had the oversight of all the universities in Nigeria. We had strategically posted the university security officers and the Nigeria police at various booths and stands and posted assistant registrars and female students at various entry points of the venue to usher visitors to their seats.

As soon as I arrived at the venue, our students stood and cheered, which greatly pleased me. Then I gave the faculty and students final instructions while the last of the visitors and dignitaries found their seats. Fifteen minutes before the official start of the events, the VC's orderly approached me and saluted.

"Dr. Ogbaa, sir. The VC has asked to see you in his office." He sounded serious.

"Am I under arrest?" I joked.

"No, sir. But I believe the matter is urgent."

"Then, let's go at once!"

"Hello, Kalu." The VC stood as I entered his office. "I want you to escort the Chief Judge of the state and his wife to their seats and then come back here quickly."

"Yes sir," I said and turned to the Chief Judge and his wife. Tipping my mortarboard, I said, "Shall we go sir, madam?"

"Yes, son, as soon as you help me to get up from my seat," the judge said.

After helping the judge up, we marched slowly to their seats.

"Where did you get your doctorate degree?" The judge turned as he shuffled along beside me.

"I received it in May 1981 from the University of Texas at Austin in the U.S., sir."

"And what did you study?"

"I studied English, sir."

"I suspected you studied abroad because of your academic regalia and the way you carried yourself when you approached us in the VC's office. I am happy to see our young Igbo people who still care about education after the civil war. I hope you inculcate that spirit in the young students entrusted in your care in this university we are inaugurating today."

"I promise to do precisely that, sir."

We reached the graduation square and I helped them to their seats. I tipped my hat for them again, turned around, and raced back to the VC's office.

"Thanks, Kalu." The VC smiled. "Now, please escort the Deputy Governor to his seat."

"Yes sir," As we approached the Deputy Governor's seat, the crowd once again clapped and cheered.

By now, the faculty and students were seated, so members of the university council began their march, with the VC by the side of the governor. Then the announcer said, "Ladies and gentlemen, please stand for the university council members."

Everybody stood, clapping and cheering loudly, then retook their seats as the announcer called on the Catholic bishop to pray, after which the crowd sang the Nigerian national anthem. Then the chairperson of the ceremony declared the ceremony open. At that point, I took a seat close to the VC. The ceremony proceeded and ended well, and I escorted the Chief Judge and his wife back to the council chambers after the chairperson asked the crowd to stand while university council members filed out.

The VC was so pleased I had performed my role as the chair of the university security and protocols sub-committee so well that thereafter he retained me as the chair of the committee in charge of most of the university public ceremonies, including graduation ceremonies, until 1989, when I returned to the U.S. on sabbatical leave.

"Good afternoon sir," my secretary, Frank, said to me. "While you were on lunch break, Mr. Okoli called to inform you that the vice chancellor wants to see you."

"Did he sound urgent?"

"I don't think so, sir. But he said I should deliver the message as soon as you come in."

"Very well. I will see him now. If any students come to see me, schedule them for tomorrow morning."

When I arrived in the VC's office, Mr. Okoli asked me to wait. When the VC came out of his inner office escorting some visitors to the door, I greeted him.

"Good afternoon, sir."

"Hello Kalu, I'll be with you in a minute."

In a few minutes, he returned. "You can come in now."

"Thank you, sir." I followed him into his office.

After we were seated, the VC turned to me. "How are things going in your department?"

"As well as one can expect in a new institution like this, sir. But I've been searching for a place where students can buy some of the books I recommended. In addition, some of them say that they lack enough money to buy most of the books and still satisfy most of their other needs."

"So, what are you doing to solve this problem?" the VC cut in.

"Well, I found a bookshop at Isinweke Market and talked with its owner, Mr. Amaobi Nnadi. He lives in New York and comes home from time to time to stock his shop. He will be able to supply some of the books we need on American literature and composition. In the meantime, I've prepared mimeographed notes of some lectures for the students. The students buy paper, and the secretary types and mimeographs the notes for them. In addition, I advised them to practice frugality with what little money their parents give to them so they can survive the way some of us survived while we were studying at the University of Nigeria, Nsukka, immediately after the civil war."

"I'm glad to hear that," the VC said. "Beginning next week, I want you and Dr. Ebeogu to start offering a 'Use of English' course to our law and business students at the Aba campus twice a week as it is offered here at Etiti campus. I've asked the head of Aba campus, Professor Onoh, to get the students ready for you. The transport officer will assign a driver for you. Adjust your schedules to accommodate this new assignment."

"I will coordinate with Dr. Ebeogu to make sure we carry out the task faithfully."

As I rose to leave his office, the VC informed me that he had decided to appoint me the hall master of the male students' hostels at the Etiti campus. Then, as if to remind me that I should not complain about being given so much work, he added: "You will be paid a monthly stipend and all the conditions of your service will be spelled out in your appointment letter."

"Sir, I'm grateful for the appointment." I shook his hand and returned to my office.

During the following weekend, however, I mulled over the demands of the offices to which they appointed and elected in succession. How successful and diligent would I be in carrying them out while simultaneously teaching my normal course load? And would I have enough time to prepare for both roles and still have adequate rest after each day's commute to and from Etiti? And, finally, Clara was pregnant again, and the government had deployed her to do her National Youth Service Corps (NYSC) program at the university as an assistant lecturer in the department of library and information science. We therefore both rode the treacherous Owerri-Etiti Road to work daily until she delivered the baby, and my family's safety weighed heavily on my mind. I decided to discuss the matter further with the VC and met with him the next day.

"Hello sir. I'd like to ask that you to authorize the works department to assign me an apartment at Etiti, so I can supervise the students more closely after hours. In addition, it will be easier and more convenient for Clara to work from there since she will need to be close to the newborn baby for breast-feeding and other infant needs."

"Oh, how is she doing with the baby?" He bent down to write something.

"They are both doing well, sir."

Smiling, he gave me the hand-written note. "Take this to the university engineer. He will assign you an apartment at Etiti immediately."

"Thank you, sir."

"Tell Clara that once you people come to live at Etiti, I will appoint her to serve as the hall mistress for the women's hostels. And say hello to her and the baby for me."

"Will do." I smiled, relieved. "And thank you, sir."

Toward the end of December 1982, the engineer assigned a two-bedroom apartment with boys' quarters to Clara and me in Achinanya Estate at Isinweke, a short walking distance to campus. We moved in after the Christmas break and Clara began her service as the hall mistress in charge of the women's hostels. Thus, both of us settled down to work on our teaching assignments and other university and community services with less stress.

My principal role as a senior lecturer was two-pronged: classroom teaching and research as well as leading the curriculum development in our department. The pioneer faculty members were Dr. Afam Ebeogu, Dr. Phanuel Egejuru, Mr. Polycarp Anyanwu, and me. And since the original department head had taken another position at a bigger university, the VC asked me to take over the leadership of the department.

"Hello friends and colleagues," I began my formal address to the other faculty members. "I'm sorry to be joining you late. The VC was aware that I had to finish teaching my fall semester classes in the U.S. before coming home to join in the efforts that all of you have already started making to build this young university. My friend and colleague, Dr. Egejuru, has given me a brief report on what you have so far accomplished with the students since November. Let me state the obvious, that what we are all to do here is an Igbo ethnic affair.

"Fortunately, Phanuel and Polycarp are my old friends, and as former students of Professor Echeruo, Afam and I were hired to help him carry out the challenging task of building the first state university in Nigeria. I believe we are all prepared to work collaboratively as we make our individual and collective contributions to the actualization of our founding fathers' dream for the students of the young institution. Furthermore, let me say that I have not come to join you as head of the department. Instead, the VC asked me to serve as a team leader in our developmental activities of the English department. I will be passing on to you whatever instructions I receive from the VC regarding the smooth operation of the department. Since we are here to conduct this new experiment together, however, it is my hope and belief that if we work in love and cooperation, we will succeed."

After exchanging introductions and pleasantries with the faculty, I outlined my vision for the program. Then, I assigned Dr. Ebeogu survey courses in drama (African and British), Dr. Egejuru, African literature (novels and plays), and I would deliver poetry (African and British) to serve our English majors. Mr. Anyanwu was assigned to teach mainly "Use of English" (Composition) to all the students at Etiti campus as a required university course. Later in the semester, Ebeogu and I took turns in teaching the course to the business and law students at Aba campus. Those courses initially constituted the first-year student experience, which adjusted in subsequent years as the administration hired new faculty members to join us.

For the next three years, I worked with the VC, Professor Echeruo, a nationally and internationally renowned English scholar, to recruit lecturers and develop curricular offerings to accommodate the growing student population. In year two, Dr. Sam Opoku joined us as a senior visiting lecturer from Ghana, and Miss Ngumoha became my graduate assistant. In year three, we hired Dr. Chukwu and Mr. Nwahunanya as lecturers, and Dr. Ben Obumselu as professor of English, who was later elected the dean of College of Humanities and Social Sciences to replace Professor Iroh. Obumselu's dual roles in the college as well as his English background necessitated that I consulted less and less with the VC on curriculum development matters. I continued to serve as the program head (*de facto* chair) of English until August 1989, still relying on the VC for the recruitment of more lecturers. By that time, I also taught American literature, African poetry, and Theory and Practice of Literary Criticism (which enabled our final year students to complete their exit research projects with expertise).

Many of the outside Nigerian lecturers thought it was risky to look for employment at our university until we produced our first batch of graduates in June 1985. However, external professors who examined our students' academic records were so highly impressed with them that at least one, Professor Dan Izevbaye of the University of Ibadan, remarked: "This is one of the few Nigerian universities where English majors write competently in English." Later, while I was spending my sabbatical leave in the U.S. they told me that because of the General Studies program we offered in the young university, our pioneer graduates took positions one through thirteen in the national civil service exams of Nigerian universities in 1986. I was proud to have served as the first director of the program.

"I found that you published many articles and book reviews before finishing your graduate studies," Dr. Ebeogu remarked. "How were you able to accomplish both tasks simultaneously?"

"That required a lot of hard work. Before going to the U.S. for my graduate studies, I taught at Alvan Ikoku College of Education where I was introduced to the 'publish or perish' theory in Nigerian tertiary institutions. I also availed myself of the opportunity to use our great American university research libraries and followed the examples of published professors like O. R. Dathorne and Bernth Lindfors, who also took me to attend many conferences on African and African American literary and cultural studies."

"You were lucky to have met the two professors you mentioned. Although our Nigerian professors emphasized scholarship and publication in the graduate school, not many of them can take their students to conferences like their American counterparts. Besides, if one wrote some articles, he or she may not find suitable journals and magazines to publish them."

"I'm sorry to hear that. Have you written some articles you want published?"

"Oh, yes. As a matter of fact, I have two or three of them I am considering sending out for publication in foreign presses."

"Then I will give you names of publishing companies that published my own articles and book reviews in the U.S., Canada, and India, which publish articles on Africana and Commonwealth literary and cultural studies."

"That's very kind of you."

"I'll give you the names of the editors, titles, and addresses of the journals and magazines by tomorrow. I don't have them here in my office. They are in my home at Owerri."

"I appreciate your willingness to help."

Within a year, Dr. Ebeogu had published two of his articles in *The Literary-Half Yearly,* an India-based journal of Commonwealth literary studies. Thereafter, Ebeogu and I became close friends, working closely together for the betterment of the English department. And as we developed, our department's reputation grew. Each time we took our students to attend the literature conferences that Professor Ernest Emenyeonu hosted annually at the University of Calabar, everybody respected the contingent from the young Imo State University. In an effort to replicate what Professor Lindfors did for me in the U.S, we often took our students to such conferences. Over the years, few other lecturers participated in our effort to promote scholarship in our department in similar ways.

In spring 1985, three years after I joined the faculty at the Imo State University, I applied for promotion to the rank of associate professor (Reader in Nigerian terms). The promotion committee of the university made a favorable premier facie case for my promotion, and the VC sent out my application files to external appraisals, who recommended me for the promotion, effective from fall 1985. However, the VC released the results belatedly in February 1988. Consequently, since the government policy prohibited them from paying any worker promoted retroactively arrears of salaries for more than one year I was only paid salary arrears of one year instead of the three years for which I was entitled.

Nevertheless, I continued to teach, conduct research and write, and maintain my contact with colleagues in American universities, especially Professor Lindfors and my literary mentor, Professor Chinua Achebe. I also continued to review books on African and Caribbean literatures for *World Literature Today: A Literary Quarterly of The University of Oklahoma*. Achebe told me about his fifth novel, *Anthills of the Savannah* (published in 1987), and sent me a review copy. My article of the new novel, "Of Governance, Revolutions, and Victims: Achebe and Literary Activism in *Anthills of the Savannah*," was later published in my edited anthology, *The Gong and the Flute: African Literary Development and Celebration* (Greenwood, 1994). My American friends continued to keep my Modern Language Association dues up to date, along with membership dues for African Literature Association, and African Studies Association. I also became a member of the Association of Commonwealth Literature and Language Studies in Nigeria.

Considering the position I occupied in Imo State University as a senior lecturer, many of my Ihechiowa clansmen expected me to join politics so I could bring home the proverbial national cake to our people. Surely, I was interested in working toward the development of our underdeveloped clan. But I made it clear that I was not prepared to play party politics. Yet, some of them continued to press the issue in private conversations.

"Dr. Ogbaa, when will you join any of the three major political parties: the Nigerian Progressive Party (NPP), the National Party of Nigeria (NPN), and the United Party of Nigeria UPN) so you can use it as a platform to serve our people?" Mr. Peter Kalu Ulu asked.

"Who told you that I was interested in becoming a politician?"

"Our people feel that since you have achieved the highest degree in your field of studies and are working in Imo State University, you can easily become a commissioner in any Imo State administration. Such a position would enable you to bring some development projects to our village and our clan."

"Do you think I cannot do any of those things without becoming an avowed politician?"

"I know you can. But not as easily as you could if you were in the corridors of power."

"Well, some of us aren't prepared to play the kind of roles you're suggesting that I play."

"Then how else do you plan to bring some development to our backward community?"

"I believe I can contribute to the academic and physical development of our community. In terms of human development, I give lectures to our secondary school and university students about how they should pursue their education to achieve the same success as I did. Additionally, I have privately approached the government and political leaders in the state to bring development projects like the supply of electricity and running water to our clan. God willing, you will soon see the results of my discussions with them. I think I can achieve the plans I have for our community development without living the life of a corrupt politician, which is the bane of our contemporary Nigerian society."

"I hope you can achieve your plans. We need the program to succeed."

Later, meeting with Chief R. B. K. Okafor, the leader of the NPP in Imo State, at Owerri I discussed how I might encourage the people of Ihechiowa clan to cast their votes for his party. I showed him the prewar map of Arochukwu District, and pointed out that Ihechiowa people counted for more than half of the total population of the six clans that constituted the district. I reminded him that my education in the U.S. gave me a status among my people, which could help to garner most of the votes from my clan for his party if he would help us reclaim what rightfully belonged to us (including land

and position). The Arochukwu people had dominated our clan politically, socially, and educationally since the arrival of the white men in Nigeria, despite out vastly larger population, and we wanted the balance of power restored.

"Why did your people allow that to happen without a fight?"

"Around 1840, the Church of Scotland sent missionaries to the old Calabar Province of Eastern Region of Nigeria. Both Reverend Hope Waddell, who was posted to its headquarters in Calabar, and Reverend Sister Mary Slessor, who was posted to Arochukwu Town in Enyong South, built the first churches and missionary schools in those locations. The people from Arochukwu clan took advantage of being the first to receive Western education before others in the district. At first, our people sent their children to school in Arochukwu, but they were later discouraged since their children were constantly kidnapped and sold to slave traders by the Arochukwu people. Additionally, our ancestors saw no need to educate the children since, as farmers, their children could work on their farmlands to feed and clothe themselves while supplementing their incomes by selling excess produce to other clans. Consequently, when Nigeria eventually regained its sovereignty from the British colonizers, the Western educated citizens of Arochukwu took over the reins of government from the outgoing British government officials. Then they excluded our people from the corridors of power. Nowadays, our people look up to a few of us, the university-educated clansmen, for guidance. If I explain to them why they should vote for your party, they will do so. But you have to promise to give them electricity and running water as the NPN agents had done to Arochukwu and Ututu clans during previous election periods in the district."

After listening to my impassioned tale of our clan's sad history, Chief Okafor sighed. "Can I see the map again?"

"Sure." I pushed it across the table.

After gazing at it a couple of minutes, he pulled a notepad from his cabinet draw and wrote a note.

"Here." He handed it to me. "Take it to the Commissioner for Works. He will tell you what to do. Good luck."

He appeared in a hurry and forgot to enclose it in an envelope. I read it and made a copy before taking it to the commissioner. The commissioner looked over the note then told me to find a vehicle and take some men from his office to our clan to survey the area for the construction of electricity and running water.

"I wonder how soon you want us to be there?" I looked at the commissioner for clarification. "I have to look for a vehicle since I don't own one."

"You need to go there in two days. Chief Okafor wants the job to begin immediately. I would have sent you and my men with one of our vehicles, but they are all deployed in the field for the week."

"Well, let me go and look for one and report back to you by tomorrow."

Later, when I showed a copy of the commissioner's letter to my clansman, Mr. Kalu Alfred, secretary to the Imo State Library Board, Owerrie, he was so excited that he offered to give us his official vehicle for our travel to Ihechiowa the following day. I asked him, however, to send another person to accompany the surveyors, telling him I was sick and needed to see a doctor that day. He and two other clansmen, Dr. Lawrence Okpii and Mr. Ekpe Okorafor, agreed to represent me in the meetings with the surveyors.

I was neither sick nor had any appointment with the doctor. I had lied because I did not want members of the NPN to know that I was also talking to the NPP and, consequently, associate me with an NPP sympathizer. In less than two months, the Ministry of Works dug trenches from the borderline between Ihechiowa and Ututu clans to my Umuchiakuma village to lay pipes for water supplies, and the government pledged N450,000 (four hundred and fifty thousand Naira) toward installation of electricity in the clan.

During the construction, I approached a colleague at Imo State University, Miss Nnennaya Ukabiala, to introduce me to her uncle and former governor of prewar Eastern Nigeria, Dr. Michael Iheonukara Okpara, so I could discuss the development of our clan with him. I told Miss Ukabiala the sad story of the deprivation of my clan, which touched her so that she took me immediately to her hometown, Nkwuegwu in Umuahia, and introduced me to Dr. Okpara and his wife in their home.

"Good afternoon Dede and good afternoon Mama," she began. "This is a colleague from Imo State University, Dr. Kalu Ogbaa. He is a native of Ihechiowa clan in Arochukwu District. He wanted me to introduce him to you. He has something important to tell you." Then she looked to my direction and nodded.

"Good afternoon Governor Okpara," I knelt. "Good afternoon, Lady Adanma Okpara."

"No, no, get up, young man!" He stretched out his right hand to shake my own then motioned me to sit on a chair near him.

"Thank you, sir." I took the seat.

"How are you, Nnennaya my daughter?"

"Very well, Dede."

"You said Dr. Ogbaa comes from Ihechiowa. What's the exact name of his village?"

Nnennaya looked at me for an answer.

"Our village is Umuchiakuma, sir."

"Oh, I know where it is. One of my young political friends, Chief Lawrence Oleh, comes from there. Do you know him?"

"Yes, I do. In fact, he comes from my compound, Nde Ngwo. And his younger brother, Onwuka Oleh, is married to my elder sister, Nwannennaya. We are in-laws."

"How is Chief Oleh doing?"

"He was well when I saw him last weekend in the village, sir."

"Okay. So what brought you to our home today?"

"Thank you very much, sir, for welcoming me to your home without any prior notice. And thank you for all you did for our clan and the Igbo people while serving as Premier of the old Eastern Region of Nigeria in the 1950s and 1960s."

Between 1914 and 1957, British administrators grouped together the Igbo-speaking clans that constituted Arochukwu territory with Ibibio-speaking clans in Itu District and Efik-speaking clans in Calabar Province for their administrative convenience, even though the Igbo did not originally have cultural connections with the other ethnic peoples. I had personally experienced the great impact of our cultural differences in 1956, when I was forced to take entrance exams at a secondary school far from home (one day to reach the examination center in Calabar, another day to take the exams, and a third day to travel back to our village). The British administrators would not permit us to take exams at a closer center in another district. I was only ten years old then, scared and alone, surrounded as I was by the Efik/Ibibio language-centered culture.

Earlier, the Igbo clans in the Arochukwu political region, under the name of Enyong South of Itu District, had so bitterly protested being a part of the district that when Nigeria gained its political self-rule in 1957, Dr. Michael Okpara, as Premier of Eastern Nigeria, created Aro-Igbo District and brought us back from the Itu District. Consequently, in October of that year, I took Eastern Nigeria Regional Standard VI Examination at a center in Ihe Central School, Obinto. That was the first of the exams for us and other elementary schools in our clan and the new Aro-Igbo District. To be united thus with other Igbo people in the region politically and socio-culturally was a great relief to our people, but Arochukwu clansmen continued to dominate us politically in the new dispensation.

"*Nna anyi*, Governor Okpara," I said. "Everybody in Eastern Nigeria sorely missed you while you were away on self-exile in Germany following the collapse of our beloved Republic of Biafra. Since then, the postwar administrations in the Igbo region have been too afraid to do anything for us since we lost the war. However, those of us who know what you did for our people two decades before the war are elated that you are home, alive and healthy. For neither the vagaries of war nor life in exile could rob us of your precious life of service. I came to you today knowing that in whatever political party you choose to belong and shine your political light, most of our people will follow you. I will solemnly swear to give you my loyalty to help you achieve whatever it takes to heal this land. You hewed the tree of community development in Igboland, now is the time for our generation to carve it."

"I have noticed your zealousness to serve our people, young man." He leaned forward. "However, I have not made up my mind on which party to join. But when I do, I will let you know."

He hardly finished the sentence, when loud noises erupted outside. Drivers honked their horns, people could be heard yelling and shouting. Then someone was knocking at the door, calling the governor by his honorific and political and chieftaincy names. Neighbors gathered and began chanting and dancing the praise songs of the governor's political heydays.

One of his servants came through the back door and announced the names of the political party officials come to pay their respects. Then Governor Okpara asked him to open the front door and usher them in. As soon as they all filed into the living room, each of the visitors knelt down and shouted: "*Onye ije ilu* (Welcome back, traveler!)"

I rose to leave, but the governor stopped me. "Stay where you are. We are not yet done." Then the visitors, representatives from five political parties, came in like carnival characters to woo him to their parties.

I sat through the meeting with all eyes riveted on me as if to ask, "Who is this man that Dr. Okpara was talking with before we came and would not let him go before talking to us?" I recognized some of the men from Imo State Headquarters at Owerri, and those who recognized me wanted to ask what I was doing there, but they dared not ask since they had already heard the owner of the house say I should remain in my seat. I surmised that some of the people must have felt I must be an important person for the governor to treat me the way he did. After they all left, we resumed out discussion.

"Since you said you are ready to work with me politically, Dr. Ogbaa," he said. "Let me tell you that other young men like you have formed what they call 'Okpara supersonic brigade.' Would you like to join them?"

"Yes, I would like to join them, sir. Could you tell me whom I should contact to brief me? I know I can write news talks to promote your political vision for our people."

"I'm happy to hear that from you. When you write your news talks, please, give them to Mr. Bob Ogbuagu for publication and tell him that I sent you."

He gave me the address of a small shop where I should send all my messages and writings for the renowned journalist. I left Dr. Okpara's house that day without asking him directly to convince the authorities to give us running water and electricity. I wanted to make that request after he had joined a political party and seen what I could do in his brigade.

Two weeks after my visit with Dr. Okpara, the media reported he was going to announce his choice of a party at the Imo State Stadium, Owerri. The day of the announcement, the Okpara supporter filled the stadium to full capacity. I was excited, hoping that he would declare for the NPP, headed by the former Governor-General of Nigeria, Dr. Nnamdi Azikiwe, and the Governor of Imo State, Chief Sam Mbakwe, both Igbo political heavyweights.

The people welcomed Dr. Okpara into the stadium with great fanfare as he mounted the podium and began his speech.

"My uncle, Chief Ukabiala, once said to me, 'Iheonukara, *first fool nobi fool, but second fool na proper foolish*' ('Fool me once, shame on me. Fool me twice, shame on you')." Everyone stood up and gave him a thunderous applause. Once the applause died down, Dr. Okpara continued, summarizing the sad political history of inept national leadership that had so negatively affected the Igbo peoples of Nigeria after they regained their political sovereignty from their erstwhile colonial masters, the British.

He reminded the audience how their fellow Nigerians chose to declare a war on our Igbo people that raged for thirty grueling months, focusing especially on Dr. Nnamdi Azikiwe, a well-known Igbo political leader, who had defected and lent support to Nigeria during the final throes of the war, thereby causing the sudden demise of the young Republic of Biafra. "For that reason," Dr. Okpara said. "I am not prepared to be fooled a second time by joining the NPP, led by the very man who had encouraged the Igbo to wage the civil war on the Biafran side, only to desert them in their greatest hour of need. To join the postwar NPP would have made me '*the proper foolish*' person. I therefore declared my membership in the NPN."

Although some people were surprised at first by his choice, many more gave him a thunderous applause since each of them deeply and personally understood his reasoning. Hundreds of Igbo people jumped out of their seats and ran to the center of the stadium, declaring their membership in the NPN, following their courageous leader's example. I was happy as well. I now knew where his interests lay, and began to plan my strategy for working through the political process in Imo State to promote the physical and economic development of my community. I was sure that if I played my cards well, our people could benefit from both political parties in the state.

Unfortunately, however, I had to put my strategies on hold, because on December 31, 1983, another group of Northern Nigerian military coup plotters, headed by Major General Muhammadu Buhari, toppled the civilian administration of Alhaji Shehu Shagari and turned the political clock of the country backward once again.

As I drove up to campus early that morning, I found faculty members and students huddled together under the shade of trees discussing the military coup in whispers:

"Who is the leader of the coup executors?"

"They say his name is Major General Muhammadu Buhari."

"Oh no. Not again! When will the Northern military officers allow the citizenry of this country to live together in peace?"

"Well, this time the coup leader has a Yoruba military officer, Colonel Idiagbo, as his second-in-command."

"Well, whether they are Hausa/Fulani or Yoruba, it doesn't make any difference, because all military leaders have the same penchant for using brute force to rule the people. Without democratically elected leaders in control of governance, there will be neither peace nor freedom in this God-forsaken country of ours. Without peace and freedom, we will continue to merely exist without any fulfilled life, and that's what we've been doing since January 15, 1966, when the country witnessed its first bloody coup."

"So, what do the coupists say is their reason to overthrow a democratically elected government this time around?"

"They say that there is corruption in government and indiscipline in the general lives of the people. For that reason, they have taken over the governance of the country so as to instill discipline in all of us."

"Wow. What a noble and patriotic act from an army that has ruined the nation for three decades!"

"It's nothing but a clever subterfuge to loot the national treasury."

"Please. That is an unpatriotic thing to say about our patriotic men in khaki. So be careful, unless you don't want our people to be disciplined in everything they do in this our blessed country," one man joked.

"Are you seriously vomiting that kind of B.S.?" another man asked.

The other pretended to frown. "*Abi*, do you see me laughing?"

Everyone burst into boisterous laughter and went their separate ways on campus. The people were worried, wondering how the army was going to wage the war against indiscipline. Were they going to arrest and imprison those who have been looting the national treasury? Were not the politicians who received contracts to construct roads and bridges, but failed to complete them, in cahoots with ex-military officers? If so, who would have the temerity to arrest and jail them for their corrupt actions? And could any civilians risk the danger of blowing the whistle against any of the culprits? Yes, even the ordinary people had these questions on their minds, but no one dared to ask them openly for fear of being shot by power-drunk soldiers who patrolled everywhere in town.

On the drive home after work, I passed a group of soldiers standing in front of the post office and the bank whipping some civilians who failed to queue up to purchase stamps and stationery or to deposit or collect money from the bank tellers. Even the *big men* who used to jump the queues to do business in the two establishments received a few strokes of the angry soldiers' whips before they learned the soldiers' order: "First come, first served."

Some in the crowd that had gathered cheered and applauded the soldiers for waging a war against indiscipline in our undisciplined nation. Still, I wondered what, in the long run, was going to change the way people had been doing business in our country, or whether the coup's ideological justification was just a temporary ploy the military adopted to support their usurpation of power from the democratically elected civilian government.

Later that evening, the head of the new military government, Major General Buhari, announced a number of austerity measures, including the banning of imported goods, especially the rice and textile materials that people produced locally, as well as the devaluation of the Naira, Nigeria's currency. While farmers cheered the government for banning imported farm produce—a measure that they believed would increase the value of their own locally produced goods—others feared that devaluing the Naira would breed inflation. They surmised that the military junta in Lagos was merely adopting the austerity measures to please the International Monetary Fund (IMF) that had recommended the devaluation. They feared that no country in the world, which had devalued their currency, ever regained its pre-austerity measure values back again. (The effect of the austerity measures of 1981: one Nigerian Naira was worth two U.S. Dollars, but in 2011, one U.S. Dollar was worth 150 Nigerian Naira in the foreign exchange [FOREX] market and more in the black market.)

Furthermore, following the announcement of the austerity measures, those businesspersons who had stocked the now-banned imported goods began to hoard them, which eventually resulted in forcing people to pay exorbitant prices for the banned goods. Additionally, such easy profits encouraged more people to smuggle goods across the porous borders of West Africa into Nigeria. In the process, packaged commodities, such as rice, sugar, beans, cement, salt, vegetable oil, and engine oil were adulterated with locally produced ones and either repackaged or re-canned with foreign containers, so they could pass as genuine foreign goods.

The newly appointed military governor of the Imo State, Major General Ike Nwachukwu, ordered his driver to stop his vehicle after they had driven a few poles past the Umuchiakuma/Achara Road junction in my village. His aide-de-camp (ADC) jumped out of the military jeep, opened its right rear door, and saluted the general, who mechanically returned the salute and stepped out of the car. The ADC shut the door, saluted again, and stood at attention, awaiting orders from the general. Passersby stopped by the roadside to watch. The presence of men in khakis always drew crowds, especially in rural areas. The general then stopped a schoolteacher passing by.

"Come here, young man."

"Yes sir." The teacher walked nervously toward the general.

"Is this Umuchiakuma Ihechiowa, Dr. Kalu Ogbaa's village?"

"Yes, it is. And Dr. Ogbaa is my uncle."

"Do you know whether he is home today?"

"No. He is not at home, sir. But we expect that he'll be home this weekend."

"Okay." The general nodded. "When he comes home, tell him that General Nwachukwu asked of him."

"Yes, sir. I'll let him know that you asked of him when he comes to visit us."

Then the general turned. His ADC briskly saluted and opened the door for him. After he entered, the ADC shut the door, saluted again, and quickly jumped into the vehicle. The crowd waved and cheered as he passed. The general returned their cheers with a sharp military salute, and they drove off.

People crowded around the teacher. "What did the general ask you?"

"He asked me whether this was Dr. Ogbaa's village and if he was home today. I told him yes it was Uncle K's village, but that he was not home today. He then asked me to tell uncle that General Nwachukwu asked of him when he comes home."

"Wow. How did the general, who was recently appointed governor, know him already?"

"You know how famous he has become since his return from the United States? Have you forgotten that he appealed to the Imo State civilian government to start the water project before the recent military takeover of the Nigerian government?"

"I didn't know that until you said it just now."

"Uncle is not one to blow his own horn in public."

"*Na true o*. Until he started driving his big brand-new Volvo, he always walked on the roads like ordinary you and me; not like the bragging, half-baked university graduates of whom we know. When uncle (my village pet name was "Uncle K," and many people who know me when I played and coached still called me uncle) addresses people in our village meetings, he speaks Igbo without a single English word in it, and yet he earned a Ph.D. in English. He is unassuming in all his ways. But when he talks with fellow big men in government, they listen closely to his words of wisdom."

"How do you know so much about him?"

"I briefly attended Imo State University, where he teaches, before I joined the Navy."

"It's true o! We need such intelligent and humble people like him in our community."

When I arrived home to visit the village that weekend, my neighbor gave me the General's message. I had expected to hear from the new governor since I had previously contacted him to express my concerns about the previous administration's neglectful representation of our clan in terms of distribution of public facilities and development projects. I had also implored him to encourage his new administration to resume the previously approved water and electricity projects.

I suspected the general had seen the open trenches for the water project along our main road and had decided to stop and talk to me in person. I recounted the communication to the villagers, who had hoped that he wanted to interview me for a job in his administration, or query me about a complaint that somebody might have filed against me. They knew by impulse that something must have caused him to stop and ask of me in our "insignificant" village.

A few weeks after the incident, I began to receive letters from the state government as one of those they named as leaders of thought in Arochuku/Ohafia LGA. However, since I lived in Etiti and came home only occasionally for visits, I did not attend all the meetings they called. But I received briefings on the meetings I missed from those who attended, and gave the board advice about government matters. Governor Ike Nwachukwu followed my advice until he moved on to another post.

A few weeks later, two military jeeps were parked in front of my apartment Isinweke when I arrived home from work, four soldiers standing beside them. As I drove into the compound, two corporals stood reading newspapers while the non-commissioned officers guarded the entrance gate. As soon as I stepped out of my car, the two corporals approached me.

"Good afternoon, sir." They saluted.

"Good afternoon, officers. What can I do for you?"

"Sir, are you Dr. Kalu Ogbaa, sir?"

"Yes, I am." I was curious, and suspicious.

"Relax, sir. There is nothing wrong." The taller of the two pulled a letter out of his file folder and handed it to me. "Sir, we are from the Government House, Owerri. His Excellency, Navy Captain Allison Madueke, sent us to give you this letter, sir." Saluting, he said, "Permission to leave for Owerri, sir."

I thanked them as they saluted then jumped into their vehicles, and drove away. A small curious crowd that had gathered in our yard slowly began to disperse. Inside the house, I read the letter from the governor's wife, Mrs. Uche Madueke, a native of Ufuma, Clara's home clan. Uche had written to invite us for lunch in the State House, Owerri.

Governor Madueke and his wife were close friends with my in-laws who had told them that Clara and I were now working back in the state. Uche had decided to invite us so that we could brief the governor on the disposition of our people, and so that she and Clara could catch up on events since they had graduated from Girls High School, Awkunanaw, Enugu, in 1974. I was excited to seize the opportunity to discuss our people's plight to the governor, just as I had with the previous governors of the state. When we arrived, Uche, the military governor's wife, gave Clara a warm embrace.

"*Nwanne m nwanyi* Clara. *Nke a bu anya gi* (My dear sister Clara. Is this you in person)?"

"*Obu mu o, ezi nwanne m nwanyi. O tego* (It's me, my dear sister. It's been long, indeed)."

"When did you come back from the US?"

"Oh, back on January 1, 1982."

"Oh, yes? And nobody heard from you all this while?"

"My sister, I inquired about you whenever my husband and I visited Ufuma, but nobody told me where you and your family were living. Without receiving your letter, we would not have known you now lived in Owerri."

Uche now turned to me. "*Ogo nno* (Welcome my in-law). I'm sorry for chatting so ceaselessly without first welcoming you formally. It's been so long since Clara and I last met. Come. Welcome to our house. Let us go to the living room."

I returned her greeting and followed her and Clara into the house. Uche asked her servants to set the table, and after lunch, she showed us to the governor's office where she formally introduced us to her husband, the military governor. Navy Captain Madueke, a light-skinned and handsome Igbo man, looked fierce and intimidating to me when I met him. But after the wife introduced me to him, he seemed to soften his demeanor as he received me, which relaxed me a little bit. Thereafter, the women excused themselves and returned to the living room. The governor and I sat down to have our own conversation.

He was a kind and receptive host, encouraging me to relate the history of my recent appointment at Imo State University and the level of my university education. Then I informed him of social and political marginalization of Ihechiowa, one of the most populous and large food-producing clans in Arochukwu/Ohafia. As I related our story, he led me to a wall map, filled with big, variously colored pins designating each area of the state where his administration was doing various developmental projects and from where they had appointed important civil servants. He asked me to show him our LGA and Ihechiowa Clan on the map. He looked closely at the map where I pointed for a moment, and sighed. There were no pins on the map to show that Ihechiowa had received any of the government benefits. He guided me back to my chair, then seated himself across from me. "If I appointed you as commissioner in my administration, will you be willing to serve?" he finally asked.

I told him I would consider it. Then he asked me to send him a copy of my updated CV to consider carefully before making his decision.

I thanked him and went downstairs to join Clara and Uche in the living room, where they were still chatting. I joined the conversation, and after telling them about my conversation with the governor, Clara and I took leave of Uche and began our journey back to Etiti.

"Are you going to send the governor your CV as he requested?"

"Surely, I will do so if God approves. I must fast and pray, first."

"How long will you fast?"

"Three days. Will you join me?"

"Of course I will, if you want me to."

"Then we will begin on Monday and end on Wednesday, before I update my CV."

"Will that be soon enough for the governor?"

"Yes. But I must seek God's approval before I apply for any job with the government."

"The governor will give you the appointment once he sees your impressive CV." Clara placed her hand on mine. "Why delay? Many people would jump at the opportunity to send their CV to the governor."

"That's true. But you know I have trusted God in all my decisions. This will be no different."

Clara and I fasted and prayed, and I sought advice from my trusted friends. A close member in our church believed that if I sent the CV to the governor, he would surely give me the appointment. But, he added, when the navy deployed the governor for another assignment, there would be a change in the administration of the state that would end my appointment as a commissioner. In addition, he reminded me that I could lose my seniority in my department at the university.

I discussed the issue with Clara who wanted me to take the job at Owerri, which could have given us some visibility in government, as well as an opportunity for me to serve my people the way I had wanted. But the sage advice of my friend influenced me to write the governor and inform him that I could not apply for the job, telling him I was preparing to spend my sabbatical leave abroad. Clara did not like my decision, but as a woman of faith, she supported my decision. I wrote the governor and he graciously accepted my decision. Instead, he appointed Barrister Kalu Uko of Achara Ihechiowa as secretary to the Arochukwu/Ohafia LGA, a position the governor felt would enable him to help our people the way I had wanted. Precisely six months after I received the message from the Holy Order, the navy redeployed Governor Madueke and replaced him with Navy Lieutenant Ikwechege as the new governor of Imo State.

I decided, instead, to work with the executive committee of the postwar Ihechiowa Development Union (IDU) to resurrect the electricity project, which the Mbakwe administration abandoned. We levied money from all able-bodied men and women according to their means, and continued the project where the government had stopped. When several people failed to pay the levied amounts, we launched a new funding drive in two other Ihechiowa clan blocs during the first and second yam harvest festivals. We also levied our clansmen in the Diaspora.

At last, we began connecting electric cables between poles along the major roads in the clan leading to the Itu electric grid in Akwa Ibom State through Arochukwu town. Thereafter, each village took it upon themselves to connect from the major roads to their streets and compounds. Many people, however, especially those of us who lived abroad, ran our country homes with electric generators, but the villages were no longer as dark as they used to be.

Even though I continued to worry about how to bring developmental projects to the Ihechiowa community, I also worked hard to develop myself professionally. The faculty in the College of Humanities and Social Studies noticed my active literary, teaching, and professional activities and elected me chair of the School of Humanities Seminars Committee in 1985, a member of the Appointments and Promotions Committee in 1988, and a member of the Postgraduate Studies Committee in the same 1988. Over time, the work overload, teaching, research activities, and other services to the university and the community, exhausted me. I needed some time to reenergize. With the help of Professors Lindfors and Achebe, I began to look for American universities where I would spend my sabbatical leave after the end of the 1988/89 academic year.

And as I planned the sabbatical leave, I also applied early in spring 1988 to the university promotions committee for promotion to the rank of full professor of English, following the publication of my first book, *Folkways in Chinua Achebe's Novels* (Zim Pan African Press, 1988). Following an established tradition, the committee made a positive premier facie case for my promotion, and recommended it to the new vice chancellor, Professor Gabriel Umezurike, who sent them out for external appraisals. Although they did not publish the outcome of the appraisals, I applied for a sabbatical leave, which they approved readily. But something more deeply devastating than a heavy workload hastened my desire to spend my sabbatical leave outside Nigeria: my father's sudden death.

At 8:45 a.m. on January 8, 1989, as I was about to conclude my discussion of Robert Frost's poem, "Stopping by Woods on a Snowy Evening," with my English class, someone came knocking at the classroom door. At first, I ignored the distraction. But when it persisted, I opened the door to find my secretary, Frank, waiting, eyes lowered.

"What's wrong, Frank?"

"Sir, your brother's wife, Kathy, and two of your cousins are here to see you," he said.

"Well, couldn't they wait for me to conclude my class discussion?"

"I told them to wait, sir. But they said the message was urgent. They needed to deliver it immediately." He handed me a hand-written note from my brother:

> Dear KO: Our dear father, Mazi Stephen Ogbaa Ikpo, passed on last night to be with the Lord. I want you to come home

immediately so we can bury him today. If I do not see you after receiving this note, I will bury him in your absence because I do not want his remains, which I could not deposit in the mortuary, to decay.—Brother Ikpo.

I looked skyward, tears filling my eyes, wondering what had happened. I had been with him four days ago in the village. He looked fine. I wiped away the tears, closed the note and asked Frank to wait for me in my office. I returned to the classroom and dismissed the students who could easily read my face and knew that something sad and serious must have happened.

When I returned to my office, my bosom friend, Levi Kamalu, an assistant registrar in the university, was already there waiting and discussing my father's death with the delegation from my village. Kathy and my cousins were also waiting in my office. They rushed across the room and embraced me, sobbing. I neither cried nor asked how Father died as they expected. Instead, I began mentally to prepare myself for the duty of giving Father the hero's burial he deserved. I would need to convince my brother, who wanted him buried immediately, to postpone the funeral.

After welcoming my relatives, I asked them to wait a little longer for me to get ready for our trip to the village. Kamalu asked what he could do to help.

"Follow me," I said.

"Sure, I'll go wherever you want. Let me inform my office assistant that I will be away from the office all day."

I walked with Kamalu to the administration building, where his office and the VC's were located, and asked him to meet me later in the VC's office. At the VC's office, I told the secretary that my father had just died, so I needed to see the VC to apply for a salary advance to help me pay for funeral expenses.

"Oh, I'm sorry to hear that, sir. Let me give you a visitor's form to fill out so I can take it to the VC for approval before I let you see him."

But I was already at his door, opened it without knocking and entered. I immediately knew I had breached protocol: barging into the room without knocking or permission. Okoli rushed in to inform the VC that he had not permitted me to enter.

"I'm very sorry, sir, for barging in like this," I apologized to the vice chancellor. "I've just been told that my father died last night.

Could you authorize the bursar's office to give me a one-month salary advance to help me pay for my father's funeral expenses in the village?"

I had hardly finished my plea for help when my voice cracked, betraying my sorrow. The VC and his cabinet appeared to have understood my uncharacteristic behavior. He quickly asked Okoli to fill out an authorization form for salary advance. I thanked the VC, closed the door, and apologized to Okoli as he carried out the VC's orders. Eventually, I got the signed form, took it to the bank and withdrew the money in Kamalu's company. Then we returned to the office, picked up my relatives then headed to my house to pick up a few things before going to my village.

By the time we got to our apartment, Clara was already home, sobbing while she prepared our lunch. When I showed her my brother's note, she wept and fell to the floor. After consoling her, I asked if she would stay home with the children, who were still in school. I told her that Kamalu would go with me and, if I did not come back that day, he would bring her all the information about the arrangements we were making for the burial.

Clara was sad she could not go with me, but she knew someone had to take care of the children in my absence. As I was about to climb into the car, Kamalu insisted that he drive. But I assured everyone in the car that I would drive carefully. We prayed for God's protection before we left Etiti and arrived safely in the village at about 1:30 p.m.

A wailing throng had already gathered in Nde Ngwo compound when we arrived. "*Ewoo, ezi nwa ya abia lewo* (Oh, his beloved son has arrived)," some said, pointed at our car. "*Kaa nwa m, ihe ukwu mere* (Sorry my son, what a great loss!)," others cried as they shook their heads.

I parked the car near our compound square as members of my agnate family watched. As I approached, they wailed uncontrollably. All the while, they wondered how I would react now that I was home to see Dimgba Eleoha whom Death made his back touch the ground the first time as it were before their very eyes. I stepped into the parlor of my father's house and saw him lying face up as if he were taking a quiet nap. Poor Mother sat directly opposite him, moaning. She had lost her voice crying all through the night and day since her beloved husband had died. When she saw me, she slowly stood and held me to her bosom, saying, "Kalu *nwa m, gben akwa* (Don't cry, Kalu, my beloved son)."

I hugged her tightly, pleading with her to stop crying and assuring her that I would take good care of her all the days of her life. I took her gently to the small kitchen stool and sat her down. When Brother Ikpo arrived and stepped across the room to embrace me, I shrugged him off and asked him to tell me what arrangements he had made for the burial. When he could not give me any clear answer, it dawned on me that he was not financially able to give Father a befitting burial. So I quickly assured all the mourners present that we would not bury Father, Ogbaa *nwa oke* Ikpo, that day, like a dog. I then communicated my plans for his funeral ceremonies, and assured them that I had the money to carry out the plans with or without additional contributions. When they heard that, they all heaved a sigh of relief.

I then moved across the room back to my father's side where I stood at attention, and saluted him in a military fashion. I thanked him for having been a most wonderful loving father to our family, especially his favorite son, and for achieving so much fame within the time he lived as a renowned leader in our community. Then, I fell on my knees, leaned against his chest and sobbed. Then I prayerfully promised to carry his torch in everything I did as long as I lived. Mother then moved closer to me where she knelt, asking me to let go. I quickly wiped away my tears to inspire courage in others who looked up to me for succor in the time of our greatest need. Then I sat down calmly and silently asked God's strength to carry out my duties.

An hour later, I was driving to the General Hospital, Arochukwu, to ask for an ambulance to take my father's remains to the mortuary. After I arrived, the charge doctor informed me that they did not have an ambulance to spare. Then he saw my Volvo car parked near his office.

"Whose car is that?" He pointed.

"It is mine."

"Wouldn't it be a great honor done to your father if you gave him a final ride in it?"

"Oh, yes, doctor!" I said, realizing the great opportunity to demonstrate the love I had for my Father, even in death. I thanked the doctor and drove back home to bring my father's corpse to the mortuary. Upon my return, I paid the hospital and tipped the mortuary attendant to take good care of my beloved father's remains until the day we would take them home for interment.

Before I left the village with Kamalu, I had a quiet discussion with my mother and Brother Ikpo and giving them some money to start paying for the rites associated with the burial. I dropped Kamalu off at Umuahia to catch a cab back to Okigwe asking him to brief Clara on what we were doing, then I drove to the Nigerian Television Authority (NTA) station in Aba to publish my father's obituary, returning late that evening.

The following day, I returned to campus and obtained permission from the dean of our college and the VC to continue the funeral arrangements. When I returned to the village, everybody was anxiously awaiting my father's obituary announcement. When it eventually aired on the Ikpo TV station during the 7:00 evening news, our family members cheered jubilantly because they rarely saw such announcements on television in our rural community in those years. After the announcement, I went to bed early to brood in solitude.

The next morning, the crowd was unmanageable and seemed to outnumber the teeming number of mourners from our village. In addition to the locals, Kamalu brought Imo State University students in two buses. Several faculty members and administrators arrived in their private cars along with many official government cars carrying administrative staff representatives from the Ministry of Information and the Ministry of Commerce and Industry, where Brothers Ikpo and Ebu worked, respectively.

The funeral procession leading to the church, where the elders conducted Father's funeral service, was led by a Presbyterian choral group, esteemed wrestlers, and cultural dance troupes. At the end of the service, the crowd that accompanied his casket to his house was so large that it made it impossible for me to observe his final funeral rites. I've often thought that maybe it was best that I was not able to see my father go down into the dark pit, never to rise in this world again.

After the burial ceremony, we entertained fellow mourners with good food, drinks, songs and dances. And for a moment, the celebrative atmosphere lightened the excruciating pent-up emotional burden my father's demise brought to my soul. Some men even challenged me to a convivial wrestling match in honor of Ogbaa *nwa* Ikpo, *ogara mgba adim uche*. I danced a few steps as I moved to the center of the wrestling arena, demonstrating his wrestling prowess, when the talking drums sent me a message similar to those I remembered they used to send to my father. The crowd cheered and shouted, "*O ya woo, o ya woo* (Like father like son)." Women from my compound rushed in to embrace me, and young men lifted me up high in the air and gently put me down to the ground again. The crowd clapped and cheered. After the brief demonstration of wrestling dance, I excused myself from the crowd to attend visitors from the university. Oh, what a day of joy. And sorrow. We said our farewells to a great man and beloved father! And it dawned on me that Father had finally completed his earthly struggles, and the joy of memories he left behind would always decorate the road of his great journey and help others by bringing them joy as they made on their own journeys down the road to heaven.

As predicted, the austerity measures the federal military government had introduced in the country were hurting the middle class and the lower socioeconomic class the most. In some segments of the country, unmitigated hunger, malnourishment, and disease were widespread and deep as that suffered by Biafrans during the civil war. Citizens who could no longer endure the suffering began leaving the country in droves for other West African and Western countries. In the media, a satirical character named Andrew began appearing on network TV:

"Hey, Andrew, what are you doing with that luggage on your back?"

"I'm checking out, man. This country is too hard to live in. Too many diseases, no affordable drugs and the food's all gone. Common people like me have no money to buy anything. Even the rich and wealthy people can't find what they want."

"Tell me, Andrew. If everyone checks out like you, who'll remain to rebuild the country?"

"Oh, I'm sure the army is doing a good job of that. Besides, many people are happy to stay where they are. But I'm checking out."

"But who are you to challenge the wisdom of the government, Andrew?" another character asks. "Did you not hear what Zebuludaya said in last night's episode of his sitcom about the poor not being given the drugs prescribed to them in the hospitals?"

"No, I didn't watch it. What did he say?"

"He said that each time a poor person goes to the General Hospital for treatment, and the doctor prescribes drugs which the government usually pays for, the pharmacist marks them 'o.s.' But when a rich person comes, the drugs automatically become available."

"What is o.s.?"

"Out of stock!"

"So how do the drugs become available to the rich people if they're out of stock?"

"Do you mean to tell me you don't know that rich people can easily get whatever they want in this country?"

"How?"

"By bribing doctors and pharmacists to prescribe and dispense government purchased drugs meant for all citizens."

"What is the army doing about it? Is it not bribery and corruption? Is it not the same indiscipline that the army claims to be waging its war against?"

"Yes. They are waging a war against indiscipline, alright. But if the army hierarchy is part of the cartel, who can wage a counter war against them? I wish I had the chance to check out of the country like you, Andrew."

But few did. While most educated people were conscious of the country's general malaise, which Andrew and Zebuludaya characterized in radio and television commercials and sitcoms, I was particularly sensitive to, and apprehensive of developments in the educational sector of our nation. The minister of education, Professor Jibril Aminu, had developed several educational policies unacceptable to academicians, compelling officials of his ministry and National Universities Commission (NUC) to implement them at all levels of educational institution in the country.

First, he recommended the teaching of nomadic education in primary and secondary schools in all the regions of the country, even though the nomads existed mainly in Northern Nigeria, especially in his native Tiv area. Furthermore, he planned to develop and impose common curricular offerings for all universities, including the state-owned institutions like Imo State University, and threatened to withhold funds and accreditation from any university that failed to adopt the common curriculum. This was indeed a serious problem for Southern academicians who had visions and missions for universities in their region, which were different from—perhaps superior to—those in the northern universities.

When the National Association of Nigerian Students (NANS) heard about the plans, they organized and carried out nation-wide protests against the Ministry of Education. Although the protests were peaceful in most parts of the country, in other areas violence flared, prompting the government to arrest and detain several student leaders and shutting down all the universities in the country. Consequently, the students engaged in further, more violent, demonstrations followed by more arrests. Soon, the actions and reactions became routine, severely affecting the standard of university education in Nigeria. Some parents even began to send their children and wards to foreign countries to acquire university educations, especially the United States.

Most troubling for me was that the national closings also closed primary schools where my children attended. The situation was so precarious that it reminded me of the civil war years in which the government shut down all educational institutions in Biafra to avoid the enemy's bombing of the students and destruction of their buildings. I had lost three precious years of college education then and did not want my children to suffer a similar fate in the so-called peacetime.

I therefore applied for two one-year replacement positions (Oral Roberts University in Tulsa, Oklahoma, and the University of Florida in Gainesville, Florida) after receiving applications from Professor Lindfors. As soon as the English Department in Tulsa received my application, they gave me an instant appointment with an annual salary that was below what I earned eight years prior in the University of Texas at Austin. Hence, I therefore waited for Gainesville to make me a better offer. But after waiting two weeks for a response from Gainesville, I finally accepted the offer from Tulsa. (On a side note, Gainesville had sent me an offer through a letter, which a jealous colleague saw in our university mailroom, read, and destroyed to prevent me from taking my sabbatical leave abroad. I found out about Gainesville's offer only after I had assumed my position in Oral Roberts University and called them to find out what happened to my application.)

Once I received the appointment letter from Oral Roberts University, I sent my sabbatical leave application to the university administration with a CV and the letter. Mr. Ogike wrote me a letter of conditional approval for the leave. He stated that the university would pay my monthly salary for one year and that the University Council was yet to decide if they would pay my transportation to and from the U.S. university or to and from a local university. According to Ogike, the Council had not yet formulated a policy on foreign travels. I decided to make my plans to leave no matter the decision the Council might make. I contacted the registrar immediately.

"Do you want to accept the provisional approval and receive whatever transportation money the Council might approve for you, or wait for their decision before you travel?" the registrar asked.

"Yes, I do accept the provisional approval, but I'll have to travel with or without getting the transportation money, unless you were able to communicate the Council's decision to me before August 16, 1989, when I plan to travel to the U.S."

"Well, then, you need to forward your decision to my office in writing, and I will carry it to the next Council meeting. The Bursars Office will be paying your monthly salary into your local bank account as we spelled it out in your letter on the matter. Once again, congratulations."

"Thank you very much. I hope and pray that the Council approves the payment so I can use it to purchase my ticket."

"Well, let's see what happens before then, Dr. Ogbaa."

I left for home happy and sure that I was going to spend my sabbatical leave in the United States. Little did I know that events in China would affect my plans to leave the country.

Oral Roberts University offered me the one-year teaching appointment to replace Professor William Epperson, the chair of the English Department, who was going to spend his own sabbatical leave in China. No sooner had he sent me an appointment letter than the Tiananmen Square protests of 1989, also known as the June Fourth Incident in Chinese, began to unfold. The protests, a series of demonstrations in and near Tiananmen Square in Beijing China, beginning April 15, 1989 and ending June 4, 1989 kept the world entranced as we watched the brave students fight against the oppressive state. But the longer the demonstrations lasted, the more Epperson and I feared they could prevent us from spending our sabbatical leave as planned. Then I received a letter from Epperson informing me that if the protests in China did not end before August, he would need to cancel my appointment since he would not be able to go to China for his sabbatical leave. The letter reminded me of my apprehension in 1976, when I received a graduate admission and a teaching associate appointment from the Ohio State University beginning from mid-August 1976 but could not travel to the U.S. because of lack of visa until January 1, 1977.

"What are we going to do, UK?" Clara asked.

"Well, we'll have to do what we usually do in times like this: fast and pray for God's intervention."

"When do we start?"

"We'll start on Wednesday and end on Friday and thereafter wait for whatever message we might receive from God at the end of our fasting and praying."

I noticed that Clara was afraid of experiencing again the kind of humiliation she went through in 1976. If I failed to go this time, I also feared, the Council might not allow me to postpone it. "Please, God, don't let that happen," I involuntarily blurted out as I thought about the situation.

I did not let anyone, not even our children know that I received the second letter Epperson wrote me. However, I wrote him back and informed him that I was convinced the incident in China would soon end to allow each of us to spend our sabbatical leave according to plan. As people of faith, all we needed to do was pray for God to make it happen. Later in June, Epperson wrote me a third letter to reconfirm my appointment and thanked me for writing him an uplifting letter, adding that the letter proved that I was indeed a man of faith. Through it all, God lowered the anxiety each of us had. I thanked Him for intervening positively on the matter.

After my father's burial, I visited Mother virtually every weekend, spending time consoling her and caring for her financial and social needs. I also arranged for family members to be with her at all times. The death of the man she was married to for well over sixty years weighed heavily on her, and I feared for her own health. My impending sabbatical to America was drawing near and I worried that she would see it as another loss. I recalled her anxiety over my last five-year graduate studies absence in America and hoped somehow to reassure her that all would be well and I would return expeditiously. I finally approached her, explaining the necessity of the long absence and assuring her that Clara would be there for her throughout the year.

"How long will you be away from me this time around?" she asked.

"My sabbatical leave will last for one year only, Nne."

"And where will you be spending it?"

"In America."

"Are sure you'll be in America for one year only? Do you remember you told me the same thing last time you went there, and yet you spent five years?"

"Yes, I remember. But it will be different this time. I'm not going to study for degrees the way I did the last time I was there."

"Are you going with the children and *Nne ogbo m* Clara?"

"No, Nne. I'm going alone. And they will be visiting you often while I'm away."

"I hope so, Kalu *nwa m*. I hope so." She looked vacantly away.

Something in her remark weighed on me. The first time I left her behind, Father was still alive to take care of her. But now, she would need to live in that lonely space of home alone. In my heart of hearts, I wanted to stay behind and help take her into her old age. But the education of my children was paramount in my mind. Consequently, I knew I might stay longer in America if I found a permanent job, which would enable me to bring the entire family over to America after my sabbatical leave. I also knew that an opportunity to teach in America would better benefit all the members of our family since I would be in a position to send them money and enable them to survive the biting economic effects of the army-imposed austerity measures. Additionally, with the extra money I could send, Brother Ikpo and Sister Nwannennaya and their children would be in a better position to take care of Mother. Nevertheless, I could not expect her to understand. Her only desire was to spend her last days with her beloved son.

I also struggled with my own sense of obligation to the woman who had sacrificed her whole life to helping me achieve my dreams. Could I forgive myself if she died while I was in America? If she lived, who could take good care of her like Kalu, the apple of her eye? Who else, besides me, could understand the feeling of loss and despair when Sister Mgbore died that year in my absence at Boy's Vocational School in 1958? In whom else could she confide when thoughts of having grown up a lonely orphan haunted her? Who else could make her face shine with joy each time she caressed it with her supple, open palms?

But what else could I do? If I spent a year and came back to the country, my children would not get the type of education I dreamed for them. Nor would we have enough money to fight the austerity measures affecting most people our native Nigeria. Nor would I develop my professional standing in such a way as to move me into positions of scholarly authority where I might be able to make a difference in the lives of my Igbo peoples.

"I'm leaving now, Nne. But my family and I will visit you every weekend before I travel to America. At the end of the month, I'll take you to Okigwe so you can rest for a while."

"*Gaa nkeoma, ezi nwa m* (Farewell, my dear child)." Mother kissed me and watched as I left to drive back to Okigwe.

A few weeks later, I was set to travel to the U.S. Clara and the children encouraged me to find a permanent job that would enable me to bring them over so we could all live happily there as a family. I told them that I would try, even though I preferred to come back after my leave to take care of Mother, and others, who needed my help.

"Give me a hug, Daddy," Nneka held me tight, refusing to let go.

"Give me a bigger hug, Daddy," Emeka said.

Then Ndubuisi, Ikenna, and Enyinna all grabbed me around both legs, crying. "Don't go, Daddy. Don't go."

Clara rocked Kelechi, crying on her shoulders and looking away as if to hide her teary poker face from me.

"Guys, what is this? You don't want me to go?"

"No. We want you to go, Daddy," they all said in unison. "But we will miss you."

"I understand. But unless you all stop crying, I won't go."

They wiped the tears off their faces, said their final goodbyes, and quickly jumped into our car. At last, Clara and I hugged and kissed.

"Take good care of the children while I'm gone."

"I will," she promised. "And you take care of yourself."

Then I boarded the taxi to the airport, watching Clara as she drove away, back to Okigwe. I would miss them terribly. But I somehow felt that this new phase of my life would bring even more extraordinary opportunities for both my family and me.

My service years at Imo State University (now Abia State University), from January 1, 1982 through August 18, 1989, were the most satisfying and fulfilling to me as both a university professor and a human being. My American postgraduate education and university teaching experiences had empowered me to render superior services to the Nigerian university inside and outside the classroom, as well as to individuals and communities in the university towns of Etiti and Okigwe, and those in my village, my clan, my LGA, and the state as a whole. More importantly, I had been given the opportunity to help individuals in my family and in my church, just as two churches in Austin, Texas had helped me when I sought financial help from them in 1978. They taught me by their example how to become a more caring and compassionate person who would strive to serve people as faithfully as I could, always conscious that the eyes of God were upon me.

Part Four

My Second Coming to America

Chapter 12

The Sabbatical Leave Years

Originally, I came to the United States to receive a graduate education. But I had also learned to teach at American universities, which prepared me to teach in Nigerian universities when I returned home. The purpose of my second visit to America was a bit different. I hoped to spend my sabbatical revising the book I had published in Nigeria, writing an article or two, and recuperating from the frantic, frenetic workload I had operated under during my previous eight years at Imo State University. I also needed to carefully consider the many sociocultural, political, and educational experiences I would encounter while serving as visiting Associate Professor of English at both Oral Roberts University (ORU) in Tulsa, Oklahoma, and Clark Atlanta University (CAU) in Georgia before deciding either to stay permanently in America (as my family wanted) or return home immediately after my sabbatical leave.

In America, I would have more opportunities to grow professionally and to make more money than I did in Nigeria. Even more importantly, America could give my children the opportunity to receive a higher quality of education than they were receiving in Nigeria. On the other hand, the racist attitudes of some professors and fellow graduate students reared their ugly heads once again, albeit subtly and subliminally in most cases. Therefore, I had to ask myself some soul-searching questions, the answers to which would help me make the right decision: Would I be able to ignore or endure permanently the type of racial discrimination, deprivation, and segregation I once experienced if I decided to stay? Would not those who depended on me for both material and moral support in Nigeria consider my staying in America a betrayal of their trust? Would I be able to live the atomistic life of Westerners in my newfound land as opposed to the communal life I used to live in Nigeria? Could I, a double minority—black and foreign—endure the life of an exile in America even though it would be self-imposed?

After mulling over these questions for more than two years, I decided in 1992 to stay permanently in the U.S. My decision was based mainly on the biting austerity measures still plaguing Nigeria, widespread national student unrest, and the discrimination from fellow Nigerians toward my Igbo people for fighting against them during the Nigeria-Biafra War, as well as the corrupt administrative practices at Imo State University. Reports I received from Nigeria in the years after we left confirmed to me that the life, which the Igbo people still suffered under in postwar Nigeria, was as painful as the life one would experience in any foreign racist society and that my decision, however painful, was the right one.

On August 21, 1989, my forty-fourth birthday, I reported for duty to Dr. Grady Walker, acting chairperson of the English Department at ORU. I introduced myself to him, watching carefully how he received me.

"Hello, Dr. Walker. My name is Kalu Ogbaa. I'm sorry that I could not be here before classes started. My flight had several rescheduling delays in Nigeria. When the airlines eventually allowed me to travel, I was also delayed overnight in Paris and another night in New York. But I'm here now." I smiled.

"Welcome to our university and department, Dr. Ogbaa," Grady began. "Yes, we were hoping that you would be here before classes began. It's a pity, however, that you had to go through all the trouble to get here, but we are glad that you finally made it. Your brother, Agwu Ogbaa, sent us the money we used as a deposit to secure you an off-campus apartment, which is within walking distance. Come. Let me introduce you to our faculty members before I take you to your office and the apartment."

"Thank you very much for procuring the apartment and for everything you and Bill Epperson did to bring me to ORU." I followed him to the general office of the English Department, where he introduced me to other faculty members then took me to my office and other important offices and buildings on campus, including Christ's Chapel, the dining hall, and the library. After lunch, he brought me back to his office and gave me my teaching assignments before driving me to the apartment, where he and I signed the lease.

The largest Charismatic interdenominational Christian university in the world, ORU's enrollment was a little over 3,000 students from forty-nine states along with a significant number of international students from fifty countries. The university offered over sixty undergraduate degree programs, and a number of masters and doctoral degrees. The Carnegie Foundation for the Advancement of Teaching classified it as a Master's University. I was highly impressed by the generally peaceful Christian ambiance of the campus environment, complemented with bi-weekly devotional services in Christ's Chapel on Tuesdays and Thursdays between 11:00 a.m. and 12:00 p.m. During those times, the administration ordered all the classrooms and most offices closed to allow faculty, staff, and students to take part in the compulsory celebrative chapel services, broadcast live through the university's television station and via satellite.

This aspect of the university life was especially satisfying because it reminded me of the activities that members carried out in our Nigerian Pentecostal church during midnight services on Wednesdays and Saturdays. Moreover, I worshiped on Sundays in a Pentecostal church, located in downtown Tulsa. At the time, many regarded Tulsa as the Mecca of Christian churches in the U.S.

However, as enthusiastic as the students were, I did not initially think that the academic standard of the university was anywhere close to those of my three alma maters: the University of Nigeria, Nsukka, the Ohio State University at Columbus, and the University of Texas at Austin. Even our newly established Imo State University in Nigeria had a higher academic standard than that of ORU. Yet, I loved to teach the students because of their discipline, dress code, brotherly love, and respect for authority. Besides, students and professors were eager to take my new literature course, "The African Novel." Moreover, as news of the course grew, others invited me to give talks on African literary and sociocultural studies to the public. My work was also highly publicized in the student newspaper and other news outlets. I was also given the opportunity to teach the course at Tulsa Community College during the 1990 summer session.

Finally, working with my department head was a refreshing change from my past experiences. One particular conversation with Dr. Walker gave me an insight into what kind of a humorous and friendly human being he was. When I received my first paycheck at ORU, I noticed that the tax they withdrew from my salary was high. Dr. Walker asked me to bring my paystub for him to examine.

"Tell me, Kalu. Didn't you say you have a family in Nigeria?"

"Yes, I did. Why?"

"I can see you did not indicate any withholdings for them in your W2 Form. Without such withholdings, your taxes will continue to be high."

"So what should I do to correct the mistake?"

"I will take you to the IRS Office in town for you to fill out social security forms to include all your dependent children and your wife."

At the IRS office, I began to fill out the form and found that it had only space enough to include four family members.

"Grady." I nudged him. "I don't have enough space here to include everybody in my family."

Grady looked at the form. "Kalu, there should be enough space for all of you. They didn't ask you to include your dogs' names in the form," he joked.

"You are right, Grady." I smiled, amused by his assumption. "But excluding my dogs, I still need enough space for eight family members: two parents and six minor children."

"Oh. Uh, well, let me get you another form." He smiled, sheepish, as if he'd regretted his bad joke.

On the contrary, the joke was hilarious. From that day on, we became close friends beyond my ORU employment. Indeed, he recommended me for the 1990 summer teaching job at Tulsa Community College.

I could not start revising my book, *Folkways in Chinua Achebe's Novels* (1988) because the ORU library did not have any African literature holdings. If I'd had a car, money, and time, I could have conducted the research at the University of Oklahoma and Oklahoma State University. I didn't. So, I reread the Achebe's novels closely and gathered new ideas, which I hoped to validate with critical opinions from books and journal articles I would later discover while doing research in bigger university libraries. Book revision today uses search engines and databases that make sources easily available outside of main university campuses. But my research was many years before such technology, therefore it took me another year in another university get to the revision. Nevertheless, during that period, I wrote an article, "Protests and the Individual Talents of Three Black Novelists," that I sent to *Phylon*, which has since changed to *College Language Association Journal* (*CLAJ*).

Furthermore, since I lacked a personal vehicle or funding beyond enough to cover my expenses, I had little social life. Nor could I afford ethnic African foods. However, just three weeks after moving into my apartment, I met a fellow Igboman who lived there.

"Hello." The man approached, hand held out to shake. "My name is Emmanuel Uche. I have seen you from my apartment. From your looks, I suspect that you are a fellow Igbo man." He smiled and gripped my hand firmly. "I also saw the name Kalu Ogbaa in the office and concluded that it was yours. Is that you?"

"Yes, it is. I came to spend my sabbatical at Oral Roberts University. One of the professors found me the apartment. I walk every day to campus, except weekends."

"Welcome, my brother. Judging from your name, I believe you come from Old Bende Division in Imo State as I do."

"Yes, I'm from Ihechiowa in Arochukwu LGA, part of Old Bende Division. What brought you to live here? Do you work or study at ORU?"

"Yes. I studied at ORU until last semester, when I graduated with a master's degree. I now work in the Marriott Hotel in downtown Tulsa. I've lived here since my student days."

"It's good to meet a fellow Igbo man. I thought I might meet one in the church."

"Which church do you attend?" he asked me.

"I have not attended any church since I came to Tulsa, and I've spent little time outside of campus. Which church do you attend?" I asked him.

"It's too bad that you have not been to any of the churches yet. If I knew you needed a ride to church, I would happily have taken you to my church, Higher Dimension Pentecostal. If you like, we can go there together every Sunday."

"I'd love to. My church in Nigeria is Cherubim and Seraphim Church. I believe I will enjoy your church if it is Pentecostal."

That weekend, Emmanuel took me to his church and introduced me to the elders. I saw similarities in the order and conduct of service in his church and mine. After the morning service, I decided to become a member of his small prayer group, and continued to attend the church with him until his employers transferred him to a branch of Marriott Hotel in San Francisco. Before he left Tulsa, however, he introduced me to a young woman who gave me a ride every Sunday to the church until I left ORU at the end of my sabbatical leave.

In the interim, Emmanuel and I would discuss contemporary sociopolitical issues in America and in our native Nigeria. The plight of our Igbo people saddened both of us. We therefore discussed how we could each improve our lives in the U.S. to enable us bring our relatives to America where they could also study and make money to send home as we did. I confided how painful it was each time I read my children's letters in which they asked me not to come home unless I was coming to bring them to the U.S. because the socioeconomic situation was so bad for most people in Nigeria. Later, when Emmanuel traveled home for Christmas, I bought many gifts, such as clothes, cosmetics, trinkets, and shoes, and sent them to my wife and children. Their letters of joy following the receipt of the gifts was a great satisfaction and delight to me.

Beginning March 1990, I began to look seriously for a permanent teaching job in the U.S. in case Imo State University did not send me a return ticket. I made it a habit of going daily to the library to read the advertised teaching positions in American universities and colleges. I applied for eight of those positions in English of which one university, located in a remote corner of Oklahoma State, invited me for an interview. They offered me the position but could not guarantee my wife a part-time job in the library. I therefore rejected the offer since there were no other universities or community colleges where my wife could get a job to supplement the salary they were going to pay. In the meantime, I continued to live in the off-campus apartment beyond the spring semester to await responses from other universities.

Toward the end of spring, I called Dr. Janice Liddell, chair of the English Department at Clark Atlanta University to ask her about the status of an article I had sent for publication. She told me that she'd forwarded it to Atlanta University where the editor of *CLAJ* operated. I took the opportunity to ask if she might have a job opening that I could fill in her department. Although there were some open positions in her department, she said the university had no money to fill them at the time. Nevertheless, she asked me to send her my CV for review in case funds became available.

After the call, I quickly upgraded my CV and mailed it to her. A week later, I phoned her to verify receipt of the document. She had, and had found it so impressive that she sent a copy to the provost for his consideration. Furthermore, she encouraged me to visit Atlanta to chat with him. Even if he could not give me a one-year visiting appointment, he might hire me to work part-time as an adjunct. I told her that I would come to Atlanta soon since I had completed my service at ORU. She gave me directions and said she look forward to meeting me.

Since the Imo State University Council had not yet resolved the issue of paying the cost of my round trip flight to the U.S., I decided to move to Atlanta and stay until the end of summer. If I got a job offer from CAU or another university, I would accept it and apply to Imo State University for a one-year leave of absence without pay, and then wait for them to send me a return ticket. That way, I would have the opportunity to finish revising the book. If, on the other hand, I did not get a job, then I would return to Nigeria before the beginning of the 1990/91 academic year and deal with the flight issue in person. I phoned Dr. Walker to thank him for his friendship and to let him know of my decision to move to Atlanta. He regretted that ORU could not hire me for a tenure-track position and wished me well in in Atlanta. In July, I paid off the balance on my apartment lease, closed my bank account, and left Tulsa for Atlanta with my personal belongings.

I arrived in Atlanta, checked into a hotel within walking distance to the Atlanta University Center (a consortium of historically black universities) and settled in for a restless night. The next morning, I went to see Dr. Liddell.

"Good morning, Dr. Liddell. How are you?" I stepped into her office and shook her hand.

"Good morning, Kalu. I'm very well, thank you. You can call me Janice. How was your flight from Tulsa?"

"Oh, very well! I arrived late last night and checked into a nearby hotel. That's why I came early this morning to see you."

"I'm glad you came. Please, have a seat." She motioned to a chair beside her desk.

"Thank you."

"As I told you on the phone, I forwarded a copy of your CV to the provost as soon as I received it. I also told him that you planned to visit us on campus as soon as possible. Now that you are here, let me call him to see if I can take you to see him."

"Thanks a lot for doing all this for me."

The provost could see me immediately. As we walked across campus to his office, Janice asked me several questions, which indicated that she had carefully read my CV. I was happy that prior to seeing me, she had noted my strengths as a professor. She also gave me the impression that she had discussed my case with the provost before my visit.

"Kalu, this is our provost, Dr. Charles Churchwell. Charles, this is Dr. Kalu Ogbaa. I'll leave both of you to talk. I have an appointment with a student," Dr. Liddell said.

"Thanks, Janice," Dr. Churchwell said. Then he turned to me. "Hello, Dr. Ogbaa; welcome to Clark Atlanta University."

"Thank you, sir," I shook his hand.

"Please, sit down. What can I do for you?"

"Thanks. I wanted to discuss the possibility of coming here to teach in the English Department. I just ended a visiting Associate Professor of English position at Oral Roberts University, where I spent my sabbatical this past academic year. I sent a copy of my CV to Dr. Liddell. Would you like to see a copy of it now?"

"No need for that." He waved his hand. "Janice told me about your visit and intention to teach in her department. As she has already told you, we have a couple of positions to fill in the department, but we cannot fill them until the president gives us the funds to do so. Will you stay for a while in Atlanta or are you going back to Tulsa after this visit?"

"Yes, I'll be staying in Atlanta for a while to see if your university or any other will hire me. If not, I'll go back to Nigeria directly from Atlanta."

"Since you'll be around, I want you to apply formally to my office for the position of a visiting Associate Professor of English and give a copy of the application to Janice. Then come back on Monday and see me. In the meantime, I'll discuss your case with the president. I hope we can hire you to teach full-time, or part-time for one year at least."

"The Office of Human Resources will give you a letter to that effect through the chair. She will let you know when she receives it. Congratulations!"

"Thank you very much, sir. You don't know how much what you've just done means to me and my family in Nigeria."

I then ran to Dr. Liddell's office and broke the good news to her. She was very pleased and asked me to give her the phone number of the hotel where I was staying so her secretary could call me to pick up the letter when they received it. When I eventually got the letter, I discovered that the salary they offered me was $11,000 more than what ORU paid me for the same rank and status.

A few days later at Dr. Liddell's office getting my teaching assignment, I met a student, who lived twenty minutes from CAU campus who helped me find an apartment. I moved out of the hotel immediately to prepare my course syllabi for the fall semester. For the first time in many months, I began to believe that my dream of staying in the U.S. just might become a reality.

Dr. Liddell called a department meeting just before the fall semester began in which she introduced me to other members of the English faculty.

"Colleagues, let me introduce our newest member to you. Dr. Kalu Ogbaa is joining us as a one-year visiting Associate Professor of English from Imo State University, Okigwe, Nigeria. This past academic year, he spent his sabbatical leave at Oral Roberts University."

They applauded and welcomed me to their department and university.

"I'm glad to work here with all of you."

With the exception of two white men and one Indian, all the faculty members were black and they all regarded the university as a black family enterprise. Although I had first embraced the black experience while studying and teaching in Black Studies Department at Ohio State University, I suddenly became aware of the strong and almost exclusive sense of community and brotherhood/sisterhood of the CAU administrators, faculty, staff, and students. In this department, everything was so Afrocentric that some of us Africans felt a little estranged by their core beliefs, vis-à-vis their peculiar African-American-specific culture. Yet, serving in the university was an opportunity for me to learn even more about the place of Blacks in America, and the world at large.

I also quickly became aware of the great importance of Atlanta as a kind of Mecca for black educational, sociocultural, and political leadership in American. Morehouse University, for example, had produced Thurgood Marshall, the first black Supreme Court Justice, Dr. Martin Luther King, Jr., the most notable and celebrated Civil Rights leader, the civil rights champion, Congressman John Lewis, and the first black U.S. Ambassador to the United Nations, Mr. Andrew Young, who served under the Carter Administration. Before the emergence of these great men, two other distinguished black men worked in Atlanta: Booker T. Washington, an educator, reformer, and the most influential black leader of his time (1856-1915) and W. E. B. Du

Bois, a towering black intellectual, scholar, and political thinker who also served at Atlanta University as a professor and founder of the black literary journal, *Phylon*, the precursor of *CLAJ* (1868-1963). They had their great debate in Atlanta, in which they sharply disagreed on strategies for black social and economic progress. Their opposing philosophies are found in much of today's discussions over how to end class and racial injustices, asking what the role of black leadership was, and what do the "haves" owe the "have-nots" in the black community.

Furthermore, as the capital of Georgia, Atlanta became the fastest developing U.S. metropolitan city in the 1990s. Even though the state governors had all been white, blacks controlled the city council, the state and city police, as well as most of the important businesses. In fact, when I taught there, the governor lived in Marietta and came to work daily in downtown Atlanta. Nowadays, average black Atlantans enjoy a better life than do blacks living in other U.S. cities. Hence, northern blacks continuously migrate from their cities down south to Atlanta.

However, I also saw what I considered unwholesome effects of capitalism as prosperous black parents neglected to instill in their children studying at the CAU campus a sense of shared responsibility for their poorer relations. While some well-off parents showered their children with expensive gifts, poor parents struggled every day to pay their children's tuition and fees. Richer parents bought their sons and daughters expensive cars, which became a distraction on campus for everybody when students equipped their fancy cars with boomboxes, blasting loud music across the quad without a sense of consideration for others who might be trying to study.

One day, I invited a young student who had formed a habit of playing loud music from his BMW as he drove around the classroom areas to my office.

"Why are you always playing your music so loudly?" I asked.

"Chill man!" he said, smiling. "Don't you know the meaning of BMW?"

"No, man, I don't! Explain it to me?"

"It means 'Be my woman.' So someone has to play the music loud to attract the most beautiful chicks around the campus."

"I'd think that loud music would chase the chicks away?"

"Oh, man! As an English professor, you don't know what I mean by chicks?"

"No, I don't, man!"

"Well, by 'chicks,' I mean pretty young women who are attracted to beautiful cars and the type of music I play. That is how to get them."

"Is that so? How come they haven't helped you earn good grades in all your courses?"

The question surprised him. He lowered his face in shame.

After our little *tête-à-tête*, I explained to him how distracting what he was doing was to him and other students. I also stressed how important it was for a student to spend more time on his studies to earn good grades than to waste it on chasing women who would definitely leave him for other men who worked hard and passed their courses with good grades. He seemed to have appreciated the advice, for he came back several other times during my office hours. He also told his rich father about me when his grades improved. Later, his father paid me a visit.

During our conversation, I jokingly asked, "Sir, since you bought your son a brand-new BMW car while he is still in college, will you buy him a jet plane when he graduates?"

He was surprised by the question. "Gee, I never thought about it."

"The next time you talk with your son, ask him to tell you the meaning of BMW." We laughed and hugged before he left.

I also discovered that there were two categories of students at CAU: first-generation college students and their families, and students who were sons and daughters of alumni. While the first category worked hard to pass their courses and make their families proud, the second worked hard as well, but their primary motivation was to graduate from college to maintain their family educational tradition. While both categories of students strived to achieve their peculiar desires, their professors had to work under enormous pressure to help them achieve success according to their parents and guardians' expectations, even when such students were not up to it. While the achievement of such desires was understandable, I personally did not appreciate the subliminal message given to professors they must give all students A's and high B's in their courses (unless they earned them) just to have good applications for admissions into Ivy League universities.

I did not become aware of this issue until after I graded and returned my first semester final exams to the students. Some of them complained that I was a hard grader. I told them I did not give away grades; instead, students had to earn the grades I awarded to them.

Later, I gave the same explanation to everybody in class. Furthermore, I paid particular attention to the grading criteria I set out in my course syllabi. Still, many of them were not satisfied. They asked why the professors who had served long in the university gave them A's and high B's in their courses, and I gave them grades, below B's in my own courses, which were similar to those they took with other professors. To make matters worse, those students who had expressed dissatisfaction with my grading standard began attending my classes late and disrupting the discussions. I eventually had to lock them out of my classrooms after giving them numerous warnings.

They continued to protest, however, until, finally, I had to meet with my department chair. After interviewing me, she concluded that I was right to insist that students meet my standards. She informed me, however, that the students were not so much disappointed in me for giving them low grades in my courses, but were scared of what their parents' reaction to the grades would be. Up to this point, I did not know that the students had been discussing me with the other professors. I decided to ask the students who were struggling in my courses to attend mandatory conferences in my office for one-on-one discussions of their work. The office conferences eventually helped them improve their performance and grades in my courses.

The Atlanta University Center Library housed rich holdings on black literature and cultural studies that I frequently used in my research. When the editor of *CLAJ* returned the article I submitted for publication with suggested corrections, I made the corrections in short time because of the rich availability of such materials. The article, "Protest and the Individual Talents of Three Black Novelists" was eventually published in Vol. 35, #2 (December 1991), 159-184. The editor featured it as one of the three leading articles on the cover page of the journal. In addition, I revised my first book, *Folkways in Chinua Achebe's Novels*, and submitted it to Africa World Press in Princeton, New Jersey, where it was published as *Gods, Oracles and Divination: Folkways in Chinua Achebe's Novels* in spring 1992. They reviewed the book in *Clark Atlanta Magazine: For Alumni and Friends of the University*, Vol. 2, No. 3 (Spring/Summer 1992): 27. The public presentation of the book attracted reporters and the media, and, along with my other writings, led to a citation in *Who's Who in the South and Southwest, 23rd Edition-Classic* (1993), *Black Writers, 2nd Edition* (1993), and *A Dictionary of International Biography, 23rd Edition* (1993).

Furthermore, in consideration of my scholarly activities, the English faculty elected me to serve on several departmental committees, including Writers Workshops Committee, English Graduate Studies Committee, and Scheduling/Evaluation Committee. More importantly, they elected me to serve as Project Director of the English Faculty NEH-Sponsored Summer 1992 Workshop. I worked diligently on these committees to ensure that my application for a tenure-track position in the department would encourage the university to hire me.

Dr. Liddell was very helpful to me in many ways, both on and off campus. As soon as I had received confirmation of my position at CAU, I had sent Clara and our children invitation letters to visit me during summer. They were all excited, but when they applied for visas at the U.S. Embassy in Lagos, the consular officials refused them. I appealed the decision and the consular officials invited them for another interview. Again, they denied my family member their visas. Apparently, I had overstayed my visa, and they reasoned that if my family was granted visas, they, too, might not come back, since I was financially capable of maintaining them in the U.S.

When I told Dr. Liddell about the problem, she advised me to go to our Congressional District representative, Representative John Lewis, for help on the matter. His office wrote the U.S. Embassy in Lagos, and they invited my family for a third interview. The officer who interviewed them told my wife that he would grant them the visas to avoid fighting with a powerful Congressman like John Lewis. Early in January 1991, my family joined me in Atlanta.

Dr. Liddell also came to my rescue by helping me to find a job for Clara once she arrived in the States. In her office, I had approached her to discuss my family's arrival.

"Hello, Janice, I wanted to thank you for suggesting that I contact Congressman Lewis about my family's visas. His office wrote a letter to the Embassy and they granted all my family members visas to travel and join me here in Atlanta. My worry now is whether Clara was going to find a job when they arrive."

"Does she have a college degree?"

"Oh, yes. She has a B.A. in English and M.Sc. in Library and Information Science. And she has been teaching as Assistant Professor of Library Studies at Imo State University."

"Wow! If you have a copy of her CV, let me have it so I can talk to people who could give her a job in the library."

"Thank you very much, Janice. I don't know what I would do without you. I'll give you the CV tomorrow."

After I gave her the CV, Dr. Liddell persuaded the library authorities to interview Clara for a job after she arrived. Once Clara joined me, the librarians interviewed her and ratified the position they reserved for her, following Dr. Liddell's appeal. Clara was able to begin work immediately. In addition, Dr. Liddell advised us to send Ikenna and Ndubuisi to Benjamin E. Mays High School, which laid a strong foundation for all their future education in the U.S., and she helped me find good elementary schools for our younger children.

Toward the end of my first year of service at CAU, Dr. Liddell made a strong case in support of my application for a regular appointment in the department before she went on sabbatical leave to Jamaica. While the administration was willing to renew my appointment as visiting Associate Professor for another year, they told me that they did not have money to fund a tenure-track position for me. The truth of the matter, however, was that the acting chair of the department, Dr. Ernestine Pickens, did not push for my regular appointment as Liddell had. From the beginning of my service in the department, I had noticed that Dr. Pickens did not like me very much. Whether it was because she was a high-yellow black who felt superior to other darker skinned blacks like me (a form of intra-racism) or because she feared that if I were hired at the rank of associate professor I could become a full professor before her, I decided to avoid the almost certain disappointment and apply to other universities.

One of the universities to which I applied for jobs was Southern Connecticut State University in New Haven, Connecticut for the position of Associate Professor of Black Literature. After reviewing my application file, the Department Personnel Committee (DPC) called me for a preliminary interview on the phone in November 1991. Then they invited me for a face-to-face interview at the December 1991 Annual Convention of the MLA in San Francisco. Following that interview, the committee invited me and six other candidates for a campus visit and final interview on February 12, 1992. I flew to New Haven on February 11, 1992 through Tweed Airport. Upon my arrival, two DPC members were there waiting to take me to the university.

"Hello, my name is Charles Fort, and this is Tony Rosso. We're your escort team to get you to campus for your interview tomorrow."

"Hello, Charles. Hello, Tony." I shook their hands. "I'm Kalu Ogbaa. Thanks for coming to pick me up. Sorry that I've arrived late. I hope you've not waited too long for me."

"No, not at all! We came here just a short while ago. Did you have a nice flight from Atlanta?" Tony asked.

"Don't ask. The flight in that small plane was rough and scary through the windy and snowy weather. I've never flown in a small plane like that before. After the interview, I plan to fly back to Atlanta through LaGuardia Airport in New York aboard a bigger plane."

"I'm sorry, I suggested that you fly that route because I felt it would be shorter and cheaper," Charles said apologetically.

"No, no, Charles! No need for you to apologize; you meant well. As you suggested, the route was cheaper and shorter. If anything, the airlines should be the one to blame for not giving us a bigger plane in which to fly."

After our initial exchange of pleasantries, Tony and Charles took me to their campus. I was so preoccupied with how well I would perform at the interviews and the meetings the professors for the first time that I rode in silence most of the ride to the hotel. However, I enjoyed Tony's views on race relations in New Haven, in the university, and in the country. And although I agreed with his condemnation of white police officers' profiling and brutalization of blacks, I was reluctant to let my guard down without first verifying his sincerity. Because of my past racial experiences in America, I was generally skeptical about trusting what any white man said about black-white relations unless and until I had known them well enough. Nevertheless, from the conversation, I had a hunch that Tony was a trustworthy man, one who could serve as a good case study in the subject, since he seemed to know so much about it.

When we arrived in the university, Charles and Tony took me to a guesthouse in its North Campus where I stayed until the next morning, when I began attending a number of interview sessions. I taught a class on Richard Wright's novel, *The Outsider*, to a graduate class followed by interviews with the DPC, the Dean of the School of Arts and Sciences, the Vice President for Academic Affairs, the President, and the Black Student Union.

Black students wanted to know what I would do to promote Black academic and cultural studies on campus if the university hired me. I shared with them my experiences in those areas in my previous universities, especially at Ohio State University and Clark Atlanta University, which I vowed to replicate at Southern. I assured them that if hired as a specialist in Black literature and cultural studies in the English Department, I would work with my colleagues and the university administration to promote the interests of all minority and international students on campus.

During my interview with the Vice President, I wanted to know if they could hire me at the full professor's rank because of my long experience—seven years at the rank of an associate professor—but he said they couldn't do that because the position was not funded at that rank. Instead, he would recommend that the president and the Board of Trustees place me on step III of professors' salary scale, which would also give me a three-year credit toward tenure. Then he advised me to ask the dean of our school to let me know what my salary would be. Tony then took me to the dean. In addition to relating my salary, the dean said that beginning in the 1992 fall semester, the university was going to raise all faculty members' salaries, which would also raise the salary they offered me during the interview.

Moreover, Vice President Anthony Pinciaro gave me two incentives to accept the job offer when the BOT approved it: a temporary job in the library for Clara until her union allowed her to apply for a tenure-track position, and an advance copy of my appointment letter before the BOT approved his recommendations. He stressed that he had never given such a letter to any candidate in the past before the university authorities' approval, but he promised to do it for me with the consent of the president. I requested the letter so I could use it for Green card applications for my family, and he agreed. Little did he know that at the time, I was so desperate for the tenure-track position almost any salary offer would have sufficed.

I received a faxed copy of the letter four days after the interview and used it to file for the Green cards. Thereafter, my family and I received the cards and became U.S. permanent residents shortly after I began working at the university.

During my two-day visit of the campus, Tony accompanied me to the interview venues, the university dining hall, and the Rotunda of the old Engleman Hall, which I immediately branded the university's "Scholars Hall of Fame," containing, as it does the names of the annual Faculty Scholar Award recipients. In addition, he showed me a trophy case in the hallway of the English Department that contained the published books and major articles by members of the English faculty, including Tony and Charles. I was so highly impressed by the display of the published works in both places that I vowed to work hard and have my own name and publications displayed as well. Overall, I knew that Southern Connecticut would be a good environment for me to carry out my future research and writing. Considering everything I experienced during the interview, I left the university campus with a great feeling of optimism.

As soon as I arrived home in Atlanta, Clara hurriedly fixed dinner.

"How did the interview go?"

"Very well," I said. "But I need to take a shower before eating the dinner."

After my shower, I sat for the dinner.

"So," Clara began. "Did they tell you the result of the interview before you left the university, or will they send it to you by mail?"

"Yes, the Vice President told me at the end of the interview that they will hire me, and that he will forward that recommendation to the president and the Board of Trustees for their ratification before writing me an official letter of appointment."

"And when will that be?"

"As soon as possible. Don't worry. The offer they made is a done deal."

Clara smiled, excited. "How do you know that for sure?"

"Because the Vice President promised to fax me a copy of the appointment letter in four days. I told him that I needed the letter as soon as possible so I can file for our permanent residency."

Clara jumped up and hugged me. "Oh, I'm glad that you will soon get the job."

"I, too, am glad that all of us will soon become permanent residents alongside Ndubuisi and Emeka who are citizens. I believe the Vice President agreed to fax me a copy of the letter because he did not want to lose me to another university."

"Wow. I can't wait for us to leave Atlanta to take up permanent jobs in New Haven!"

"Oh, that is not the end of the good news. They will give you a temporary job immediately in the library, and the salary they offered me is a lot higher than what I'm being paid here in Atlanta. Besides, they gave me Step III of associate professors' salary and a three-year credit toward tenure, which means we'll not be going back to Nigeria at the end of this academic year."

"Oh, UK. We have to give special thanks to God for His mercies and blessings to us."

"Yes, we will, as soon as I can arrange it with the elders of our church. In the meantime, we'll conduct a midnight thanksgiving service here at home for His manifold blessings unto us."

I asked Clara not to share the news of my employment in New Haven with anyone yet so that the English Department would assign me a summer teaching load. I continued to do my job quietly, eventually telling the acting chair, Dr. Ernestine Pickens, in July that I was leaving the university to take up a tenure-track position at Southern Connecticut State University in the fall semester. Instead of regretting the university's failure to give me the tenure-track position, she was happy that I had found a job elsewhere. I thanked her and my colleagues in the department, as well as the university administration for allowing me to work there for two years. In addition, I wrote a letter to express my heart-felt gratitude to Dr. Janice Liddell, who made my employment at CAU possible, and followed it up with a phone call during the fall semester. And though I did not receive any severance pay, due to my temporary employment status, Clara did since she worked on a regular job appointment for the library. On August 15, 1992, we left Atlanta with our children for New Haven, Connecticut. I knew that Father was smiling down on me from heaven, and finally started to feel that all the tools, talents and traits that I had toiled and labored to develop such that my life would be worth the faith he had placed in me were finally coming to fruition. I was beginning to sit *with* my father around that circle of great wrestlers, holding my head high and proud just as he had.

Chapter 13

From Permanent Residency to Citizenship

Before moving to New Haven on August 15, 1992, I contacted Cyprian Ukah, a fellow Igbo man living in New Haven, by phone about renting a house for our family. After we arrived, Cyprian took us to the house, an old brick-walled colonial surrounded by other houses with vinyl walls, located on the northern end of Ella Grasso Boulevard. I sent Clara and the kids to lunch at a nearby Burger King and suggested they visit the schools where Ikenna and Ndubuisi, and the younger children would attend. I stayed behind with the driver to offload the truck and begin arranging the house.

"Who will show us the schools?" Clara was anxious after the long, difficult flight from Atlanta.

"Mr. Cyprian, the man who rented the house for us." I motioned to Cyprian, who smiled and nodded.

"Yes, I'll take the kids to see the schools. First we'll eat lunch." Cyprian guided them into the car.

"Thanks, Cyprian. And be careful with the kids. This is a new city for all of us."

When they returned, Clara immediately expressed her deep concern about the appearance of the schools. Graffiti and racial slurs covered the brick walls of Hillhouse High School.

"What kinds of children live here, UK?"

"I promise I'll find a better school for Ikenna and Ndubuisi. Please. Don't worry."

But she insisted that we go back to Atlanta where the children attended better schools. Cyprian also informed us that the only way to move to a different school would be to move from New Haven to Hamden, where the children could attend Hamden High School. I reminded Clara of the old saying that the hood does not make the monk. If it turned out that their teachers did not teach them well in school, then both of us would have to reteach them at home in addition to helping them with their take home assignments. I reminded her that going back to Atlanta was not an option. We had to adjust to life in the new city.

The steady stream of college students transiting through town made it clear that New Haven was an important university town. College buses were busy conveying students to and from the campuses of Yale University, Southern Connecticut State University, University of New Haven, Albertus Magnus College, and Gateway Community College. Since our house was only a five-minute walk to Southern, we felt as if we were living in the middle of the university campus. Students lived in apartments and houses all around us, giving me an opportunity to inspire my children to study hard so that they might themselves find their future at one of the area universities. In addition, Clara and I took them regularly to the Buley Library at Southern, especially during the weekends. Ikenna, the oldest, then in eleventh grade, immediately began to dream of attending college at Yale. Indeed, each child developed their own individual aspirations depending on their interests. As proof of their scholarly desires, they all made A's their first school year in New Haven.

Before classes began, I went to our department and introduced myself to the new chairperson.

"Hello, my name is Kalu Ogbaa."

"Hi Kalu. I'm Bill Gustafson. Please, sit down. We've been expecting you." He motioned to a chair in front of his desk.

"I know. I had to finish my summer teaching at Clark Atlanta University before moving up here four days ago. Since then, my wife and I have been unpacking, arranging the house, and registering our children in school."

"That's fine, Kalu. We're happy to have you here. What was the weather like in Atlanta?"

"Oh, very hot and humid, which is usual during this time of the year."

"If so you'll like it here. Our weather is usually milder than that."

"But I heard it is usually very cold over here."

"Not all the time as you can see now. Our weather gets very cold—sometimes chilly—only during the winter. Even at that, it gets that way in the northern parts of the state like Hartford."

Bill said I'd been assigned a four-course teaching load: two courses at the freshman level and two at the sophomore level, and asked that

I develop courses at the upper-level and graduate levels for approval by the University Undergraduate and Graduate Curriculum Forums. After assigning me an office, mailbox, and copies of the Undergraduate and Graduate Catalogues, he walked me to the University Police Station to pick up a parking decal, and toured the classroom blocs where I would teach my courses. When we finished the tour, I thanked him and headed home to begin preparing course materials.

The following week, I met Tony in his office before my first class to let him know that I was ready to start teaching.

"Hello Tony. How are you this morning?"

"Hi Kalu. When did you get in?"

"Oh. We arrived seven or eight days ago. I would have called you, but I didn't have your phone number."

"Well, I'm glad you accepted the job. Welcome to Southern."

"Thank you for all your help when I came for the interview. I hope you will continue to guide me until I get on my feet."

"You're welcome, Kalu. I'm glad I could offer some help to you."

Tony caught me up on the burning campus issues of the day and stressed the importance of applying for service on major department and university committees. His readiness to assist me, even though he did not know me well, helped to build my trust in him. He also informed me that Governor Lowell P. Weiker had recently directed the presidents of the four-campus state university system to include multicultural studies in their curricular offerings, necessitating the hiring of faculty members like me. By the time I had arrived, the battle for the inclusion of Human Diversity courses in the university's curricular offerings had been already raging in the faculty senate for months.

Tony, already knowing my passion for racial equality, took me early in the semester to the first Senate open forum where I made an impassioned presentation in favor of the implementation of the proposed campus-wide Human Diversity program. I asked everyone to look out the windows at the various colors in nature. Now, I told them, look at everyone around you. They're all dressed in multicolored clothes. If both nature and people enjoy such a wide variety of color, I continued, how much better would it be for our faculty to reflect such a variety of colors in the courses?

Despite months of unnecessary acrimonious debates on the issue, however, proponents of the proposal lost. The senate decided to leave such decisions up to individual departments to define and adopt whatever they considered appropriate human diversity courses to them.

The English Department had to make few changes. Even prior to my arrival, Professor Kenneth Florey was already teaching several courses in African American Literature. He hewed the wood that I came to carve, as it were. He and I collaboratively worked to develop several new courses in Black Literature concentration, which I added to the current course offerings in African Literature to fill out our new seminars in English and World Literature.

Over time, the university curriculum forums approved all the courses I developed at both the graduate and undergraduate levels. The courses serve to this day as important fulfillment of the multicultural studies that Governor Weiker envisioned to help promote a level of understanding among various ethnic and racial groups in the state and, perhaps, in the country. Over the years, the department personnel committee (DPC) has recruited three additional professors and several adjuncts to teach Africana literary and cultural studies in our English Department. Only two incidents occurred which slightly marred my first months at the university.

First, when I asked the English Department secretary to show me how to operate a new copier machine in our general office, she told me she could not help me because it was not part of her official duty. Then, when I asked if she would copy the teaching material for me, she again refused to assist me. I thanked her, believing my experience was the normal procedure, and left to look for someone who could help me copy the material. But when I returned, another professor was teaching a graduate student how to operate the machine. I said aloud, to one in particular, how disappointed I was that the professor could teach a graduate student how to operate the machine but I could find no one to help me, even though I was new to the department.

At this point, the secretary shouted: "Leave my office."

"No, Madam, I'm not leaving," I said. "This is a general office, which belongs to the staff and professors of the department. As you can see, my mailbox and the copy machine are both here. I would not have come to this office if they were not installed here for our common use."

"If you don't leave the office now," she continued. "I'll report you to Mrs. O'Connor, the president of our staff union. You cannot come here to harass me in my workplace."

"Make your report to whomever you like. I'm not leaving the office until I've made copies of my teaching material. That is why the machine was installed here."

Here, I was wrestling with distinct cultural differences between America and Nigeria. In Nigeria, a secretary would have been glad to copy the teaching material for me or any other professor. In addition, in my home country, it would have been unheard of that a secretary would dare order a professor out of a departmental office as this secretary did.

I was further baffled that the professor, not the secretary, reported the incident to the union president. She claimed that, as the director of Women's Studies program at Southern, she worked for the interest of all women on campus. After receiving the complaint, Mrs. O'Connor, the president of her union, quickly forwarded it to the Vice President for Academic Affairs, Dr. Anthony Pinciaro for review.

Tony volunteered to attend the trial with me as a representative of my union, Association of American University Professors (AAUP). The meeting included Dr. Pinciaro, our department chair, the dean, Mrs. O'Connor, and various other witnesses. After hearing the testimony from both sides, Dr. Pinciaro dismissed the harassment charges. But he admonished me, saying I should have left the office when the secretary asked since it was her primary workplace. He also advised that I avoid any future arguments with the secretary.

After hearing the judgment on the case, and noting the total absence of blacks among the witnesses, I recalled the similar treatment Nigerians had given to my Igbo people back home—the same kind of treatment that had driven me into self-exile here in America. Thank God, I thought, the decision was not worse. Emotionally, however, the incident reminded me of other various forms of segregation and deprivation based on my race and national origin I'd experienced at American universities. But since I was determined to settle in the U.S. as a latter-day immigrant to afford my family a better life, I decided to adjust and, to this day, bear up under many American cultural mores that are alien to me.

Thereafter, I avoided the general department office unless accompanied by a faculty member. Fortunately, I soon met two friendly secretaries whose department offices were adjacent to ours. Mrs. Virlinda Billups in the Psychology Department, and Mrs. Kathy Yalof in Grants Office at Engleman shared a fax and copier they allowed me to use whenever I needed. Since that year, I have developed close friendships with both women, especially Kathy who was reassigned to the Office of the Provost and Vice President for Academic Affairs, and became my point woman there. My many friendships with her and many other women on campus gives the lie to the assertion that I disliked or disrespected female employees, as that unfortunate incident seemed to portray.

As if emboldened by the outcome of the case, however, the department secretary continued her negative attitude toward other people in the department, which eventually led to her reassignment in the Chemistry Department three months after the incident. I later learned of her release from service in the university and quietly wondered what the professor now thought of encouraging the secretary—perhaps unknowingly—to treat people like me with disrespect and insensitivity.

The second incident involved salary negotiations. When I received my first paycheck, I discovered that the Payroll Office had based the payment on Step III of the old associate professors' salary rate and not on the new rate. I decided to meet with the dean to discuss the matter.

"Good morning, Dean Smith."

"Good morning, Kalu. How can I help you?"

"I've just received my first paycheck and discovered that my pay was based on the old salary scale. I was wondering if you inadvertently forgot to remind Payroll to pay me according to the new salary rate now that it has been implemented for everybody."

"I believe, Kalu, they must have paid you what we agreed when you negotiated your salary with me. I trust that they paid you exactly what was written in your appointment letter."

"The point, sir, is that what you and I agreed on in the presence of Tony Rosso was not reflected in that letter."

"And what was that, Kalu?"

"That when the new salary, which was awaiting the government's approval at the time I attended the interview, was implemented, my salary would be adjusted and paid accordingly."

"I'm sorry, Kalu. I don't recall the conversation. So I cannot write Payroll to adjust your salary at this point."

"Thank you, sir. I'll talk to Tony to see if he remembers the conversation, for he was present when the conversation took place in your office."

"Let me know what Tony says about the incident, Kalu."

I thanked him and met with Tony later that day to discuss my meeting with the dean. Tony said he would be happy to tell the dean he was a witness to the negotiation that included the adjusted pay rate. He then called the University System Central Office to seek clarification about the new salary rates and their effects on new hires in the 1992 fall semester. The Central Office verified my position. Once Tony presented the facts to the dean, he reversed himself and asked Payroll to pay me according to the new salary rate.

The role Tony played in resolving both incidents, and the help he gave me during my initial interview showed him to be a friendly colleague and reliable ally. I often sought his wise counsel before carrying out my plans at the university. I soon realized the root of my alliance with Tony came from a wrestling lesson I had learned from fighting Ogbonnaya Obi, the left-handed wrestler who I later befriended and teamed up with to fight and defeat our enemies. As with my one-time left-handed enemy, white people had also been my enemy (because of my experiences with the brutality of Great Britain and the USSR in support of Nigerians who fought against the Igbo people (Biafrans) during our civil war). After meeting and interacting with Tony, however, I transformed that internalized anger and hate into ever-abiding love and respect for him and, coincidentally, others. As a result, in my course on African American Literature, I much enjoyed teaching Maya Angelou's poem, "Touched by An Angel":

> We, unaccustomed to courage
> exiles from delight
> live coiled in shells of loneliness
> until love leaves its high holy temple
> and comes into our sight
> to liberate us into life
>
> Love arrives
> and in its train come ecstasies
> old memories and pleasure
> ancient histories of pain.
> Yet if we are bold,
> love strikes away the chains of fear
> from our souls.

We are weaned from our timidity
In the flush of love's light
we dare be brave
And suddenly we see
that love costs all we are
and will ever be.
Yet it is only love
which sets us free.

Letting go of the general postwar anger and animosity I harbored against white people, which my interaction with a man like Tony made possible, liberated me from self-imposed segregation.

Before the liberation really took hold in me, however, a professor from another department at a welcome party for new faculty members asked to which department I belonged.

"English," I said.

"I heard that some professors in your department quarrel among themselves so much that one or two of them have suffered heart attacks and had to undergo open heart surgery. Are you sure you'll survive in that environment?" He chuckled.

"Thanks for giving me that information. I'm sure there are good professors still teaching in the department in spite of their raging *civil war*. I experienced a bloody war in Biafra and survived it. So I don't think the conditions in the English Department are such that I could not survive any troubles that might come my way."

The man grimaced, sipped his coffee, and moved away to another spot in the party. He must have thought he was doing me a favor forewarning me about the dangers of working in a department of unfriendly colleagues. But I have never been intimidated by the actions of bullies—and I wasn't going to start then. However, the incident did pique my curiosity. So I asked Tony and Charles enlighten me as to whom I might avoid or trust among our colleagues. After our conversation, I thanked them for their candor, and recalled an Igbo proverb about a cautious duck.

Once upon a time, the duck came to a strange land where he stood on one leg, with the other one up, and surveyed the area. He stayed in this position, ready for quick flight, until he was satisfied that the area was safe. Then he lowered the second leg and stood firmly on the ground. For a long time after coming to America, I had also stood on one leg, maintaining the duck's cautious attitude to protect myself while I dealt with the social and cultural challenges I met in this new land. And even after I came to Southern, I only slowly learned to trust people, and only then after I had verified the motives of those around me.

During the first few faculty meetings I attended in our department, I witnessed the bickering between professors, the divergent ideological and philosophical divide between them as they argued like Democrats and Republicans in the U.S. Congress. I maintained a position of impartial observer, conscious that each expected me to join their side. My first impulse was to join Tony's camp. But I maintained my neutrality for about three months, sitting on the fence as it were, until I found myself agreeing with Tony on almost every issue under discussion, both within and outside the department. He was, and still is, an honorable man whose ideas and wisdom many people acknowledge openly. Soon we were attending meetings together everywhere on campus, which resulted in helping me to understand university politics and policies within a short time.

I worked hard enough during my first year at Southern, in the areas of teaching, scholarship, and service, that my application for renewal received high commendations from the administrators. In addition, the good reviews that stemmed from the strong cultural critique contained in my first U.S. book publication, *Gods, Oracles, and Divination: Folkways in Chinua Achebe's Novels*, attracted the attention of many editors and publishers who invited me to write several books and articles on African sociocultural issues for their presses. I took up the challenge and published a few things for them, which brought me some accolades and visibility in our university.

Unfortunately, however, while things were going well for me professionally, my home life was falling apart. My seventeen-year marriage to Clara hung precariously in the balance. We both had become unhappy, despite my professional successes, and I sensed that another metaphoric wrestling match of life was lurking in the corner like a bookie threatening a fighter into a match-fix—no way to win.

Clara filed for a one-year separation in April 1993, and kicked me out of our home. After paying our rent and utility bills in the house she and the children were staying, and our additional car payments, I had no money left to buy food for myself, let alone rent an apartment. I ended up sleeping in my car after working late every day. I managed to buy bagels for lunch with change I found in my car and office. I brushed my teeth, "dry cleaned" my body in a men's room adjacent to my office and prayed God help me get out of the problem soon.

One day, I met a man during one of the president's dialog sessions I believed from his looks to be Igbo and decided to ask him for help.

"Hello, I'm Kalu Ogbaa, from the English Department. Are you a fellow Igbo man?"

"Yes, I am. My name is Obiora. How are you, sir?"

"Well, I'm alright."

"But you don't sound alright to me." He eyed me, questioning.

"Yes, you're right. I'm not alright. I have a problem."

"What's wrong, if I may ask?"

"If you have a minute, let's go to my office where I can tell you all about it."

"Please, let's go at once, and let me see if I can be of any help to you."

We sat down, and I briefly told Obiora about my situation, adding that I needed a place to stay for a few days after each day's work until I received my next paycheck to rent a place off-campus. I was so desperate, I was not ashamed to ask the favor from a fellow Igboman, even though I'd only known him briefly. I relied on our ethnic Igbo apothegm that had always worked for us in times of war and peace: "*Onye aghala nwanne ya* (Never neglect a brother or sister in trouble)."

Although Obiora was in a tenuous position since he was the director of a student residential hall in which he also lived and allowing me to take refuge in his rooms, even for a short while, was illegal, as a true Igbo man he decided to help me in spite of the potential risk of losing his job. Nevertheless, he took me in on the condition that I come very late at night and leave early in the morning each day. I agreed.

In the end, it worked out well. I was able to take showers and eat one square meal every day. I was lucky and grateful that Obiora accommodated me when I desperately needed someone to help me endure the pain of the loss of my beloved wife and my own home.

At the time, I debated going back to my job in Nigeria while the authorities there would allow me to continue my position and thereby avoid suffering the humiliation of being divorced. But I decided against it, not wanting people to see me as a deserter. Instead, I'd stay on to protect and educate our children, which is what I'd desired to accomplish before bringing them to America.

"How can you do that when the children have all been taken away from you?" I said to myself.

"Surely you can. Are they not living in the same city as you?"

"But they are not living under your roof where you can control them as you used to."

"It doesn't matter. They'll always enjoy your company whenever and wherever you visit them, however short the time you spend with them might be," I argued.

"What makes you think that your soon-to-be ex-wife will allow them to get close to you as they used to?"

"You shouldn't fear to visit with them wherever you may be. Your love will overcome any animus their mother may have against you."

No. I'd rather not go back to Nigeria. I'd stay here in the U.S. and fight for reconciliation with Clara and the children. If that failed, then I'd fight at least for the children's education and protection wherever I'd be, which was the main reason for my second coming to America. Copping out without a fight would be cowardly. Besides, how would I explain to my people in Nigeria that I, Kalu Ogbaa *nwa* Ikpo the great wrestling champion, was forced to abandon his children in the U.S. and return home without them? *Tufiaa kwa!* Surely, that would be the height of cowardice and disgrace. I'd not allow it to happen. As far as I was concerned, the situation was another wrestling match I was determined to take on boldly. However, I'd first make sure that I anchored my professional life and practice on a solid ground at Southern.

I redoubled my effort to get into and work on as many department and university-wide committees as I could manage while still working toward promotion and tenure. Both areas of concentration helped me dwell less on my failing marriage, which weighed heavier on me than anything I'd known before. In addition, I became closer to my students, seeing them as an extended family. But during the weekends, the shadow of my failing home life descended upon me like a dark pall. I was especially sad and miserable on Fridays when friends, students, and colleagues asked me what I planned to do during the weekends and I found myself coming up with imaginary parties and activities that I dreamed of attending with my family. Then I'd hide in my office and read, weep, and pray. I found some measure of peace, comfort, and spiritual sustenance reading religious and inspirational books.

My one great day was Sundays when I could see the children. But after a few weeks of taking our kids to worship in United Church of

Christ on the Green in New Haven, Clara suddenly decided to attend the same church, but not in our company. I wondered if she purposely intended her presence in the church to create a conflict of interest for me, for she had a restraining order that banned me from being a hundred yards near her. I could not worship in any church she attended no matter what her intentions were.

Hence, the next Sunday, I took the children to Saint Luke's Episcopal Church, also in New Haven, where Ukah once took me. Three weeks after I made the change, Clara refused to let me take them, despite my legal right to keep the children from Friday afternoons through Sunday evenings. When I dropped by to pick them up, she was ushering them across the driveway, saying, "*Ngwa, baa nu na moto*, Get into the car now!"

Ndubuisi hesitated, but the other children hopped in as soon as their mom issued the order. I was left to attend church alone. After three consecutive Sundays of this routine, I decided to stop trying to pick them to avoid fighting with her over the issue. Although the heartache that followed each disappointing episode was almost unbearable, it was also a terrible mistake since Clara used it against me each time she talked to the children about their *uncaring* dad. Soon, some began believing that I didn't care about them.

I didn't press the issue because I feared fighting her would make her angry and jeopardize any chance of our reconciliation. Besides, I assumed that she simply missed the children just as I did when I went without them. To further complicate the issue, the children feared that she would scold and deny them privileges at home if they disobeyed her—a fear that trumped my visitation right.

Therefore, I approached my colleagues, my pastor, and friends for their help in resolving the matter amicably. In spite of numerous attempts to make peace, however, Clara failed to change her mind. Her attitude made me so angry that I could no longer relate closely with the children nor take care of them as much as I should have. The gap between Clara and me widened as I lost the children, and became a sad and angry man. I finally decided to seek the intervention of God over the situation, which was rapidly spiraling out of control.

Then, the third week of December, 1993, I traveled to Nigeria to collect research material for the book I was working on. But more importantly, the trip afforded me the opportunity to discuss my marital situation with members of my family, especially Mother. The story of my separation with Clara devastated her since both she and

Father had regarded and loved her, as they would have their own deceased daughter, Sister Mgbore. Mother encouraged me to do everything in my power to prevent the divorce from taking place. She even volunteered to come to the U.S. with me to try to dissuade Clara from going through with her plans, believing that Clara could not disregard her plea for peace and reconciliation. Unfortunately, I could not afford to take her back with me. But she sent Clara a strongly worded letter through me, imploring her to stop the divorce proceeding.

Then, early on the morning I was set to leave, Mother approached me.

"Nne. Shall we pray now? I'm ready to return to the U.S.," I said.

"We can pray. But I don't want you to leave." She held me to her bosom.

"Please, Nne, I have to drive to Owerri today and leave my car with Mr. Kamalu before I can fly out of the country tomorrow morning." I held her at arm's length.

"Please, don't go today, Kalu *nwam*. Stay with me for this one more day. Then you can go back to America tomorrow. Could you do that for me, please?"

"You are scaring me, Nne. Do you not want me to go back at all? What is wrong, Nne? Tell me." My eyes welled with tears.

"Yes, I want you to go back. It's just that I've been missing you every day since you left the country without me."

"Then I'll stay with you today. But I'll have to leave early in the morning for Owerri or else I'll miss my flight. I promise that when I get to the U.S., I'll work on getting you to America with me."

"Thank you so much." She kissed me and smiled as we walked back into the house.

The following morning before leaving, Mother held me tightly again, crying. "God be with you till we meet again."

"Nne, what do you mean by 'til we meet again'? Tell me, are you sick?"

"Oh, no. I'm not sick! I'm just praying that God should be with you until we meet again."

I left the village low in spirit. I knew that Mother had missed her baby child, *odu nwa*, all the years I was away. But I wondered, why she bid me farewell with the words of the song we usually sang in church before the interment of the dead? I prayed that God not let

Mother die in my absence just as Father did in 1989. Little did I know that death of another kind awaited me after my return to America.

One late wintry afternoon, while I was playing cards with my son Ndubuisi, I heard three loud knocks on my apartment door.

"Who is it?" I asked.

"It's the court bailiff. Could you open the door, please? I have something for you to sign," the voice outside answered.

"Just a minute," I opened the door.

"Are you Kalu Ogbaa?"

"Yes, I am. What's wrong, officer?"

"There's nothing wrong, sir. I'm just serving your papers. Could you sign here for it, please?"

"Yes, of course." I took the package, signed the receipt, and returned it to him.

"Thanks. By the way, your wife wants you to return Ndubuisi to her immediately."

"Thanks. I'll do that."

As soon as he left, I sat down to open the package and Ndubuisi approached me. "What is it, Dad? And why does Mom want me home?"

"I don't know, son. Let me read the document to see what it is all about."

I opened the package, which contained the divorce papers and a court date, then showed them to Ndubuisi. The news devastated both of us. I never thought that Clara would file for divorce to consummate the separation she filed almost a year ago. I had hoped she filed for separation as a way of calling attention to our marital problems.

"What are you going to do, Dad? Are you going to allow Mom to divorce you?" Ndubuisi's voice quavered with passion.

"I don't want the divorce, but I don't know that I can talk your mom out of going through with it. It appears she has already made up her mind to divorce me after the separation date expires."

"Please, don't let her divorce you, Dad. I want all us to live together as we used to in Nigeria."

"As I said before, my son, I don't want the divorce. I promise you that I will do everything I can to stop it. But according to the way divorce is handled in America, which is quite different from how it is done in Nigeria, only your mom can stop it. If we were in Nigeria, I would be the one to file for divorce if I needed to and not the other way round. That means since I never wanted us to live apart from one another, I would never have sought divorce from her."

Ndubuisi asked again, "Why does Mom want you to take me home immediately?"

"I don't know, son. Maybe, as a custodial parent, she wants to begin immediately to exercise her rights over all of you. Nevertheless, I have to take you home now to avoid getting into any legal trouble from her. Maybe we'll get some answers to your questions from her."

After Ndubuisi heard all that I said, his attitude and mood changed immediately. Like me, he had hoped that before the legal separation date expired, his mom and I would reconcile our differences. On the contrary, however, the divorce papers she served on me seemed to indicate that she wanted divorce, which scared both of us.

As I drove him back to their house, Ndubuisi refused to speak or look at me, even when I tried to start a conversation with him as I normally did whenever we rode together on visitation days. When we arrived at their house, Clara refused to talk to me. I left her house sad and devastated. When I called the next day and asked for Ndubuisi, I was told that he was sick and could not talk to me. And we never again were able to talk as father and son again. He never fully recovered from the shock of the news of the divorce. I cannot relate the depths of his sorrow and pain in this memoir, but I'll continue to carry the sorrowful memory of it until I return to my Maker.

At the time of the divorce court proceedings, I still did not contest it, hoping that Clara would change her mind. She did not. The judge granted her the divorce at 2:02 pm on March 22, 1994. Until the divorce, I had never understood the full extent to which my behavior toward Clara had hurt her. In Nigeria, we'd had our fights and misunderstandings, like other married couples. But our parents, our friends, and our church had helped us to settle them amicably. Here in America, though, it was a different. One woman in particular, who had been divorced for eleven years before we met her, continually pried into our relationship and seemed not to be interested in creating harmony between me and Clara, but discord. It was almost as if she wanted to make Clara her disciple instead of being her true friend.

Another revelation was the way my children felt about me by the time of the divorce. During the one-year separation, our children did not live with me, which led them to feel liberated from my strict discipline. I never permitted them to be away from the house after 7:00 p.m. unless they were engaged in officially scheduled school activities. In that case, Clara or I would accompany them wherever they went. I played cards with them after dinner before we studied together at our dining table until it was time for them to go to bed.

Although the discipline produced good academic habit for all of us, little did I realize that the children felt socially choked because I was always with them in the house. They preferred to live as free as other children of their age did with their less strict parents. Their safety in a dangerous city like New Haven was a primary parental responsibility for me. Ironically, that responsibility put me in a dilemma that now reminds me of the Igbo cautionary proverbial saying that a man may worship Ogwugwu to perfection and yet be killed by Udo. Ogwugwu and Udo are both sea goddesses, whom a man must worship with equal devotion at all times. If he pays more attention to one and less to the other, he suffers the ire and punishment of the less-worshiped one. Yes, I, Kalu Ogbaa *nwa* Ikpo the great wrestler, succeeded in teaching my children to become great students. However, I woefully failed to see that the Igbo man's control of his children and wife that I learned from my father in Nigeria, which I transplanted to America, would bring my downfall. I learned the lesson too late for me to change. Indeed, the children were ostensibly happy that their mother divorced me.

Although the realization is belated, it has led me, as the head of the family, to accept total responsibility for my divorce, which brought about a loss of love and cohesion in my once proud and lovely family unit. I sincerely regret it, despite my great successes in other areas of my life.

Then, ten days after the divorce, I received the news I had dreaded to hear since returning from Nigeria during the second week of January 1994. I woke to the phone ringing at five in the morning.

"Hello. Who is calling this early?"

"Good morning, sir. This is your namesake, Kalu Alex in Savannah, Georgia."

"Good morning, Ogboo Kalu. Is everything okay? You've never called me this early before." I was apprehensive.

"I'm calling because of the news that Ogboo Kalu Ulu brought for you. He is here with me." Alex handed the phone over to Ogbonnaya Kalu Ulu.

"Good morning, sir. How are you?"
"Good morning, Ogboo Kalu. *O dikwa mma ee*, Is everything alright?"
"I'm sorry to say that all is not well."
"What's wrong? Tell me. Please, tell me. Is it Nne? Please, please tell me that it isn't Nne."
"Yes. It is your mother that died, sir. I'm sorry."
"Oh! God. Why? Why now?" I paused, absorbing the shock of the sad news.
"Are you there? Sir, are you still there? Tell me. Are you still on the line? Hello, hello, hello. Are you still there?"
"Yes, I'm here." I quietly sobbed.
"Take it easy, sir. I know the news is too painful to bear. But it is done. Please, bear it like the strong man we've always known you to be, and tell me what to tell your people at home."
"Thank you both for the news." I composed myself the best I could. "Were you told the cause of Nne's death?"
"I don't know everything. But your brother Ikpo said she complained of acute pains in the abdomen. They rushed her to the Christian Hospital (a small clinic) in our village for treatment. The doctor had operated on her without making adequate preparations or taking precautions before and after the surgery. Consequently, your mother bled to death."
Mother's painful death broke my heart. I asked Ulu to instruct Brother Ikpo not to rush her burial, to embalm and keep her until I returned to give her a befitting burial. I wired money to Brother Ikpo for pre-burial preparations and called Clara to tell her the sad news. She and Ikenna came to console me in my studio apartment.
Ikenna wept for Mother, and Clara volunteered to go with me to Nigeria for her burial. When they left, I began singing dirges, recalling Mother's words when last we visited: "God be with you till we meet again." Could it be that she foresaw her death but decided not to tell me about it because of the immeasurable love she had for me, her *odu nwa*? The answer to continues to elude me each time I think about the last days I had with Mother before she died.
Clara's company during Mother's burial in Nigeria gave me, and my kindred family, some hope that she might call off the divorce and allow us to remarry. If not for our sake, we should do it for the sake of our children. When we returned to the U.S., I made a more serious effort to pursue reconciliation. I invited Dr. Umachi Nnukwu

Umachi, my clansman who lived in Detroit, to make peace between us. Others joined in the efforts, including Professors Cyprian Ukah and John Nwangwu. Two years later, Uchenna Nwachuku, a professor of Counseling and School Psychology at Southern, joined them in their efforts. Each time we met, Clara would agree to our reconciliation, and then add that she must talk to the children about it first. But later, she would say the children did not want us to remarry. Nwachukwu told her that she shouldn't base her decision upon what the children wanted, because marriage was a parentocracy. If she made up her mind to remarry me, the children would go along. But it soon became obvious to everybody that she did not want to change.

So, after four years of separation, divorce, and failed reconciliation efforts, I gave up any further hope for a prospective remarriage. I often struggled over these years with the fear that my failed marriage was, at least at some level, plagued by the very same character flaws that had plagued my father's marriage to Mother. But all through the years, I had striven to place the family first and practice the kind of patience, compassion, and gentleness that I never received from Father. There is, however, something to be said about the difficulty of breaking the bonds of blood, and I suppose there were times when I let my guard down and allowed Father's habits and behaviors to influence my own actions and reactions as concerned familial relationships. Could I have done better? Perhaps. But, now, I had to move on and pray God if I were given the opportunity to begin again, I would learn from those mistakes and do better. I finally told Clara and the children that I was disappointed and sad that we could not reconcile, but I would accept their decision. I also decided it was time to date other women and try to mend my broken life.

Chapter 14

A Second Chance on Marriage

The thought of marrying and living with any other woman in the same city as the children while Clara was still alive was an awkward an unsettling idea for me. I was also uncomfortable contemplating seeing her with another man. But, surely, it wouldn't be possible to avoid the embarrassment of such a situation while we both worked at Southern. Then one day, it happened.

Clara's car was in the body shop, and she had asked me to bring my car to her house so she could drive it to work in Bridgeport. I arrived at her house at 7:30 a.m. and waited for almost an hour without seeing her. When she finally arrived, she was with a man. I stepped out of my car and waited as they approached.

"This is Kalu." She motioned to me. "Kalu, this is my friend, Clarence. He gave me a ride from a body shop."

Clarence and I shook hands as we said hello to each other. Then Clara walked inside her house with him and closed the door. I waited fifteen minutes for them to return. Then I walked to her front door and knocked several times. I heard the bolt on the door turn and lock, and then Clara drew the window shade aside.

"This is to let you know that it is all over."

Just like that; short and sweet. Then the shade closed, and I was left standing speechless, stunned.

Later that month, I attended a cultural meeting of the Association of Nigerians in Connecticut (ANC) where we were planning a celebration for Nigerian Independence Day that took place in October. It was not the first time I'd attended such a meeting, but the first time without Clara. As I exchanged greetings, members of the group who still didn't know about our divorce asked me about Clara and our children. Their reactions were understandably mixed. Some felt sorry for me and volunteered to help find me another woman to marry. Others encouraged me to continue trying to persuade Clara to remarry me because we were good for each other. But after having so long and sorrowfully trying to reconcile without success, I was ready and determined to find someone I might marry as soon as possible.

At the Independence Day celebration, I met two women whom I much admired. I exchanged phone numbers with each and began a correspondence with both. They each visited me separately from New York, but in the end, each of them was worried about my ability to support them while still paying child support for the six children from my previous marriage.

I perfectly understood, and therefore ventured to approach other women. But every one of them had the same worries. Prompted by these initial rejections, I turned to my pastor, Rev. Victor Rogers of Saint Luke's Episcopal Church, for his advice about two other members whom I didn't know well, but had admired from afar. He promised to get back to me with a recommendation after prayer and meditation on the matter. In the meantime, I approached a woman who lived in my apartment complex, also a member of the church, and asked if she would like to join me for a dance at a local nightclub.

"Good evening, Sister Yvette. How are you today?"

"Good evening, Kalu. So you know my apartment, huh?" She smiled.

"Yes. Of course I do."

"Have you been stalking me?" she joked.

"No," I said. "But what if I had been?"

She smiled again. "Please, come in and have a seat." She motioned to a chair next to the window. "Coffee or beer?" she asked.

"No, thank you. Just some cold water will do."

"Only water? You've got it." She returned briefly with the water and sat opposite to me on the couch.

"Thank you very much."

"For the water?" She waved her hand. "No problem. So, you don't drink beer at all?"

"No. Members of my church don't drink anything alcoholic."

"Oh. Which church is that? Saint Luke's Episcopal Church?"

"No, no! I mean my church in Nigeria."

"What kind of church is it?"

"A Pentecostal church, but I attend Saint Luke's now because we don't have a branch of the church in New Haven. But we have one in New York City, where I worship occasionally."

"Oh, how nice! What is the church's name?"

"The Eternal Sacred Order of Cherubim and Seraphim."

"Wonderful. Maybe you'll tell me more about it someday."

"Thanks. I'd be happy to tell you all about it whenever you like."

Yvette was already in a serious relationship, but she and I attended a West Indian nightclub twice with one of her girlfriends who showed some interest in me—but for whom I could never be serious. When Yvette introduced me as a Southern Connecticut State University professor, she thought I must be a scientist.

"Do you teach biology?"

"No," I said. "Why do you ask? Are you interested in studying biology?"

"Yes, I like biology." She laughed and added, "Especially the hairy type."

"Oh, I see." I was a bit irritated, and confused. "I teach English; the plain type."

She laughed, again, then slugged down a shot of whiskey and staggered back to her seat. I was not impressed.

Yvette and I continued to attend church together until she moved to Hamden. We continued our friendship even after I remarried and introduced her to my new wife and daughter with whom she developed a relationship, visiting with us occasionally both at home and at Saint Luke's Episcopal Church.

I finally decided to go back to Nigeria in hopes that I might meet someone with whom I might find a second life in marriage. I phoned Brother Ikpo and the head of our church in Umuahia, Senior Apostle Onyenze. They fasted and prayed for God to choose a suitable woman for me and found Glory Eke Uche, a young intelligent woman from our village. And though I worried she might be too young for me, I decided that if I explained myself well enough to her and her family to win their consent, it would prove God's will in the matter. Christmas break, 1995, I traveled to Nigeria to collect research material for a book project, and stopped in our village to meet Glory in person.

Glory and her family already knew who I was when I arrived. We'd all grown up in the same village, and by our local standard, I was already famous as the first and only university professor from our village at the time. Her father, Chief Eke Ogbonnaya, was a towering figure of both wisdom and physique, a member of Ihechiowa Clan's Eze-in-Council, the First Olumba of Ihechiowa, a man of letters, and one of the richest elders of our village. As my mentor, he had taught me many of the Igbo cultural exegeses I used in my analysis of the four novels of Chinua Achebe in *Folkways in Chinua Achebe's Novels*. Over the years I'd given him Christmas gifts, and on one occasion money for Glory while she was still in school. Still, I worried that other villagers might discourage Glory from marrying me because I was an older man, a divorcee, and a member of a denomination of a church that was different from hers.

A few days after I arrived, I was talking with a friend, Amoji Okoro, when Glory and her half-sister, Rosaline, dropped by briefly to thank me for money I had given her during her school years. Glory was mature and stunningly beautiful, and as they turned to leave, I asked them to visit again. Four days later, they were back for a more relaxed and convivial conversation.

"Good afternoon." Glory and Rosaline nodded and smile as they entered my house.

"Good afternoon to you both." I gestured to the couch. "Please, have a seat."

Once they were settled, Glory turn to me. "How was your flight from America?"

"Oh. Very pleasant, thanks. It was not my first time, and you pick up some good tips after traveling abroad some. Thanks for asking. May I offer you a drink?"

"Yes. A soft drink," Glory answered for both.

"Nnukwu," I called to my half-brother. "Bring some maltina, maltex, or whatever soft drink is available for Glory and Rosaline."

"Yes, sir," Nnukwu ran for the drinks and returned in a few seconds.

"Your father tells me, Glory, that you have just started teaching. Do you like teaching as a profession?"

"Yes. I like working with the children."

"Oh. That's good. Where is the school?"

"It is in Amanta, Abiriba, in Ohafia LGA."

"That's wonderful. But with all that teaching, when will you find time to get married and have your own children?"

She smiled. "I've not thought much about marriage yet."

"Is that so? Do you mean to say that men have not already asked you for marriage?"

"Yes, they have. In fact, they started when I was still in secondary school. If I had succumbed to their pressure, I wouldn't have had the opportunity to attend the Nigerian College of Education and become the elementary school teacher I am now."

"A very wise decision, Glory. So, what else do you want to achieve before marriage becomes a priority?"

"Don't get me wrong. I'll think of marriage seriously when I meet the right man."

"I'm glad you think that way. As you may already know, Clara and I were divorced back in March 1994. I have come back to Nigeria this year to collect research material for a book I'm working on, and to look for a girl I might marry. I wonder if you might have any suggestions for me."

Glory lowered her eyes, and sipped her drink. "I'm very sorry to hear of your divorce," she said. "As you know, I'm too young and inexperienced to offer you any suggestions on marriage. Maybe you should ask more experienced people to help you find someone suitable."

"Thanks, Glory. I'll do that."

Then she and Rosaline rose to leave. "Thanks for the drink. We have to go now."

"Why are you leaving so soon? You have not even finished your drinks."

"I know." Glory nodded in thanks. "But we have to go now to cook dinner for my father."

I stood, thanked them for their visit and walked them to their home gate. By the time I had returned to my house, I was determined to approach Glory and her family to ask for her hand in marriage.

Before I left Nigeria, I made my intensions known to Glory and her family. Though they did not give me an answer, I was fairly confident that they would say yes, and therefore asked Senior Apostle Onyenze and Brother Ikpo to handle any arrangements for me in my absence from the village.

But not all went well. As I had feared, some members of the Presbyterian Youth Association accused her father of supporting her marriage to an older and divorced man because his family simply wanted to enjoy the riches of an American professor. At first, Glory succumbed to the pressure and initially rejected my marriage proposal. However, her brother, Kalu Eke disagreed with the Youth Association and persuaded her to rethink her position. After months of discussion between Senior Apostle Onyenze and her family, Glory finally agreed to marry me. Chief Eke and Senior Apostle Onyenze registered our traditional marriage on November 25, 1996, in Umuahia Municipal Court. On January 4, 1997, Glory joined me in America as my wife.

For the first time in more than six years, joy and happiness returned in my life. I returned home after each day's work to enjoy the embrace, good cooking, and intimate conversations with a lovely and loving bride. My life couldn't have been more enjoyable.

Glory quickly acclimated herself with her new culture and environment, meeting with neighbors and learning her way around the new city. Three months later, she was pregnant with our first child. But that didn't stop her from beginning her college education during the first summer school session, which started in late May, 1997. She struggled a little at first, mostly due to the difficulty of understanding the American accents of her instructors. I helped her with homework assignments and took care of our home chores while she studied. In the end, she passed three of her courses with high grades, but was disappointed with the fourth course grade of D+. I assured her that it was a passing grade in the university's grading system, and that she could make it up as she progressed through the system.

I was always proud and happy to attend social functions with Glory, including Nigerian cultural meetings, Nigerian Independence Day celebrations, wedding ceremonies, and above all, church services at the Saint Luke's Episcopal. One of our female church members took me aside one day and asked if Glory was a professional model.

"No. Why do you ask?"

"Because, apart from being very beautiful, she always dresses well, like a professional model each time she comes to church."

"Thank you for the compliment, but she is a model only for me," I smiled broadly.

"Well, the Episcopal Women's Association is planning a fashion show to raise money for the church. I was wondering if you and Glory could like to take part in it to exhibit the beautiful Nigerian dresses she's been wearing to church this summer."

"Thank you for inviting us. I will be happy to participate since it will benefit the church. And I will ask Glory, but I'm sure she will also agree. Nevertheless, let me ask her first."

She thanked me and we parted. A few weeks later, Glory and I took part in the fashion show alongside other members of the church. The show was a great success, raising a significant amount of money for the church. Coincidentally, since then our clothing budget has increased to ensure that Glory, our children, and I continue to appear in our Sunday best whenever we attend services at church.

In other areas of our family life, Glory has been a good partner, working hard at home and on her outside job to support our efforts to train our young children to become as successful as the children from my first marriage. She tolerates my human shortfalls and inadequacies, which Clara could not do. For instance, when she first arrived from Nigeria, I was living in a one-bedroom apartment. After seven months, we moved into a two-bedroom apartment in anticipation of the birth of our first baby, Uchenna, who arrived on Thanksgiving Day, November 27, 1997 (we had a double celebration that day). During those initial months, we never dined out. Neither could we afford to entertain ourselves with many outside visits with friends. But she never complained. She knew that I was still paying child support for six children and struggling to maintain a modicum of happy, good life for our young family. She has never ask for much from me. Instead, she cheerfully accepted whatever I could give.

I succeeded in attracting several small research grants from our university and eventually made some reasonable royalties from the three books I had previously published. These two sources of added income enabled me to buy a house in 1998, one year and seven months after Glory arrived in the country. However, before buying the house, I told her what I was thinking about doing. At first, she was afraid that I might not be able to make the monthly mortgage payments on the property. Nevertheless, I assured her that I depended on her to make it happen. She wondered how she could be of any help to me while she was nursing a baby and attending college without a job. I told her that if she continued loving me as she did, without asking for much, we assuredly could make it. She did precisely as I asked, and I worked my utmost best to keep my side of the bargain.

By March 1999, Glory, who had trained as a certified nurse's aide (CNA) at the New Haven branch of the Red Cross Society, also landed a full-time job. She attended college classes full-time in the day and worked full-time as a CNA at night, from 11:00 p.m. to 7:00 a.m. I cooked for the family, cleaned the house, and took care of Uchenna, driving him daily to and from the daycare center on weekdays. We relaxed a bit on Saturdays and Sundays but maintained our busy schedules even after Adanne was born in 2000 and Ekeoma in 2001. She finally quit the night job when she was admitted to graduate school in fall 2004. I was the proudest husband in the crowd when she graduated in spring 2006.

Since then she has been working as a social work clinician with a Master's degree in Social Work. She contributes all her salary toward running the household. And there lay the source of our peace and happiness as a couple. We struggled together to live life fully, no matter how little or much we earned. Thus, I was able to pay off my mortgage in 2009. Since then, my financial focus has been saving as much money as I can toward the payment of our young children's future college education.

But our blessings have been multiplied. For when the Federal Government of Nigeria paid my pension entitlements in Nigeria, I was able to use the money to build a one-story house in our old village, adding to the bungalow I built after I married Clara. With both houses, the two sides of my big family would always find adequate accommodation whenever any of us visit home in Nigeria. Meanwhile, my sister and her children occupy part of the old house and help provide security to the entire compound.

In fact, when Glory and our three children visited Nigeria in 2004, the children so thoroughly enjoyed the new building and our people that they refused to return to America. They only agreed to return with us after we promised to take them back as often as possible. Besides, we told them, after their college education, they could return to work in Nigeria if they so chose. And they could live in our home and enjoy their cousins' presence all year round. When we took our fourth child, Kalu (KK), to the village in December 2011 for my father-in-law's funeral, he used the opportunity of the trip to explore the village and get to know our relatives. In addition, we chat on the phone with members of our extended family in Nigeria whenever possible, and the children seem more proud as Nigerian Americans ever since we introduced them to their Nigerian roots.

All in all, Glory and I have lived a good married life. That is not to say that life has been easy. No, that is far from the truth. The age difference and the imbalance in our individual academic attainment and intellectual interests have often been a source of tension. And I still have to stay vigilant about the ghosts of Father's attitudes concerning marriage and parenthood. To listen as much as advise. To spend as much time with my family as I do with my career. To lend a modicum of respect to opinions and ideas with which I may not agree.

To allow both my children and my wife to be wrong. And, maybe most importantly, to allow myself to be wrong. For, in many ways, the one thing I most struggled to overcome with Father was his seeming inability to accept me just as I was and to encourage me to discover who that man might be through a deep consideration of the great ache in every human: the need to be loved. Thank God, Glory and I have both developed enough patience and tolerance with each other to enable us to maintain a harmonious balance in our relationship.

In some ways, ironically, we also owe our loving and open relationship to Clara, who told Glory on her arrival in the U.S. that our marriage would not last more than two years because of my inherent violent nature. Conscious of that ill omen, Glory and I quickly learned to discuss our problems as friends so as not to enthrone Clara a prophet of doom. Specifically, on my part, I am always sensitive to, and watch out for, the mistakes that Glory makes which seem similar to those that Clara made in our marriage that I neither tolerated nor forgave—an attitude that partially led to our divorce. Hence, I have learned to respond to such mistakes differently whenever Glory makes them. Because of my changed behavior, Glory has also learned to deal with my shortcomings and to forgive them out of her love of me. By the grace and love of God, I will not fail the trust of the woman that loves me so much, nor plunge myself into a dark hole of another divorce. So help me God.

Chapter 15

Southern Life

As I reflect on where I've been and what I've been through in my academic and spiritual journeys, from my small rural village of Umuchiakuma Ihechiowa in Southeast Nigeria, to my appointment at Southern Connecticut State University, I thank God for giving me a father, teachers, and professors, who gave me the attention, tools, and desire to succeed.

My employment at SCSU began in fall 1992, and I have since gained many personal rewards and academic successes. The journey, however, has not been without its heartaches. As with everything in life, the light is always balanced with the darkness. As my professional life has moved along at a smart pace, my family relations, particularly those with my children from my first marriage, proved more difficult to reconcile.

Once Glory arrived in America, I introduced her as my wife to Clara and the children. Clara stayed for a time with the children in Hamden, about half a mile from where Glory and I live. I had chosen the location of our house so that I could help take care of the children whenever needed. Ndubuisi, Emeka, and Enyinna would occasionally walk the short distance from their home to visit my new family. Each of them, separately, lived briefly with us, and I had high hope that we could maintain such an arrangement until they all came of age.

Clara, however, found a new job in Texas, and soon my contact with the children was limited to phone calls and brief, infrequent visits. Even Ikenna, once he finished his medical degree programs at Yale and Rutgers, headed south to the Bello College of Medicine at Houston for his Residency program. The lack of regular physical contact with them, especially with Ndubuisi who needed me most, was devastating. Clara eventually returned to Hamden, which made it possible for the children to visit with Glory and me whenever they came to town. Regrettably, Ndubuisi never came back to visit me in Hamden like the other children.

Then, on December 8, 2009, I received a telephone call from Nbubuisi, which later turned out to be the last conversation I would have with him. He still had the same spirit of independence, fierce loyalty, and convictions that he'd always had.

"Hello Dad, how are you doing?"

"I'm okay, except that I'm tired because I've had a long day of teaching. What about you, Son?"

"I'm blessed as always. I called you earlier today, but little sister Adanne told me you were still on campus. How did your classes go?"

"Very well. Thanks. It never really changes. You know that. And how was your day?"

"Not too good. That's why I called."

"What happened, Son?"

"I received a summons to appear in a San Antonio court."

"Why? Did you commit a crime? Tell me."

"No, Dad. You know I can never commit any crime that would send me to court."

"Then what is it about?"

"Well, I went to preach the gospel of our Lord Jesus Christ to my neighbors in our apartment complex. Some of them reported me to our apartment manager, accusing me of disturbing their peace."

"For preaching the gospel to your neighbors ... ?" I cut in, angry.

"Yes, and none of them talked to me first about it. The manager gave me a quit notice, which I refused to sign. So he sent the notice to the court for them to evict me. I will be going to San Antonio tomorrow morning for the hearing."

"Have you told Ikenna and Enyinna about it?"

"No. I have not, Dad."

"Why not, Son?"

"Because there's nothing to it. You know me as a man of peace and love, who would not cause trouble for anyone. If they didn't like me preaching to them, they should have told me, and I would have stopped. I think the manager just wants to rent my apartment to a white man. I was the only black man living in the complex."

"Please, Ndubuisi. Talk to your brothers. As you know, they both have beautiful homes in Kyle and Austin. They'd be glad to accommodate you until you find another place to live."

"I'll let them know about my court case, but I don't want to leave San Marcos. I belong to a wonderful Pentecostal church with members who love me dearly. I'll not be happy away from the church. I love it here, Dad."

"Very well. But talk to your brothers, and call me as soon as you return from the court to tell me how the judge handled the case."

"I will. Good night, Dad; I love you so much."

"Good night, Son. Be careful as you travel to San Antonio. And may God bless you!"

The next evening when I returned from work, Adanne said that Ndubuisi had tried six times to reach me on phone. He'd promised to call again later.

Adanne was thrilled because Ndubuisi had talked to her, Uchenna, and Ekeoma for more than three hours, promising to buy each of them an iPod for Christmas. She was so impressed and pleased she called Ndubuisi her most beloved elder brother. I was very tired and told her that I would talk to Ndubuisi the next day unless he called back that evening. He did not call.

The following night, October 10, 2009, I received a call. The voice on the other end of the line wailed and screamed uncontrollably.

"Oh my God! My brother, my brother, my brother...."

"Who is this?" I yelled trying to stop the screaming so I could understand.

"My brother is dead. They have killed him. They have killed him."

"Please. Please. Who is this? And who did they kill?"

"Dad. This is Britney, Enyinna's girlfriend. Something terrible has happened. Enyinna will call you back when he collects himself." Then she hung up.

I was frantic. I dialed Enyinna and he picked up. "Tell me, Enyinna! Which of your brothers is dead, and who killed him? Tell me! Oh tell me who killed him!"

"Dad. The San Marcos Police has just come to give me the news...."

"What happened? What happened to my son, Ndubuisi? Who killed my beloved? Oh God! What sin did I commit to earn me this kind of punishment? Who killed him, and for what reason? Is it for preaching the gospel of our Lord Jesus Christ? When was it ever a crime to serve God as a committed Christian? Tell me Enyinna. Tell me what has happened to my beloved."

At 4:30 that evening, Ndubuisi had just finished playing basketball and was crossing a major road to get to his apartment. A twenty-year old college student, driving without a license in a borrowed uninsured car, struck and killed my son. According to the passenger in the car, the driver did not see Ndubuisi even though he'd shouted, "Watch out!" The driver slammed the breaks, but it was too late. He got a ticket for driving without a license. No other charges were filed.

I fell to the floor, helpless. The whole family, led by Adanne, rushed in to find out what was the matter. As soon as I told them, they all joined me in a chorus of lamentation. We cried, and cried, and cried, huddled together on the floor. No words, just tears. Words lost their meaning.

The next morning, December 11, 2012, Clara and I traveled to Texas, and joined the rest of our family and members of Ndubuisi's church to give him the kind of burial he deserved. We buried him on December 15. I came back to Southern the next day, graded my students' finals, and then settled down at home to weigh the full impact of my loss, our loss. I realized that Ndubuisi's death had brought the whole family together for the first time in years, which attested to the quality of his life as a unifier. It also came to me that God had just exacted from me a human tithe, the choicest of all my ten children. As a faithful Christian, I saw my *tithe* as a path through my suffering. And as I thought about Ndubuisi, the following song echoed in my ears and gave me some little measure of relief:

> Safe in the arms of Jesus,
> Safe on His gentle breast,
> There by His love o'ershaded,
> Sweetly my [Ndubuisi's] soul shall rest.

Still, for more than a year, I was severely depressed. Nevertheless, my second daughter, Adanne, stayed by my side, comforting me. And my two other sons, Michael and Enyinna, gave me much love and comfort that helped to mitigate the impact of the loss. I also turned to fervently reading the Bible, along with spiritual books by Elisabeth Elliot, Billy Graham, and Joel Osteen, which finally helped me to move out of the depression.

I also began experiencing good dream visions in which Ndubuisi and I continued our usual happy father-son relationship. We'd play cards together, sing Cherubim and Seraphim songs, and discuss Bible stories just as we used to in life. I felt wonderful every day that followed a night I dreamed about him. And although he is my "cross of snow," he will continue to live in my heart until I cross the narrow sea to join him and the rest of my departed friends and family, who are now enjoying their perpetual rest above.

The primary focus of my life for years before Ndubuisi's death had been my career at the university. Southern Connecticut State University was primarily a teacher training college for Connecticut State schools. My appointment as an associate professor of English at a rank I had held for four years in my home university in Nigeria and three years while I was on sabbatical leave in the two American universities led me to wonder how soon I would be promoted in order to regain my lost seniority. I realized that whatever losses I'd suffered, moving from one university to another required me to work even harder on my new tenure-track position and make Southern my final professional destination. I was determined to achieve both promotion and tenure within a relatively short time, no matter what obstacles I would face in the process of realizing the dream. Additionally, I reminded myself that everything important I ever achieved in the past involved some forms of struggle, like the many wrestling matches of my youth.

Over the years, Southern had evolved into a modern, diversified center of higher learning, expanding both its undergraduate and graduate programs and opening up entirely new fields of study and research. And beginning at our first faculty orientation, I learned that the criteria for evaluating faculty for promotion and tenure included teaching, research/creative activity, and service, in that order. The importance of teaching, which serves as a constant reminder to all professors that the original concept of building the institution was to train teachers for the state, was made abundantly clear to us.

Even though I perfectly understood and appreciated the administrators' commitment to maintaining the founders' purpose for building the institution, I worried that the heavy teaching load—four courses per semester, with a high teacher-student ratio in every class—would take me more time and energy than any other committed professor could give while at the same time excelling in the other two evaluative areas: research/creative activity and service.

Teaching was not such a problem, but grading papers and giving weak students the close individual attention they needed was. The five office hours per week required by the school in which to hold conferences with students who needed help was not enough time for me to personally deal adequately with all of the students' writing problems. I had to set aside more time.

Fortunately, my teaching experiences at Alvan Ikoku College of Education in Nigeria helped me to understand the educational needs of students at Southern. In addition, my heavy teaching load with high teacher-student ratio at Southern were similar to those I encountered at Imo State University also in Nigeria, and so I was able to adjust quickly to my new situation at Southern. And luckily, most of the courses I would teach were similar to those I had taught at Columbus, Austin, Tulsa, and Atlanta.

Consequently, my research/creative activities hardly suffered. I had already made a name for myself after I published *Gods, Oracles and Divination: Folkways in Chinua Achebe's Novels*. Many scholars, students, and general readers in the fields of Comparative Literature and African/Black Studies popularized the work. Consequently, publishers invited me to contribute articles and other books to their journals and book series. Subsequently, I contributed *The Gong and the Flute: African Literary Development and Celebration* to The Greenwood Press's "Contributions in Afro-American and African Studies, Number 173, Series" in 1994; and *Igbo* to The Rosen Publishing Group's "The Heritage Library of African Peoples" Series in 1995, which won the New York Public Library's "Books for the Teen Age 1996" Award. Hence, I was able to apply for tenure and promotion to the rank of full professor and received both awards with effect beginning fall 1995.

Soon thereafter, I received other invitations from acquisitions editors of publishing companies for more articles and books. I contributed *Understanding Things Fall Apart: A Student Casebook to Issues, Sources, and Historical Documents* to The Greenwood Press's "Literature in Context" Series, 1999, which won the 1999 Southern Connecticut State University Faculty Scholar Award; *The Nigerian Americans* to The Greenwood Press's "The New Americans" Series, 2003; *A Century of Nigerian Literature: A Select Bibliography* to Africa World Press, 2003; *General Ojukwu: The Legend of Biafra* to The Triatlantic Books' "African History Makers" Series, 2007; and *Blood and Bravery: Voices of Biafan Veterans of the Nigeria-Biafra War*, 2010, which served as a sequel to the biography of General Chukwuemeka Odumegwu Ojukwu, the Biafran strongman.

The publication of each of these books was important because they underscored that a self-imposed exile in America could still tell the stories of the homeland and the oppressed Igbo people in Nigeria. *Igbo* tells the story of my ethnic group alongside fifty-five other African peoples included in the Heritage Library of African Peoples. *General Ojukwu: The Legend of Biafra* and *Blood and Bravery: Voices of Biafran Veterans of the Nigeria-Biafra War* is an insider's tale of the brutality of Nigeria, Great Britain, and the USSR against the Igbo—known then as Biafrans—who were in combat for their survival along with other ethnic peoples of Nigeria during the Nigeria-Biafra War (1967-70). Ironically, without living in America, I could not have had the resources or enjoyed the scholarly atmosphere in which to conduct the research on those traumatic events.

I also wrote other books and articles to promote my national Nigerian cultural heritage to other immigrant citizens of all nationalities in our newfound land, the USA. *A Century of Nigerian Literature: A Select Bibliography* was written to enable students and scholars of Nigerian Literature to more easily find the sources they needed for their research. I also contributed *The Nigerian Americans* as a means of distinguishing the identity of Nigerian immigrants in America, which is separate from those of other Black Americans. In doing so, I emphasized Nigerian Americans' peculiar contributions (in all areas of human endeavor) to this country.

Since their publication, student affairs units of high schools, colleges, and universities, as well as the U.S. State Department and the courts have used *Igbo* and *The Nigerian Americans* as useful sources of information about Nigerians, helping them to understand better the Igbo and Nigerian cultures, especially when family cases in courts were involved. Defense lawyers have occasionally consulted me in trials involving Igbo or Nigerian clients.

I only mention these publications here because I value my contribution to the Nigerian (indeed, Igbo) cultures and civilization through literature most highly. If the works accurately represent the cultures as I intended them to do, I can feel that the money and love my people and the Nigerian federal and state governments invested in me through granting me scholarship awards in Nigeria and America, as well as my Nigerian, especially Igbo, upbringing and education, have not gone unrequited.

Southern also made it possible for me to be creatively productive. Between fall 1993 and spring 2012, I received eleven awards of reassigned time for research—three or six credits per semester—from the English department and the Dean of the School of Arts and Science, as well as two sabbatical leave awards from the university administration to conduct research for the books. Within the same period, I applied twelve times for the Connecticut State University-Association of American University Professors (CSU-AAUP) Grant Awards and received one eleven times. While each grant amount was not large, it partially helped me financially to conduct the research in America, Great Britain, and Nigeria.

That my work has brought some visibility to Connecticut State University System is also rewarding. I am also humbled that my colleagues, who nominated me three times for the Connecticut State University System Professorship award, did so primarily because of their respect for my research activities and publications. In addition, I'm highly honored that the publications have garnered accolades and honors from *Who's Who in America; Who's Who in American Education; Who's Who in the World; Who's Who in the South and Southwest*; and *Annual Fellow of International Biographical Association*, editors of *The Writers Directory, Black Writers,* and *Dictionary of International Biography*.

All of these awards and accolades serve as evidence of my determination to carry the torch Father lit for me during my youth in our village. At the time, neither he nor I could have imagined how long and far into the world I would carry it. Today, however, my biographic volumes and my published works serve as a witness to a writer and professor whose pride and happiness my father would have enjoyed for carrying his torch in this manner if he were alive today. A life of scholarship and service is all he ever wanted from me. And at the end of this match, I know he would be proud.

As to my service to the university and community, I've served on academic committees every year, sometimes as a chairperson and other times as a regular member. Some of the committees include the Connecticut State University System's Professorship Advisory Committee for Southern Campus in 2001-2003, 2003-2006, and 2008-2010; the SCSU Faculty Scholar Award Committee in 2001-2003 and 2008-2010; Chair of the English Department Student Award Ad Hoc Committee; Chair of the Connecticut State University System's Board of Trustees Research Award Committee for Southern Campus; Chair of the English Department Sabbatical Leave Committee; Promotion and Tenure Committee; Distinctive Programs Grant Review Panel; the Hardship Department Evaluation Committee Pool; and, the SCSU New Faculty Mentoring Pool.

But what I treasure most are the services I have rendered to minority and international students on campus, just as I had promised the black students who interviewed me for my appointment in 1992. I became their official faculty advisor both in the department and on campus as a whole, attended the Black Student Union meetings every week during the university community hours, and worked with Student Supportive Center. I also introduced myself to Mr. Richard Farricielli, a director in the Student and University Affairs Division. From my close associations with administrators, I was able to draw their attention to the particular needs of minority and international students on campus. The students were so satisfied with the help they received, they began encouraging other prospective minority students to come to Southern. All our combined efforts have helped to increase the enrollment of minority and international students since I came to the university.

Additionally, while working with those students, other students, from the Caribbean and Africa, drew my attention to the intra-racist attitude that some African Americans were showing toward them. I spoke against such behavior at the BSU meetings, admonishing every black student to work together as brothers and sisters for the benefit of all. But when the Caribbean students could no longer tolerate the purported intra-racism, they asked me to help them form their own separate organization. With my help, they formed the West Indian Academic Society in 1996. I served as their official academic advisor for five years. Later, the African students asked me to help them form their own separate organization. I did, and they named it African Students Organization. I also became their official academic advisor. Once the three black student organizations found their feet, I decided to visit and advise them occasionally until other faculty and staff members took over. Even after their organizations were established, I continued to advise individual black students academically, especially during the registration periods, and many of them continued to depend on me for help in their courses in Africana literature.

I also tried to help the Student Affairs Unit in the recruitment and retention of minority faculty at the university, serving as a member of the university's Minority Recruitment and Retention Committee (two years as chairperson), and mentoring the majority of new minority faculty members under the SCSU New Faculty Mentoring Pool program. Whenever I hear students and faculty members tell me they benefited from the wealth of experience I accumulated while serving in the four universities as an international student and faculty member before coming to Southern, I feel a great sense of satisfaction that I am now in a position to help light other people's candles with the torch Father lit many years ago for me to carry. Once again, he would have been well-pleased to see me pay forward the service of helping other people wherever I could.

My life and service beyond the university campus have been equally exciting. As one of the Nigerian elders in Connecticut, I helped our people to found the Association of Nigerians in Connecticut (ANC), to foster healthy sociocultural interactions and cooperation among Nigerians residing in Connecticut, and to disseminate information about political, economic, and social issues in Nigeria to our community that would enable us to maintain a link with our homeland. We held monthly meetings in members' homes and discussed the burning issues of the day in Nigeria, as well as America, which affected us as Nigerian Americans and permanent residents. We also used the platform to condemn people coming to the country illegally or overstaying their visits, and those who came with student visas but failed to stay in the colleges and universities where they gained admission. Collectively these activities could tarnish the image of all Nigerians as a community in America. Speaking against them was a way to help end them.

I used my status as a university professor to advise Nigerian parents occasionally about academic issues affecting their children and wards, including what such children must do to succeed, especially at the university level, and to reduce their dropout rates.

Collectively, ANC organizes annual cultural dances and fashion shows as a means of exhibiting an aspect of the Nigerian culture, which is distinct from the collective Black or Africana culture and in America. In addition, the organization plans and hosts Nigerian Independence Day celebrations in America and invites officials of the Nigerian Embassy and Consulate General in Washington, D.C. and New York to discuss contemporary issues affecting Nigerians. The officials use the opportunity to resolve passport and visa problems that some of our members and their families might have. In addition, ANC sends some of its members to the two American cities as a pressure group that asks the federal government of Nigeria (through its consular officials) to address current atrocities that affect the people in our homeland, including rigged elections, misuse and abuse of petrol money by the political class, and the destructive activities of the Islamic fundamentalists (known as Boko Haram), which the federal government in Abuja has not been able to stop. Some of us even take trips to Nigeria and take part in discussions at national conferences, rallies, and colloquia, which the government and non-governmental organizations (NGO) arrange, to help find better ways to solve the problems.

As an Igbo elder, I have played an active role in the formation of an Igbo ethnic sociocultural organization called Igbozue of Connecticut. At the end of the Nigeria-Biafra War, the Igbo people in the Diaspora formed many such organizations to assist the parent pan-Igbo cultural organization, Oha na Eze Ndigbo, whose primary duty is to promote the unity and progress of the Igbo ethnic peoples of Nigeria politically, economically, socially, and culturally. Igbozue subscribes to working for the achievement of the goals of Oha na Eze in Connecticut. We carry out many functions, similar to those of the ANC, but with emphasis on the particular needs of the Igbo people, which occasionally creates conflict for some Igbos who belong to both organizations. Such conflict, I confess, is one of the reasons why I have not recently played an active role in the ANC. For I prefer a situation in which all Nigerians can maintain their memberships in ANC, while the Igbo continue to maintain our memberships in Oha na Eze, which transcends local Igbo needs in Connecticut. I still hope to find a way in which all of the Igbo can resolve the conflict and thereby strengthen both the Nigerian national and Igbo ethnic organizations in Connecticut.

Overall, despite Ndubuisi's accidental death, which could have happened wherever we lived, my life at SCSU has been positive. The university environment has greatly helped my professional development, such that I received tenure and promotion to full professorship in three years' time. To date, I have published seven books, and I have friendly colleagues in my department (especially Tony Rosso), who have helped me to become productive in my scholarly activities.

My employment at Southern has also enabled me to improve my home life. Glory has used the free tuition offered to spouses and children of university professors to study for her bachelor's and master's degrees in Social Work, which qualified her to work as a clinician in downtown New Haven. Ndubuisi, Emeka, Enyinna, and Kelechi used the same tuition waiver opportunities to study at Southern before they withdrew to study elsewhere. Furthermore, any of the four younger children I have with Glory will be free to use the same tuition waivers to study if they choose to do so at Southern.

The stability of my employment as a professor, the family I have been able to raise, the great friends I have made over the years, and the community services I have rendered to my fellow Igbo people and Nigerians in the Greater New Haven Area, as well as those living in my homeland, could not have been possible if I were not employed at Southern Connecticut State University. For all these manifold blessings, I thank the Almighty God in the high heavens.

Conclusion

I started working seriously on this book after publishing *Blood and Bravery: Voices of Biafran Veterans of the Nigeria-Biafra War*. At the time, a dear friend asked, "Kalu, now that you have published a second book on the Nigeria-Biafra War, are you going to write another to create a war trilogy?"

I told him that my next writing project would be based on my personal life, without fully realizing then that my story was, in the main, the story of struggles that reflected, among other issues, the tensions and anxieties of many Nigerians living in a fragmented war-torn country. It was also the strory of my struggle to move into the modern, twentieth-century, world outside the homeland, while at the same time maintaining a close connection with the familial, cultural, and political ties of my ancestors.

"Will that be your memoir? If so, why do you want to start writing it now? Are you sick or planning an early retirement?" the friend asked, deeply worried about me.

"Oh no, I'm neither sick nor planning any early retirement!" I assured him. However, I also told him that I wanted to write my story while I could still recall with clarity all the important incidents in my life. Memory, as we all know, is a tricky thing; we lose some of it as we grow older. The more the incidents taking place in our lives become distant, the more our memories of them become cloudier. That was why I could no longer defer carrying out this book project, which has been on my mind for a long time.

Little did I know then that, like the soldier coming home after a long tour of duty abroad, I was going to strip myself naked so as to see the scars and wounds of my life struggles all over my metaphoric body. Writing would remind me of the pains I suffered and endured as each individual incident occurred—incidents of traumatic accidents, family struggles with poverty, and deaths. Nevertheless, I had to confront and tell of them if my story was to be truthful. It occurred to me that the traumatic side of memory was why my friend wondered why I would choose to write my memoir now, which he seemed to have felt I should re-experience only when I was retired or close to death. If that was his thinking, then he did not understand that, in addition to the deep-seated pains and sorrow, my story would also relate the joys and satisfactions of strong family bonds, dedicated love, and cultural enlightenment, as well as a record of the numerous personal triumphs and achievements in my life.

I wrote the book partly to demonstrate, in practical terms, the importance of the Igbo apothegm, "It takes a village to raise a child," as it positively affected me as an individual. For me, life began with this guiding principle, passed on through the village elders, who coined and adopted it all through the ages. As shown in the discussions in all the chapters of the book, my academic and spiritual journeys, which began in my rural village of Umuchiakuma in Southeast Nigeria, were influenced greatly by the foundations of character the village laid for me. There, I acquired at a very young age its value system, the Igbo morality, worldview, and oral educational system, which have continued to influence my values, even now. To give some balance to my upbringing, my father and teachers complemented my oral Igbo values with written Christian morality, Western worldview and education, when I became a Christian and student in the church and school the Church of Scotland Mission established in my village.

As sad but curious as it was for me to leave the village that raised me as a child to pursue further education, I'm so glad that the separation launched me into a global village (including America), where I now live. It was then that Father figuratively handed me his torch to carry and shine back its light to the homeland. Thereafter, he watched out even from a distance until his death in 1989, to see how well I held it up and how strong it would reflect back. The previous year, however, something happened that revealed his great pride in the way I had been carrying his torch.

Father had been staying with us several days in Okigwe while undergoing medical treatment. After he had recovered, he asked to be taken home, and so we drove him to a village in Akara Isu Motor Park, to catch a taxi. Father got out of the car to stretch his legs. When a charter driver offered to find him a car to take him home, Father told him that I was taking care of the arrangement. Then he proceeded to tell the man how proud he was that his son and daughter-in-law were both lecturers at the newly established state university, and how his own flesh and blood would one day travel the world as a great Igbo man. When I returned with his taxi, he said nothing about the incident as he got in and headed back to our village.

On the ride back to Okigwe, however, Clara related how proud Father was of my achievements, saying: "*A furum na oku owa m munyere nye di gi na ero nke oma* (I see that the torch I handed over to your husband to carry continues to burn well)." We both laughed with satisfaction at Father's gracious, revealing remark, and I secretly looked forward to a day when I could say so about my own children's endeavors in life.

Currently, some of them have become famous in their own professional fields. My first son, Michael, acquired a Bachelor's Degree in Economics from Imo State University, Okigwe, and a Master's Degree in Business Administration from the University of Liverpool in the United Kingdom. For the past thirteen years, he has served as a manager in Guaranty Trust Bank, Lagos, the third largest bank in Nigeria. He is married with four sons. Ikenna graduated from Yale University with a Bachelor's Degree in Psychobiology, and a Medical Doctorate from the University of Medicine and Dentistry, Robert Wood Johnson Medical School, in Piscataway, New Jersey. He is currently a medical director (clinical development) in Lexicon Pharmaceuticals, Inc. in Houston. My first daughter, Nneka, graduated with a Medical Doctorate in 2012 (I give much credit to Clara for her hard work and encouragement, which contributed a lot to Ikenna and Nneka's ultimate successes). And, my son, Enyinna, is a finance director with a Hyundai Car dealership, as well as a successful hip-hop musician, in Austin, Texas. Like Michael, he has fathered a grandson for me. If any of them fail to serve our extended family and village community as Father and I did, that won't be because of they lack the wherewithal.

But there have also been disappointments, in spite of these achievements. Attempting to raise my children in the American cultural and social dynamic under the strict discipline of my father caused conflicts between me and Clara and some of the children, conflicts that resulted, ultimately, in our divorce. Ironically, however, the experiences of our failed marriage helped me to work more diligently on my career as a means to earn enough money and lend support to their upbringing and to the successful second life, which I've gained with Glory. The pain of the failed marriage also helped me to reassess my own worldview and to reach out to Clara and our children in such a way that has helped us to developed more lasting and stronger familial bonds.

In that vein, it has also made me a stronger and better husband and father to my younger children. I have learned to balance my original Nigerian life and values to those I have acquired in America. And because of the remarkable strides in my academic and professional journeys, which have earned me accolades and awards, I have been able to provide Glory and our young children, Uchenna, Adanne, Ekeoma (Chief), and Kalu (KK), the opportunities for success in their educational progress.

All told, my spiritual, academic, and professional journeys over the years have been incredible in a variety of ways. My dearest hope is that I have carried my father's torch well. I have used those strategies and moves I learned early in the wrestling circle of our rural village to help me grapple with the reversals, take-downs, and holds that life threw at me, consistently progressing to the match, win or lose, with great strength and fortitude. And after receiving the torch of champions, I have learned to carry it high so that others, including my children, can clearly see the signal and follow the path I am handing over to them. And although I have not come to the end, have not been counted out, it is with great gratitude to God, my father, my teachers, and my friends that I can say, for now, that all is well with my soul.

Acknowledgments

I could not have written this book without the extraordinary support and encouragement of a number of people.

My heart-felt gratitude goes first to my lovely and dedicated wife, Glory. Being married to a man who was married before is scary enough; being married to a professor who is also writing his life story, which is full of private anguish and deep-seated pain, in spite of publicly acknowledged achievements and accolades, requires immeasurable patience. Not only did Glory take care of our young children while I was reliving and writing about the traumatic incidents in my life, she gave me all the emotional support I needed to strive along, even as she also worked on her own stressful job as a social work clinician. What she did every day to keep our young family together made me know fully that Glory was a lifelong partner that God sent to show His grace on me. I pray fervently that God should enable me to requite her love as long as I live.

I want to express my gratitude as well to Tony Morris and Steve Larocco for proofreading and editing the typescript of the book. The critical comments they made on chapters of the script caused me to reenvision or even discard some of them. I could not be happier with the overall outcome of their painstaking work.

The following colleagues also offered invaluable critical reactions to this memoir at its many drafting stages, and I am grateful and humbled by the generosity of their individual responses. They are Mike Shea, Scott Ellis, and Patrick McBrine. I hope they will be pleased with the outcome of the work they saw in progress.

I express a special gratitude to Vivian Shipley, my Muse on campus, and to my bosom friend and soul brother, Tony Rosso, who has been on my side through the thick and thin of my life at Southern Connecticut State University. I cherish his deep brotherly love for me all through the years we worked together as friends and colleagues.

I would also like to acknowledge, with honor and humility, the following teachers from elementary through graduate schools in Nigeria and America, who encouraged me to excel in my academic pursuit and professional development: Arunsi Ikoro, Eleke Nwankwo, Frank Okereke, Agwu Kalu Ogwe, Azu Irondi, Michael Echeruo, Chinua Achebe, Emmanuel Obiechina, Oscar R. Dathorne, Emmanual Odita, and Bernth Lindfors.

Finally, my heart-felt gratitude goes to my first wife Clara who strongly supported my struggles to build a better life for our family, from Alvan Ikoku College of Education, through Graduate School in America, to Imo State University. I share the glories of my achievements with her. And I give thanks and praise as well to my village elders and church leaders—too numerous to name individually—for their spiritual and material assistance which enabled me to overcome all adversities, trials, and temptations as I embarked on my academic and spiritual journeys, and to our Merciful and Almighty God, who makes everything possible.

Index

A

Abia State University, 218 also see Imo State University
Aburi Accord, 81
Achara, Eze Ogo, 85–86
Achebe, Chinua, 3, 114, 154
Adebayo, Olu (Lieutenant), 98, 100
Advanced Teacher Training College (ATTC), 78, 80, 82–86
Afo Market Days, 8
AICE Tablet, The, 122
Aja, Onoh, 5
Ajah, Kalu, 129
Akanu Ibiam National Ambulance, 84, 96
Alfred, Kalu, 129
Alvan Ikoku College of Education (AICE), 120–121
Amaramiro, Alex, 87, 91–94
Aminu, Jibril, 213
Anyanwu, Polycarp, 189
Apartheid, 157
Arochukwu, 194
Arunsi, Enyia Mgbore, 65-66
Association of Nigerians in Connecticut (ANC), 276
Atlanta University Center, 227
Awah, Alicho (Corporal), 68
Awah, Eme (Professor), 103
Azodo, Lt. A. C. C., 86

B

Balewa, Abubakar Tafawa (Alhaji Sir), 79
Bello, Ahmadu (Alhaji Sir), 79
Biafran Organization of Freedom Fighters (BOFF), 86
Black Festival of Art and Culture (FESTAC), 156–157
Boston College, MA, 78
Boys Vocational School (BVS), 61
Bridget, Mama, 68–69
Buhari, Muhammadu (Major General), 199, 201

C

Chiowa, Elder Kalu, 24
Church of Scotland Mission, Umuama, 31
Clark Atlanta University, 221, 226, 228
CSM Primary School, Umuama Ihe, 31, 53

D

Dathorne, Oscar Ron, 10, 152, 154, 191
Dike, Thomas Okoro, 77
Dimgba Eleoha, 9
Dimgba Ikwun, 9

E

Eastern Nigeria Consultative Assembly, 82
Ebeogu, Afam, 180, 189, 191
Echeruo, M. J. C., 112–114, 170–171, 180, 182, 190
Egbuna, Obi, 114
Egejuru, Phanuel, 180, 189
Egudu, Romanus, 112
Eleoha Ihe Primary School, 77
Emenyonu, Ernest N., 131
Eternal Sacred Order of Cherubim and Seraphim, The, 88-96, 102

F

Federal Military Government (FMG), 97
Folkways in Chinua Achebe's Novels, 207
Fourah Bay College, Sierra Leone, 109

H

Harbor, Jonah (Rabbi), 88

I

Ididep, 66
Ihe Central School, Obinto, 77
Ihe Youth Association (IYA), 85
Ihechiowa Development Union (IDU), 206
Ikoro, Teacher Arunsi, 31, 48, 50
Ikpo, Okore, 45
Ikpo, Robert Ebu, 21
Ikpo, Stephen Ogbaa, 4, 19, 44, 135
    banishment, 23
    conversion to Christianity, 23
    death of, 207
    funeral of, 211
    member, Church of Scotland Mission (CSM), 24
    poisoning, 58
    wrestling, 10–11
Imaga, Joseph Kalu (JKIMA), 84
Imo State University, 170, 178-179, 218, 221-227
Irondi, Azu, 121, 131
Itu, 67

K

Kalu, Alex, 254
Kalu, Eke, 84
Kalu, Emmanuel Ekpesu, 109
Kalu, Okwaraeke, 54

L

Lewis, John (Congressman), 233
Liddell, Janice, 226–227, 229, 233
Lindfors, Bernth, 114, 160, 168, 191
loan scholarship program, 105–108

M

Madueke, Allison (Captain), 204
Madueke, Uche, 204
Maimalari, Zakari (Brigadier), 79
Mgbogo, Nne Udo, 20
Mmagu, Amos Ota (Chief), 93
Muse, The, 112

N

National Association of Nigerian Students (NANS), 213
National Youth Service Corps, 116
Ndolo, Thomas, 88
Ndu, Acha, 45
Negritude, 156
Nwachuku, Uchenna, 256
Nwachukwu, Ike (Major General), 201
Nwangwu, John, 256
Nwankwo, Christian, 128

INDEX

Nwankwo, Eleke, 54, 59–60
Nwankwo, Joshua (Deacon), 128–129

O

Obi, Ogbonnaya, 4–6
Obiechina, Emmanuel, 112, 115
Odita, Emmanuel Okechukwu (Professor), 131–132
Ogbaa, Adanne, 148, 263
Ogbaa, Agwu, 102
Ogbaa, Chukwuemeka, 147
Ogbaa, Clara Kalu (née Onyejiaka Nwankwo), 126, 129, 141
Ogbaa, Daniel, 148
Ogbaa, Darren, 148
Ogbaa, David, 148
Ogbaa, Derek, 148
Ogbaa, Ekeoma, 148, 263
Ogbaa, Enyinna, 147
Ogbaa, Glory (née Eke Uche), 146, 148, 259
Ogbaa, Ikenna, 147
Ogbaa, Ikpo Stephen (Brother Ikpo), 15, 19, 60, 88, 104
  at Kalu's marriage, 129
  at school with Kalu, 40–49
  death of mother, 255
  father's funeral, 208–210
  in 1962, 139
  Kalu's return, 173
Ogbaa, Kalu, 145, 148
  1999 Faculty Scholar Award, 146
  and family at funeral of father, 145
  and roommates, UNN, 141
  and soccer team, 138
  as teacher at Imo State University, 144
  at ATTC, Owerri, 140
  at Ohio State University, 142
  burns, 25
  graduation, 141, 143
  head injury, 26
  malaria, 68
  naming ceremony, 21
  Pentecostal Church, 87–94
  with Brother Ikpo, 139
  with Clara, 141
  with family in 1958, 138
  with Glory, 146
  with wife Glory and Family, 148
  young adult, 137
Ogbaa, Kalu (KK), 148, 264
Ogbaa, Kelechi, 147
Ogbaa, Mgbore, 19, 65-66
  death of, 70
Ogbaa, Michael, 148
Ogbaa, Ndubuisi, 147, 167
  death of, 269–270
Ogbaa, Nneka, 147
Ogbaa, Nwannennaya 19, 28, 65
Ogbaa, Ogonnaya Stephen (née Nwagbara Uche), 16, 19, 49, 136
  death of, 29, 255
Ogbaa, Sandra, 148
Ogbaa, Uchenna, 148, 263
Ogbonnaya, Eke (Chief), 259
Ogbuta, Orie Ikechi, 16
Ogoro, Kalu (Chief), 33
Ogoro, Umachi Kalu, 69
Ogwe, Agwu Kalu, 62, 71
Oha na Eze Ndigbo, 277
Ohio State University, 132, 151
Ojiuko, Kalu, 109
Ojukwu, Chukwuemeka (Emeka) Odumegwu (Colonel), 79, 81–82
Ojukwu, Chukwuemeka (Emeka) Odumegwu (Colonel, Governor), 97
Okereke, Frank Nwankwo, 71, 77
Okereke, Ukobasi, 76

Okorafor, Ekpe Ekpe, 76
Okorafor, Ovuonu, 16
Okore, Mgbore Teacher, 28
Okoro, Agnes, 60
Okoro, James, 73–76
Okoro, Kalu, 102–103
Okoro, Kalu (Chief), 21, 102–103, 105–106
Okoro, Martin, 84
Okpara, Michael Iheonukara (Governor), 195–198
Okwuagwu, Thomas Ikpe, 24
Oleh, Imaga, 105–106
Oleh, Kalu, 107–108
Oleh, Lawrence, 129
Onuoha, Eme, 76
Onyenze, Senior Apostle, 259
Oral Roberts University (ORU), 221
Organization for African Unity (OAU), 81

P

pogroms, 80
polygamy, 23–24
Presbyterian Primary School, Kpirikpiri, 78

R

Republic of Biafra, 82
Rosso, Tony, 234, 244, 277, 283

S

Saint John's Catholic Church, Umuchiakuma, 32, 53
Saint Mary's Catholic Church, Umuye, 32
Southern Connecticut State University, 234, 267

T

Things Fall Apart, 3, 114–115, 154

Tiananmen Square protests (1989), 215

U

Uche, Teacher Agwu, 107
Uche, Emmanuel, 225
Uche, Nkwocha, 16
Ude, Ikpo, 15
Ude, Ikpo Ogbonnaya, 15
Udo, Eni *nwa*, 45
Uka, Kalu, 112
Ukabiala, Nnennaya, 195
Ukah, Cyprian, 256
Ukoha, Isaac, 9
Ukoha, Ukoha Kalu, 76, 80, 82
Ulu, Nne Mgbokwu Kalu, 20
Ulu, Ogbonnaya Kalu, 84
Umachi, Umachi Nnukwu, 255
Umuchiakuma, 15
  founded, 16
  Ihechiowa, 7
  Nde Abaka (compound), 15
  Nde Akwara (compound), 15
  Nde Ngwo (compound), 7, 15
  Nde Uche (compound), 15
  water/electricity, 193–195
Umuchiakuma Ihechiowa, 267
United Church of Christ on the Green (New Haven), 249
University of Nigeria, Nsukka (UNN), 102, 110
Uro, Abaka, 21
Ututu/Ihe High School, 101
Uwakwe, Eke, 61, 73
Uwakwe, Simeon (Colonel, Commander), 86
Uzomah, Cosmas, 129

W

Walker, Grady, 222
West Indian Academic Society, 275